President Lincoln review the troops in Washington, D.C.

- To Terry -
6.18.14

This Special Edition
of
September Suspense
Lincoln's Union in Peril
is
905 *of 1,000*

Dennis E. Frye

Dennis E. Frye

September Suspense

September Suspense

Lincoln's Union in Peril

Dennis E. Frye

Antietam Rest Publishing

Harpers Ferry, West Virginia

September Suspense: Lincoln's Union in Peril

Published in the United States of America by

Antietam Rest Publishing
P.O. Box 246
Harpers Ferry, WV 25425-0246
www.antietamrestpublishing.com

Dust Jacket Cover Image: "A Gallant Color Bearer" from *Harper's Weekly,* September 20, 1862

Antietam Rest Publishing logo image: "The Signal Officer Off Duty" by Edwin Forbes, 1864

Endsheet image: *Frank Leslie's Illustrated Magazine*

Library of Congress Control Number: 2012938497

Dedication

Mentors teach and sometimes preach, but most important, they endlessly give themselves to you for your betterment. I dedicate this volume to my mentors.

Dwight L. Scott,
Coach, Boonsboro High School

Millard K. Bushong, Professor, Shepherd College

Donald W. Campbell, Superintendent,
Harpers Ferry National Historical Park

Paul R. Lee, II, Division Chief,
Harpers Ferry National Historical Park

Thomas W. Richards, Chairman,
Association for the Preservation of Civil War Sites, Inc.

Colonel Ben and Alice Cheaney, my in-laws,
The Greatest Generation

John and Janice Frye, my parents,
Generations in Washington County

Sylvia Bento Frye, my spouse,
My companion & Texas Bride

Many people like newspapers, but few preserve them. Yet the most interesting reading imaginable is in a file of newspapers. It brings up the past age with all its bustle and everyday affairs, and marks its genius and its spirit more than the most labored description of the historian.

— *Savannah Republican*, September 3, 1862

Table of Contents

Introduction

Americans are addicted to news.

Our appetite is insatiable. We crave it. We demand it. We spend hours absorbing it.

It crawls across our televisions. It streams into our computers. It alerts us on our smart phones. Tablets tantalize us with blogs. It blasts on Talk Radio. It's 24/7 on cable. The feel and smell and ink of the newspaper delight those who remember a tablet only as a pill.

Anywhere, anytime, the news is there for us.

Instantaneous news is today's norm. The 21st century has conquered delays in delivering all forms of communications. We need *not* seek the news. It comes to us. And if we like the news, we share it. Nearly one-seventh of the earth's population shares news via Facebook. So many people move news through social media — confined only by the speed limit of how fast you text or how well you type — that revolutions have occurred in places where people thought revolution impossible.

I remember one day when I was isolated from everyday news. It was September 11, 2001.

As an associate producer for the Civil War movie *Gods and Generals*, we purposely selected filming sites removed from modern civilization — especially without cell towers. Director Ron Maxwell wanted to "feel" the 19th century on set; and for the 3,000 reenactors that I managed, we wanted them to "live" in the 19th century.

On September 11, I left our period Civil War encampment and drove to a rural post office (producers were permitted to have cars) somewhere on a back road in the heart of Virginia's Shenandoah Valley.

I had no idea what was happening in "this" world, as I spent most of my waking hours in 1861, 1862, or 1863 (we moved from year to year, from film day to film day, depending upon which actors were scheduled that day). It was about 8:50 a.m. I turned on my car radio. No music. Only news on every channel. Something had just happened in New York.

I entered the post office to buy a thousand stamps, making the day for the post mistress. The radio was on in the background, and I listened to the news reporters describing the scene at the World Trade Center, as I aimlessly put stamps on reenactor notices. The announcers thought it an obvious accident; tragic, indeed, but an accident.

Then I *heard* it — the fiery crash into the second tower. I didn't see it, but I could visualize it through the graphic words and near hysteric voice of the announcer. I'll never forget those seconds. It was my "Pearl Harbor" moment.

I rushed back to the movie's base camp. On my car radio, I heard about the plane slamming into the Pentagon. I didn't know details, but I knew we were under attack.

Because of the movie's complete isolation, no one knew what had happened. At that moment, I became the equivalent of Wolf Blitzer. Everyone wanted to know the little bit that I knew.

We immediately stopped film production, and huddled around the few car radios we could find. Reception was miserable. We were far from FM stations, and the AM stations kept fading in and out. I didn't actually see the horrifying spectacle until near midnight, when I returned to my hotel room to watch it on television.

Imagine yourself being isolated from news on the day that changed our modern world.

Americans loved news during the 19th century, too. But it didn't travel fast. Unless you were a telegraph operator (the 19th century form of texting), nothing was instantaneous. And telegraph wires don't move the news as quickly as wireless networks.

The newspaper was the only form of news. It appeared daily in the big cities, though many did not publish at all on Sundays, out of respect for "the day of rest." Local communities boasted their weekly paper, sometimes with more than one paper serving a community. Population didn't drive the need for competing papers. Politics did. During the Civil War era, newspapers tied themselves to political parties — serving as the party trumpeters to the masses, much like MSNBC versus Fox News (although today's news channels claim no political affiliation). And, as today, editors weren't afraid to express their opinions. They used stronger and more colorful language in the days when a duel — rather than a lawyer — settled a defamation case.

Newspapers are the last frontier of Civil War research. Tens of thousands of books have been written on the Civil War and Abraham Lincoln, but newspapers usually are not cited as sources.

One reason has been inaccessibility. Most newspapers are in curators' collections, and very difficult to locate. Even if you happened to discover a period paper, the original is so brittle, no curator worth the title will let you handle it. The fragile nature of newsprint is another problem for historians. Many of the newspapers are gone, withered away by sunlight, moisture, fire, or bugs. Newspapers, unlike the stone tablets of antiquity, are not designed for eternity.

Then there's the microfilm or microfiche machine. What's that? Now it's in the Smithsonian, but it used to be a roll of photograph negatives that you passed under a magnifier. You stuck your head into a hood to view an image projected onto a black and white mini screen. What person of sound mind would subject oneself to such torture? Most historians, of sound mind, did not.

Then came the invention of digitization, the home computer, and the worldwide web. Curators and librarians figured out how to place their papers on the internet so that historians could utilize them. A research revolution was born.

I like Civil War newspapers. They offer a plethora of new discoveries, fresh perspectives, and frank expressions. Newspapers were the first social media. Their stories represented their societies. Their pages included personalized accounts of women and men; blacks and whites; new immigrants and generational immigrants; slaves and freemen; wealthy and impoverished; laborers and capitalists; mechanics and inventors; farmers and teachers; rural inhabitants and urban dwellers; leaders and followers. Newspapers had their slants, but they were inclusive. Each newspaper freezes each day in time. They offer, for the historian, the best and most comprehensive glimpse into the day-to-day lives of average Americans.

Even better, they often copied articles from one other — especially if the editor disagreed. They never plagiarized, always gave credit; but the wonder is you can often read numerous newspapers by only reading one. My favorite example is the *Philadelphia Inquirer*. Politically neutral by the standards of the day, it consistently copied accounts from a myriad of city and local newspapers — North and South — often with its own accompanying commentary. This saved me hundreds of hours of researching different perspectives. The 1862 *Inquirer* editor consolidated the perspectives for me.

You feel history when you read an historic newspaper. It takes you there. It becomes your time machine. You're living the moment with them, and you experience their drama, their trauma, and their triumphs.

History is people — not dates, not facts, not memorized texts. We must remember that history does not create itself, but people create history. Newspapers bring us closer to people, and allow us to be there when they make their history.

I just shared my philosophy in writing this book. I chose *suspense* as part of my title because when you read their papers of September 1862, Americans were paralyzed with suspense. Every day, their futures could change, perhaps spectacularly. Drama pervades this volume, because drama invaded their lives. Everyone felt the tension. We were at war with each other. No one knew the outcome, but the newspapers recorded the drama, diligently and intelligently, day by day.

These newspapers, along with diary entries and daily correspondence, tell the story as it's happening. That was my goal: share their story as it occurs. What did they know at that moment? How did they react to their moment? What were their options? Why did they choose this decision?

Through the use of daily contemporary sources, you not only feel with them, but you begin to think along with them. You become part of their existence — at least momentarily.

The best way to achieve this connection is through use of their own words. Let them tell you their story. They are marvelous story-tellers.

My job in *September Suspense* has been to discover their stories. I'll string their stories together, but then get out of the way. Let them speak for themselves.

Civil War historians have a tendency to define a "primary resource" as a person who experienced the action or event that made history. No argument from me. My peeve is with primary sources that chronicled their participation *long after the event had occurred*.

My good friend Ed Bearss, former chief historian of the National Park Service, once illustrated this point for me. Ed served as a marine during World War II, and was badly wounded in the South Pacific during the Battle of New Britain. I once asked him if he attended his unit's reunion. "Yes," Bearss growled, "but I stopped going." Why? I asked. "Because every year more and more became a bunch of damned liars!"

Memory has its ways of distorting history. Civil War veterans created their own distortions, some through fading recollections, but others through intention. Good historians work hard to discriminate between good and bad sources, but in the field of Civil War scholarship, too often we have accepted the "primary resource" as truth, without careful examination.

One of my favorite examples illustrating this problem was at the Antietam Battlefield. For several decades, a small exhibit welcomed you at Bloody Lane, under the bold quotation, "The End of the Confederacy was in Sight." The premise was that the U.S. commander could have ended the Civil War right there, and the quote came from a primary source: Edward Porter Alexander, a

Confederate ordnance officer, who wrote a terrific personal narrative nearly 30 years *after the war*.

How much do you remember from 30 years ago? While once conducting some research on nearby Harpers Ferry, I made a startling discovery: Alexander *was not at Antietam during the battle*. How could he know if the end of the Confederacy was in sight? To the credit of my NPS colleagues at Antietam, that questionable source of interpretation no longer exists.

So, I've attempted to avoid "primary sources" of accounts written years after the fact. I've even tried to brush away accounts written months afterwards. Too much reflection time can change the historical record, and alter the story significantly.

No historian can attain absolute truth. Even the people who write *the very day* about their moment in time insert their own prejudices, stereotypes, and interpretations into their memoir. It's natural — we're human. We are immediate filters of the historical record, persuaded by our own backgrounds and beliefs.

In *September Suspense: Lincoln's Union in Peril*, we will share history's imperfections together. But we'll come as close to their reality as we can.

CHAPTER 1

September Suspense

Everything combines to prove that the revolt is culminating in its strength. Upon the next few weeks hang interests of appalling magnitude.

— *Baltimore American and Commercial Advertiser,* September 4, 1862

It's September 11.

The United States is under attack.

Foreboding news bombards the president. Danger stabs Washington. The Army stands at full alert.The Navy patrols the Potomac.

Abraham Lincoln is under siege in September 1862.

The Civil War had been raging across America for 17 months. The summer had been bloody — bloodier than any summer in American history. United States forces had attempted to capture the enemy's capital at Richmond, Virginia, but they had failed. A stubborn Confederate army under Gen. Robert E. Lee had stymied their efforts.

Lee's Rebels had inflicted mass carnage on President Lincoln's army. In seven stunning days, bullets and shells fired by Lee's Southern gunners had killed and wounded nearly 16,000 U.S. soldiers — equal to half the American casualties in *all seven years* of the Revolutionary War. Mangled bodies littered the Richmond landscape. New York farmers now were bloated corpses. Pennsylvanians fumbled without arms or hobbled without legs, amputated victims of modern warfare. Massachusetts mechanics bled their puritan blood into Virginia's bright red clay. Ohioans breathed their last to reunite the *divided* states of America. Cries of "On to Richmond" — spurred by impatient politicians and an imprudent press — had turned into tears and fears for innocent widows, siblings, and orphans.

Except for the grieving families and growing graveyards in the North, the war seemed far away. The battlefields belonged to the South. The target cities were Richmond and New Orleans and Charleston and Savannah. The states being conquered were Virginia and Tennessee and Mississippi and North Carolina. The conclusion was certain: the rebellious Confederate States of America would submit. The industrial machines and population power of the United States guaranteed victory. No other outcome seemed possible.

Then, astonishingly, the war abruptly moved.

The compass shifted north. Instead of Richmond, Washington became the centerpiece of contention. Gen. Lee raced his army toward the United States capital. He crushed a Union army blocking his path at Manassas, only 30 miles from the White House. Then he diverted. Instead of assaulting fortified Washington, Lee splashed across the Potomac River. Now he invaded Maryland, threatening Washington from the north. The Rebel chieftain frightened Baltimore and Pennsylvania. A Confederate tsunami surged onto the unstained soil of the North.

Invasion!

Pennsylvania's governor sounded the alarm. "Their destination is Harrisburg or Philadelphia," Gov. Andrew Curtin wrote in a distressed message to President Lincoln on September 11. "Send here not less than 80,000 disciplined troops. . . . Order from New York and States east all available forces here at once." The governor then issued Mr. Lincoln a challenge: "The time for decided action by the National Government has arrived. What may we expect?"

Curtin's plea to the president ended with passion and conviction. "It is our only hope to save the North and crush the rebel army. . . . Do not suppose for one instant that I am unnecessarily alarmed."[1]

Gov. Curtin was not alone in his alarm. "Citizens of Pennsylvania! Your services are demanded for the defense of your State," wrote the *Philadelphia Inquirer*. "Emboldened by real or imaginary successes, the enemy has crossed your boundary line, and now, with expectations buoyant of plunder and rapine, is marching towards your State Capital."

The *Inquirer* personalized its plea. "The present and future prosperity of our State, the welfare of our cities, and the safety of our homes and families, depend upon an instant and unanimous response." The paper exuded urgency. "Before another morn dawns upon us, every military organization in the Commonwealth should have marched against the enemy, and every loyal and able-bodied man should have prepared himself to follow in the glorious path of duty and patriotism."

The City of Brotherly Love editor finished with this warning: "Let no citizen hesitate in this hour of need. The foe is cunning in his devices, rapid in his movements, and while we hesitate he is advancing." It was not too late. The Rebels could be repulsed. "It remains for the loyal men of Pennsylvania to crush their hopes and destroy their infamous calculations."[2]

Women of the town of York, astride the suspected warpath toward Philadelphia, understood the emergency. Hourly they heard reports of railroads ruined, bridges burned, crops destroyed, cattle driven off, and in some instances, citizens murdered. The violence of war was coming to their doorsteps. No fit and dignified man could stand idle. To ensure against cowardice, the York women bonded, devising a plan to encourage maximum enlistments in the Pennsylvania militia. "When a young man sends up his card," announced the determined women, "if there be no Lieutenant, Captain, or Colonel prefixed to the name, let the first inquiry be: 'What regiment does he belong to?' If the answer be, 'None,' refuse to see him until he has enlisted."[3] How could a man of decency sustain such dishonor in the mores of Victorian America?

Certain of Confederate intentions — and desperate for troops to stop them — Gov. Curtin dispatched an urgent request to the

Mayor of Philadelphia on September 11. "We need every available man immediately. . . . Stir up your population tonight." The governor dictated specific instructions. "Form [your citizens] into companies, and send us 20,000 men tomorrow. No time can be lost in massing a force along the Susquehanna to defend the State, and your city. Arouse every man possible, and send them here."[4]

"*Here*" was Harrisburg. Marching men gathered throughout the streets of the Quaker State capital in response to Gov. Curtin's state-wide appeal for home-grown troops. Drum beats sounded "to arms!" Fifers whistled *Yankee Doodle,* remembering the patriots of 1776. Three companies of infantry formed uneven ranks within the State Capitol grounds, while nearby artillerymen practiced loading their polished cannon. Citizen soldiers from all parts of the state converged upon Harrisburg, responding to the governor's General Orders Number 35. "In view of the danger of invasion now threatening our State . . . it is deemed necessary to call upon all able-bodied men of Pennsylvania to organize immediately for the defense of the State, and be ready for marching orders upon one hour's notice."[5]

One hour's notice! From citizen to soldier. From home front to warfront. The governor called for 50,000 volunteer militiamen to rendezvous, bringing with them "the best arms they can secure," with each man carrying 60 rounds of ammunition. Would they come? "Everyone was whispering some dark forebodings in the ear of his neighbor," recalled a capital dweller. "'Pennsylvania is in danger!' The Rebels are coming on to Harrisburg!''[6] The governor's call solicited a remarkable response. "I met in [Harrisburg] the best men of the city," observed an out-of-town newspaper correspondent. "Merchants, lawyers, physicians, and all branches of profession, practicing the soldier." He witnessed determination, stoic seriousness, and "the light of battle upon their faces."[7]

East of the Pennsylvania capital, Philadelphia was also in a state of panic. America's second largest city believed its capture was "a favorite hope of the Rebels."[8] "The invasion of this Commonwealth has long been a proclaimed project of the Southern traitors," stated the *Philadelphia Inquirer,* "an infamous cause [for] devastating the farms of Pennsylvania and the warehouses and banks of Philadelphia."[9] The *Inquirer* righteously reasoned that Harrisburg was "of little importance," other than disrupting railroad traffic. *But Philadelphia — now she was a prize of war.* "Philadelphia is an object of intense desire to them," explained an editorial. The Rebels targeted the city "on account of the immense stores they would secure here, the damage they would inflict upon us, and the prestige which its occupation would give to their desperate cause."[10] Proof that Philadelphia was *the target* came with a Confederate announcement to dictate terms of peace in Independence Square. "We now know the worst."[11]

Philadelphia trembled at its woeful lack of military preparation. "We are lamentably deficient in the elements of self-protection," complained the *Inquirer*. No one expected the tentacles of civil war to grasp the birthplace of American independence. "In such an emergency what is our condition?" Not good. The city had no fortifications. No generals. No gunboats. No consolidated forces. No guns in position or plan of defense. "How is all of this to be remedied?" queried the press.[12] The *Inquirer* offered its own solution: Dust off a military engineer's study from the previous year and impress city workers to build fortifications. "The highway, water, gas, and other branches of the City Government have an immense body of laborers employed on works which, at a time such as this, are idle mockeries." The paper challenged the City Council to order the temporary discontinuance of all such works "and direct that hands employed should be transferred to the erection of defenses."[13]

Mayor Alexander Henry agreed something must be done. He declared, "The critical period of the war, as far as the safety of this city is concerned, is now upon us. . . . Much may depend on the amount of realization of the impending danger that exists on the part of our citizens."[14]

Several prominent citizens decided not to depend upon the local response. Presidents of Philadelphia's largest banks, worried about their deposits, appealed directly to the President of the United States. "In view of the inadequate organization of its local troops and the deficient means of defense against a hostile army . . . [we] earnestly entreat Your Excellency to create a military district of this city and the adjacent country, and to assign a general of known capacity to the command thereof, with instructions to adopt whatever measures of security may be needed in the present crises."[15] The calendar read September 11. Anxiously, the bankers awaited President Lincoln's response.

ABRAHAM LINCOLN HAD PROBLEMS more pressing than Philadelphia. Five hundred miles to the west, another U.S. city prepared for Rebel attack.

Cincinnati seemed shocked. September opened with the Queen City bustling with business, its steamboats transporting tons of trade up and down the wide Ohio River; and its iron-horse railroads blessed by a geographic nexus between East and West. Now Ohio's largest city was dormant, its stores shuttered, shopping suspended, and its factories closed. Within one week, Cincinnati had transformed from a modern metropolis into a gloomy and deserted place.

A Confederate army had lunged across east-central Kentucky, marching at unfathomed speed, catching Cincinnati and U.S. military authorities by surprise. Sirens sounded when the Rebels arrived within 20 miles of the city. Twenty miles was just one day's march. Nowhere had the enemy inched closer to a major U.S. urban area. Nowhere was a hub of U.S. trade and commerce in greater peril. Nowhere was a United States city in more danger.

Ohio Gov. David Tod issued an emergency proclamation: "Our Southern border is threatened with invasion. . . . [Have] all the loyal men in your counties at once form themselves into companies and regiments, to beat back the enemy."[16]

Into this dire situation arrived Union Gen. Lew Wallace. Eighteen years before he authored his best-selling novel *Ben-Hur*, Wallace was writing orders to save Cincinnati from the Confederates. His first words were not poetic, but portending. "[It] is but fair to inform the citizens that an active, daring and powerful enemy threatens them with every consequence of war."[17]

Reports circulated in the newspapers that the Confederates were determined to arrive in Cincinnati within the week. "They seemed all to be terribly earnest on this subject, and will, no

Abraham Lincoln
(Frank Leslie's Illustrated Newspaper)

doubt, fight most desperately for the possession of the city," claimed a recently released prisoner of war from Indiana. The soldier alleged the Rebels were destitute — "almost naked with the exception of a few rags and tatters" — and desperate for provisions and clothing. Warehouses were their inspiration, he said, and they would "be allowed to sack and plunder at will, when in their hands." He had heard both officers and privates grumbling that they were "completely tired of the war, and most heartily curs[ing] those who had plunged them into it." Yet the Confederates exhibited no hints of quitting. "They have been made to believe that the only way in which the matter can be settled is by the complete subjugation of the North."[18]

Gen. Wallace determined such subjugation would not happen at Cincinnati. Confronting the emergency, he issued instructions impressing the local inhabitants into fortification construction. "The labor ought to be one of love," Wallace contended. Love for your country; love for your city in its hour of peril. The no-nonsense general announced his policy. "The principle adopted is — citizens for the labor — soldiers for the battle."[19]

Not every resident was enamored with Wallace's edict. "None are exempt, from the millionaires to the beggars," revealed an onlooker. "This, of course, causes some little grumbling among the upper classes." Noting that even the rich were compelled to perform an equal share of the labor, the observer marveled: "Their threats and growls do no good; go they must. . . .They who, perhaps never worked before, must work now."[20]

To ensure maximum labor was available from the citizens, Gen. Wallace proclaimed martial law, and ordered every business in Cincinnati suspended and closed. Liquor establishments first were forced to lock their doors, and if any refused, "the stock on hand would be confiscated for sanitary purposes."[21] This action enraged "hundreds, almost thousands of dram drinkers and habitual loafers," and the German portion of the community became indignant that their "supply of lager was so suddenly cut short." Resistance was useless, however. Laggards were rounded up at police stations and hustled off to help construct the forts. Even the army's contractors spent every other day "digging for Uncle Samuel's benefit."[22]

With business suspended, soon every shop, store, and grocery was devoid of customers. Even the food markets were extin-

Lew Wallace, defender of Cincinnati. *(Frank Leslie's Illustrated Newspaper)*

The Confederates threaten Cincinnati, the largest city on the Ohio River. Mustering the Militia (top). Troops crossing over the Ohio to defend the city from Kentucky (middle). Citizens impressed to build fortifications (bottom). (*Frank Leslie's Illustrated Newspaper)*

guished. With doors closed and blinds down, it appeared contagious disease or epidemic had driven the citizens to seek some safe retreat. "Whole families began roaming the streets, with baskets on arms, trying to "buy, borrow, or beg the wherewith to sustain the inner man."[23]

As local citizens labored on a circle of fortifications, militiamen from throughout Ohio raced toward the Queen City. Volunteering for 30 days in response to their governor's urgent plea, they assembled as a special guard for the defense of Cincinnati. Each came carrying his own gun and accoutrements. Some arrived with rifles, others with shotguns; some came equipped with old-fashioned powder-horns and bullet pouches. "It strongly reminds some of the good old days of 1776, when men were gathered from the field and shop without being allowed time to bid farewell."[24] Many boasted they could kill a squirrel at 150 to 200 yards, and though entirely undisciplined in the face of a veteran Confederate army, they looked forward to testing their marksmanship behind the newly built fortifications. "You will no doubt hear a good account of the riflemen of Ohio," anticipated an impressed journalist.[25]

Pennsylvanians hoped to emulate the model of Cincinnati. "We see an illustration of what may be affected in a few days," the *Philadelphia Inquirer* wrote with admiration. "Lines of fortifications created, an army extemporized, and an entire city placed wholly on a war footing." The editor concluded the energetic and sudden action in Cincinnati was due to a sense of immediate danger. "The foe is at the door, and the household is alarmed. The work of the last few days is the out birth of near and imminent peril."

The *Inquirer* writer discovered "one of the latent reasons why we have allowed this Rebellion to linger so long. We have not thought ourselves to be in danger." Much had changed, indeed, since the final days of August, when "we saw only the skirts of the war cloud as it spread darkly over the distant sky. We would not believe that it was sailing slowly to our own zenith."[26]

Before day's end on September 11, proposed Confederate peace terms suddenly appeared in Northern newspapers. Sunset found citizens wondering what this portended. Was the country on the verge of permanent division? Were the flag's 34 stars soon to be reduced? Six days shy of the U.S. Constitution's 86th birthday, was it destined to become a political artifact? Were the opening words of its hallowed preamble about to face extinction?

We the People of the United States, in Order
to form a more perfect Union . . .

CHAPTER 2

Abraham's Abyss

The next sixty days will determine the question whether we are to maintain the supremacy of the Government, or whether the Rebellion will prevail.

—Parson William G. Brownlow, September 8, 1862

September started shamefully for President Lincoln's government.

Thousands of wounded United States soldiers suffered in Washington, their care limited, their limp bodies crammed into makeshift hospitals throughout the capital.

The Capitol building, with its half-finished dome dominating the city's skyline, had been transformed from a sanctuary of democracy into a sanatorium to prevent death. The rotunda, Senate and House halls, and corridors of the Capitol, had been converted into hospital wards with "cots and beds being placed in every available place."[27] No American ever envisioned the Capitol "admirably adapted for hospital wards," yet its large halls and passageways were "well ventilated, easily kept cool or heated, and well supplied with water."[28] Seats formerly occupied by U.S. Senators from the South — men who now headed the Confederate government or served as Confederate generals — served as stretchers for wounded U.S. soldiers. "Only two short years ago who would have thought such ever could have been the case."[29]

Work on the Capitol dome ceased. Construction crews traded their hammers and wrenches for rifles and bayonets, organizing into a temporary militia company to meet the emergency — protecting Washington from attack. Clerks from government departments and bureaus dropped their pens and papers and stuffed their hands with powder and bullets. Employees of the Interior Department elected their chief clerk their captain. The Census and Indian bureaus mustered 73 men apiece into the rank and file. The Auditor's Office of the Treasury Department offered a clerical corps, and a company of nearly 100 recruits in the Patent Office answered the urgent call. The bookbinders at the Government Printing Office began organizing for war, and the Office of the Postmaster General boasted 87 eager enrollees and 30 reserves. All totaled, nearly 1,800 clerks, organized into almost 20 military companies, left their government offices to prepare themselves for the battle to save Washington.[30]

Noticeably missing were volunteers from the War Department. They, understandably, were "so pressed by [their] current duties as to be unable to answer the call." In their place arrived an offer from a Washington-based patriotic organization: the veterans of the War of 1812. These wrinkled and grizzled 60-year-olds, who had fought the British 40 years previously, tendered their services to the War Department, where their "proffer was graciously received."[31]

Wall Street noticed the capital chaos, and it dampened the ardor of investors. "The nerves of Wall Street were considerably shocked by the alarming rumors," reported a market observer.[32] Uncertain traders whip-sawed stock prices up and down, depending upon the latest telegram that arrived in New York. Market specialists sensed an "unsettled feeling apparent among the operators."[33] All suspected "another great battle somewhere on the line of the Potomac as inevitable, and as upon the result hangs the most momentous issues."[34] Some stocks plummeted. Baltimore and Ohio Railroad stock caved 10 percent as sellers sensed danger from the proximity of the Confederate army. Gold prices also fluctuated, and Street insiders insisted movements in the precious metal "serve now, more completely than stocks, to indicate the momentary changes of public feeling."[35]

Washington's street scenes hardly inspired confidence. The provost marshal scurried about, impressing anything on wheels. "All available hacks, omnibuses and other vehicles, including express and store wagons, were pressed into the service of the government for public purposes." The principal public purpose was to convey thousands of wounded from the nearby battlefield of Manassas. Over 8,000 U.S. soldiers had been injured battling Robert E. Lee's Confederate army during the final three days of August, and the mass casualties overwhelmed the army's ambulances. Surgeons were inundated with the wounded, forcing Washington to plea for physicians. Trains loaded with doctors soon began arriving from New York, Pennsylvania, Massachusetts, Delaware, and Maryland. City police in nearby Baltimore began gathering names of persons who could assist in nursing the Washington wounded, tallying nearly 500 in one day.[36]

The Ladies' Soldiers' Relief Society of Washington worked day and night to prepare lint, bandages, and compresses. "They have made a good use of their linen sheets," noticed one observer. "Many ladies of the city have made liberal contributions from their private stores. In fact, the people of the District are acting nobly, and not a few men have volunteered as nurses."[37] Churches welcomed the wounded, and residents opened their homes. "Many citizens of Washington have taken convalescents from the hospitals to their houses, so that the wounded could fill their places."[38] The medical department identified one of the largest estates in the city, the palatial residence and grounds of banker W. W. Corcoran, as a location that could accommodate 500 hospital tents. Georgetown's seminary buildings became the recuperation point for officers.[39]

Trains brought thousands of worried family members into the city, who wandered Washington's streets searching for the hospitals of their beloved. Where was Jacob Leonard of the 21st New York, whose shoulder had been injured? Did James Davis of the 3rd Pennsylvania, whose arm had been amputated, reside here?

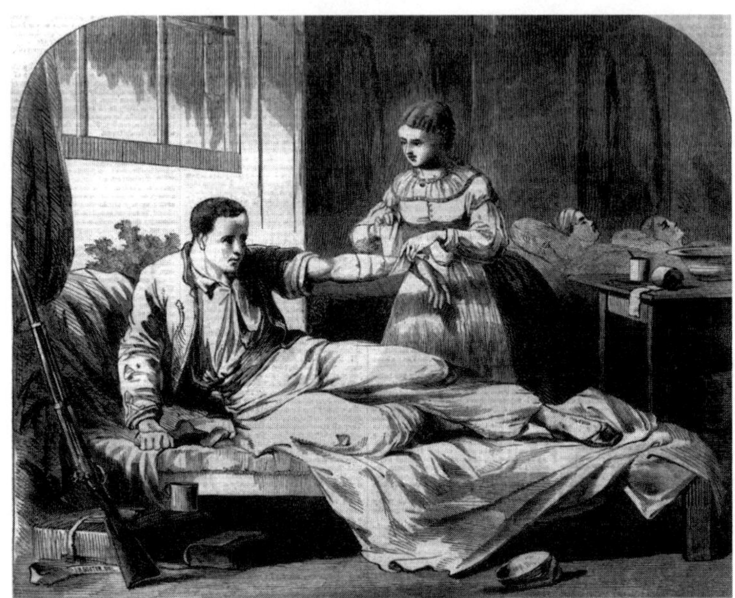

Women offered care in unprecedented numbers at Northern hospitals in Washington, Baltimore, and Philadelphia following Union defeats in the late summer of 1862. Previously, women nurses seldom were permitted to treat men due to strict Victorian mores. (*Harper's Weekly*)

Can you inform us of the location of Isaac Norrill of the 2nd Maine, who suffered a wound in the neck? Any idea where we can find Robert Fowler of the 25th Ohio, with a debilitated leg? On occasion, a newspaper announced the exact location of wounded soldiers. At Third and C Streets, where Isaac Newton and his wife resided, 14 soldiers from New York, Wisconsin, Ohio, Indiana, and Massachusetts were recovering, as identified in a brief notice in the *Philadelphia Inquirer*. Mostly, however, the Northern papers reported a daily ledger of casualties that included thousands of names in dozens of columns, with fates and locations unknown.[40]

At least the wounded still were breathing. Dead men — thousands of Abraham Lincoln's soldiers — filled battlefield graveyards and hospital cemeteries. Many of the corpses never returned home, moldering in mass graves in their tattered blue uniforms, without individual identification. Men with names became souls now "unknown." Regiments that had marched from their cheering communities 1,000 soldiers strong now limped along with fewer than 400 still standing. Battlefield casualties and malignant diseases had wiped out two-thirds of the muster rolls. Diarrhea, dysentery, tuberculosis, measles, and small pox had ravaged the ranks, killing more men than bullets. The war, projected to end in three months, now approached its 500th day, and Lincoln's army was running out of soldiers. Lieutenant John Mead Gould of Maine described the depreciation graphically: "a skeleton Corps, of skeleton Divisions, of skeleton Brigades, of skeleton Reg[imen]ts, of truly skeleton men."[41]

Bleak letters home became the norm. "I have set down to write you what to do if I should be so unfortunate as to fall on the field of battle," Lt. Col. Henry Barton Stone of the 5th Connecticut Infantry informed his wife. "If I am killed, I wish to have [my executor] settle my affairs, pay all my debts, and with the remainder buy a small place for you and the children, where you could live comparatively comfortable with the pension you would receive from the Government." Sensing a premonition, Stone explained. "You must not think strange that I write you thus, for it is my duty to you all; as it could not be done after I am killed." Then he calmly comforted his spouse. "Be of good cheer. If it should please the Lord to take me from you, He has promised to be the widow's God, and Father to the fatherless." Col. Stone concluded with a vision. "And if we meet no more on earth, I hope to meet in heaven, where there shall be no more wars, or rumors of war, and the weary are at rest." Stone was slain two weeks later, at a place named "Slaughter Mountain." His portending letter appeared in newspapers throughout the North.[42]

A mournful song that symbolized the war's relentless losses chorused in churches and parlors throughout the land. *The Vacant Chair* evoked the emptiness of the seat at the daily dinner table.

We shall meet but we shall miss him.
There will be one vacant chair.
We shall linger to caress him
While we breathe our ev'ning prayer.

When one year ago we gathered,
Joy was in his mild blue eye.
Now the golden cord is severed,
And our hopes in ruin lie.[43]

Despite the remorse, the depleted ranks of the army needed more men. President Lincoln called for 300,000 volunteers on July 1; but fearful of failure, the Congress adopted a measure never before employed in the United States — the draft. Many citizens considered this to be a usurpation of individual liberties and contrary to the Constitution. It appeared an act of desperation by a despotic administration. Men of drafting age began to run to escape registration. The Lincoln government reacted by imposing martial-law regulations that restricted travel from city to city or across state lines. The *London Times* mused that "the land of self-government and unlimited freedom is now ruled by a force that is creating terror." Referencing the draft, and comparing it to a type of Northern slavery, the British paper ironically perceived, "Involuntary servitude is now the lot of the white race."[44]

Commentary from the Mother Country was not the principal concern Abraham Lincoln faced from across the Atlantic. British and French leaders considered the United States so weakened by the war that they contemplated intervention, not with their armies or navies, but with their mediators. The *London Times* argued that "the North cannot conquer the South . . . and the time for compromise of some kind has arrived. . . . The worst settlement of the dispute cannot be so fatal as the continuance of the war." The *Times* drew an analogy between the frail position of England during the Revolutionary War and the uncertain future of the U.S., and exclaimed, "It is time the North followed the example of England."[45]

Such suggestions were anathema to President Lincoln. How dare the English! How could they consider the United States incapable of victory? Yet current evidence sided with the South. The Southern capital had been saved. The Southern army had defeated Lincoln's legions just outside of Washington. Southern offensives had kicked the Federals out of Virginia and Kentucky and much of Tennessee, and were threatening invasions of Ohio, Pennsylvania, and Maryland. "If such reverses do not teach the North to reconsider its course," opined the *London Times*, "we do not see how political wisdom can be learned or political error retrieved."[46]

Politics at home presented more of a problem for President Lincoln than politics from abroad. Election season had arrived, not for the Chief Executive, but for members of the U.S. House of Representatives. Here Lincoln's Republican Party held a majority, but now came the first large-scale election since the war had commenced. All knew it would be a referendum on the war. Democrats anxious for a return to power pointed to reverses on the battlefield as proof of Republican mismanagement and incompetence. Peace Democrats, derisively coined "Copperheads," campaigned aggressively on a platform of immediate negotiation, with some even advocating a cease fire. Important governorships and state legislatures, too, were facing voters — the local results crucial to Lincoln's ability to continue the war. Early results from Maine, the home state of Lincoln's vice president, did not herald hope. As votes were counted during the first week of September in the "I Lead" state, Lincoln's Republican allies saw their tallies diminished by thousands.[47]

Even the president saw signs of defeatism. Near the White House, a journalist spotted a regiment of U.S. cavalry "who presented the most miserable and outré appearance I ever witnessed. . . . In plain phrase, they were a disgrace to themselves and to the army." He described the men as "in want of uniformity of equipment," and sorry specimens of soldiers. "In the dirt and disarray of their uniforms and accoutrements, there were all the painful evidences of absence of discipline and of inefficiency." This absence of discipline particularly offended the observer. "There was hardly a man who did not lounge upon his horse instead of sitting on it; scarcely two who carried their sabers alike, and certainly not one who showed a decent presentable soldierly appearance." His diatribe continued with respect to the horses. "If the men looked bad, their horses were worse. Such a collection of spavined, half starved equines I never saw together before.

There was not an animal in the lot that would have sold at the horse market for ten dollars — the majority [was] only fit stock for a [residue] factory."

The analyst then identified a systematic problem. "As for the men whose appearance provoked these remarks, they must, in the dirt and disarray of uniform, and mounted upon such miserable animals, have lost their own respect and held their officers in contempt." He concluded by offering the army his advice: "Learning men to take pride in their appearance, and to present a neat soldierly appearance, may appear to be a very small thing, but it is the corner-stone of discipline and efficiency."[48]

Efficiency was not the army's present forte. "The men would have starved today had it not been for the sutlers," recorded Lieutenant John Mead Gould in his September 3rd diary entry. "We rec[eive]d no rations. Funny thing it is and very creditable to our Quartermaster's Department that we starve in sight of our Capitol."[49]

Weariness was another worry. Three consecutive days of fighting, followed by a fourth when the Confederates pursued the withdrawal from Manassas, had regressed into nerve-racking nighttime retreats, exacerbated by an untimely rainstorm and miserable mud — all conspiring to deprive the soldiers of sleep. Many marched despondently in the darkness, experiencing "confinement, privation, discomfort, and torture."[50] When orders finally arrived to "stack arms," Lieutenant Gould recalled his men "actually dropped as if shot and were instantly asleep. . . . Cold, hunger, and sore limbs were nothing." Gould exclaimed, "Sleep, sleep!" hypnotized the brain and body so much that he "didn't care if all creation fell into the hands of the Rebels."[51]

Fatigue further weakened the army's constitution. Chaos ensued in the ranks during the retreat from Manassas as tired men slowed, separated from their commands, and suddenly found themselves marching astride strangers. Confusion reigned. Where is my colonel? Where has my sergeant gone? Why can't I find my regimental flag? What's become of my mates? "The whole movement was in confusion," recounted a Baltimore correspondent. "Regiments were separated from their brigades, divisions lacking whole brigades, batteries straying from the commands to which they were attached, cavalry cutting columns in two, and making no end of mischief in all directions." He concluded, "No circumstances could have made such a march — a retreat from a Rebel army upon the capital — anything but gloomy."[52]

Many soldiers simply dropped by the roadside during the retreat, no longer able to continue. This brought them disparagement and discouragement. Branded as "stragglers," they were chastised as weak and ill-disciplined, regardless of their physical exhaustion. Some stragglers had reputations of immoral hellions, charged with battlefield cowardice or laziness, but these were the minority. Most simply were lost. "Large crowds of stragglers continually line the roads in the rear of our army," revealed one observer. "The sidewalks, stoops and yards of houses in [Washington] and its neighborhood being filled with them every night."[53] This produced a most negative impression. A writer with the *New York Post* labeled straggling "an evil so great that it most dangerously affects the very safety of the army." The reporter directed his blame, however, not at the stragglers, but at its root cause: the army's absentee officers.[54]

Officers in the all-volunteer army often considered themselves privileged, and often came from privilege. Most officers in the Union ranks were not West Point graduates, and most had no previous military experience. Town mayors now were leading infantry companies. Local bankers, who purchased uniforms for neighborhood patriots, now commanded regiments. Fire chiefs and police chiefs now had commissions in the army. Most were dedicated to the war effort, but many resisted or ignored the discipline necessary in their novel martial roles.

"If we want to succeed in the field, we must have strict discipline in our armies," opined the *New York Post*. "Our soldiers are brave, and the majority of them fight well; but they fight under the most serious disadvantages." Disadvantage number one was an ill-disciplined officer corps. "The first evil which the Government and the people must unite to check at once is the absenteeism of officers," declared the *Post*. The paper proclaimed (with purposeful exaggeration) that one-half to three-quarters of officers during the recent campaign were missing, "being at home, at watering places, or elsewhere taking their ease." The writer complained that colonels "only reappeared to take charge when the wreck of their commands returned" to the capital's defenses. The newspaper further charged that brigadier generals were "leaving their brigades in the very face of the enemy, and wandering off unblushingly to enjoy themselves." Nowhere did the *Post* name names; nowhere did it identify culprits. But it did yield a prediction: "We cannot expect to beat an enemy drilled to perfection, zealous and strictly disciplined, while such laxness is permitted in our own army."[55]

A Maryland newspaper confirmed the problem. "The multitude of men wearing shoulder-straps now in this city [Washington] is somewhat astonishing," reported the *Baltimore American and Commercial Advertiser*. "There are companies of Brigadier Generals, regiments of Colonels and Majors, and a good-sized division of Captains and Lieutenants. They swarm everywhere." The Baltimore critic, while strolling down a Washington avenue, conducted his own officer census. "One man out of every three you meet wears shoulder-straps, and in the corridors, public rooms, and billiard saloons of the hotels their number is still more preponder[ant]." Considering the army's recent defeat —- and the capital's uncertain future — the Baltimore writer concluded: "I cannot but think there is something both wrong and disgraceful in this. . . . Certainly this is not one of those halcyon periods when officers can justify idling their time away in the cities."[56]

DESPITE THE BAD APPEARANCE in Washington, and the certain hyperbole of the news reporters, the majority of officers had remained with their ranks and had fought bravely with their men at Manassas. But they had their own burrs. Officers began complaining, loudly and publicly, that they and their army were victims of incompetent commanding generals.

Abraham Lincoln had expected victory when he appointed Maj. Gen. John Pope as commander of the newly organized U.S. "Army of Virginia" back in July 1862. The elevation of Pope inaugurated a new strategy for the president. He would advance two armies against Richmond from two different directions. Pope's army would move toward Richmond through northern and central Virginia; the second would thrust forward from the east, via the river approaches to the Confederate capital. This "pincer" movement would entrap Richmond between the jaws of two powerful armies, forcing a speedy collapse of the Confederacy.

Robert E. Lee had wrecked Lincoln's plans. The Confederate chieftain outmaneuvered, out-generaled, and outfought his adversaries in just eight weeks; by September 1, his victorious army crouched menacingly within a day's march of Washington. Lee's feats were remarkable — one of the most exceptional turnabouts in world military history — but he received a significant assist through the incompetence, insubordination, and infighting of Lincoln's generals.

"I must ask to be relieved, unless General Pope is removed," uttered an unidentified general to a Baltimore correspondent during the retreat from Manassas to Washington. "I cannot see my men murdered." Carl Schurz, who commanded a division in the battle and who did not remain anonymous, said: "I have lost a thousand men. I dare not go to the hospital and look in the faces of those wounded men, who, I know, have shed their blood bravely and in vain."

Maj. Gen. John Pope was disgraced at September's outset, leaving President Lincoln without a general in command. (*Frank Leslie's Illustrated Newspaper*)

Vanity was Pope's principal flaw. He acted as the antithesis to Lincoln's humility. Blinded by his ambition, Pope displayed his weakness to his men. But they practiced patience and gave him a chance. Then Pope's arrogance, his certainty, and his self-righteousness brought disaster at Manassas. "There was mismanagement everywhere, because at headquarters there was incompetence, confusion, no settled plans, no head." The soldiers found solidarity in their anger. "The army was not so much disheartened as enraged — willing to fight, but not willing to be sacrificed — denouncing, with a unanimity that had no exception, the incapacity which had caused their defeat."[57]

Pope ignited his own demolition. He ignored evident dangers, though his men sensed trouble. When the Confederates reached his rear, he refused to believe it. When they massed in his front, Pope refused to accept it. When the Rebels commandeered his flank, he failed to see it. When subordinates offered their advice, he declined to accept it. Pope never understood that an army was more than himself. His mishap at Manassas destroyed the tentative trust and faith his own army had offered him. "Half the strength of an army is confidence in its commander," remarked a sage columnist. "That confidence is not given to General Pope. The opinion of his troops is unanimously against him." Pope's future was hopeless. "There is no dissent or disagreement," observed the critic. "They will not, cannot, fight again under Pope with confidence. The Army of Virginia demands a general."[58]

Abraham Lincoln determined the generals. Considering the consternation caused by Pope and his humiliation of an entire army, some began questioning the president's sense of character and his judgment of military leaders. "The latest experiment in generalship is the most immediate and disastrous failure," wrote a Baltimore editor. "Once more the National army gather[s] about the National Capital, and the defense of Washington is the strategic signal of the [war]."[59]

A dead captain influenced opinions on Pope, more so than any critic. Captain Thorton Brodhead of the 13th Massachusetts Infantry, whose last letter to his family circulated on front pages and editorial sections in newspapers throughout the North, pleaded for Pope's eviction.

Dictated on the Manassas battlefield, just before he expired, he cried for a competent general. "I have fought manfully, and now die fearlessly," he announced to his brother and sister. "I am one of the victims of Pope's imbecility. . . . Tell the President would he save the country he must not give our hallowed flag into such hands." His words then swelled. "But *the old flag* will triumph yet. The soldiers will re-gild its folds, now polluted by imbecility and treason." He then made his final request to his brother. "John, you owe a debt to your country. Write! Show up Pope's incompetency and [other generals'] infamy, and force them from places where they can send brave men to assured destruction. I had hoped to live longer, but I die amid the clangor of battle, as I could wish."[60]

PUBLIC CHARGES OF A GENERAL'S incompetency and imbecility, combined with the stinging defeat of Manassas and the ignominious retreat to the capital, tormented and taunted Lincoln's leadership. Complicating matters for the president, Gen. Pope — now ensconced safely behind the defenses of Washington during the first week of September — refused to accept blame for the Manassas disaster. No! The fault was not his. The cause: *treason by Gen. McClellan*.

President Lincoln had selected Maj. Gen. George Brinton McClellan as general in chief of all United States armies during the fall of 1861. Fashioned as a "Young Napoleon," McClellan had finished second in his West Point class of 1846, and had shined during the Mexican War as one of Robert E. Lee's brightest military engineers.

Now Lee and McClellan, both proud Americans, were fighting for opposing countries. Lincoln charged McClellan with the capture of Richmond; Lee prevented his success. Frustrated by McClellan's failure, Lincoln ordered "Little Mac's" Army of the Potomac back to Washington in August 1862, to assist Pope with his offensive operations. McClellan became a general without an army. He was incensed. Feeling spurned, ignored, and unappreciated by the president, McClellan pouted over Pope. To the president, he acted indignant, irreverent, and even insubordinate.

Maj. Gen. George B. McClellan was selected by President Lincoln to lead the army despite opposition from his cabinet and McClellan's controversial past. (*Harper's Weekly*)

Referring to Lincoln often as "the original guerilla" and "an old stick," McClellan privately denigrated the president in letters to his wife and closest advisors. "What a specimen to be at the head of our affairs now!" McClellan scoffed. He considered Lincoln of inferior intelligence, a mindless meddler, and inept at grasping military matters. "He really seems quite incapable of rising to the height of the merits of the question & the magnitude of the crisis."

McClellan even personalized his disdain for the president. "I can never regard him with other feelings than those of contempt — for his mind, heart & morality."

McClellan's epithets extended to Lincoln's cabinet as well. "I have lost all regard & respect for the majority of the Administration, & doubt the propriety of my brave men's blood being spilled to further the designs of such a set of heartless villains." He believed the president and his men had done "all that cowardice, folly & rascality can do to ruin our poor country — & the blind people seem not to see it, but to submit like serfs to the lash." Some McClellan supporters even encouraged an overthrow. "I have commenced receiving letters from the North urging me to march on Washington and assume the Govt!!"[61]

Rumors circulated throughout Washington that a moping McClellan had sabotaged Pope's Manassas operation, purposely slowing reinforcements to Pope to ensure his defeat and to strike back at the president for taking away *his* army. Circumstantial evidence indicated that McClellan's officers moved lackadaisically to the battlefield, and responded slowly to Pope's orders once upon the field. Some professed that McClellan conspired to destroy Pope, thus to regain his reputation and compel Lincoln to return him to command.

The president's cabinet conspired, meanwhile, to prevent McClellan from ever again resuming command of any army anywhere. The Secretary of War and Attorney General prepared a petition for the president, signed by most cabinet members, declaring McClellan treacherous, dangerous to the country, and impossible to trust. "It was evident there was a fixed determination to remove, and if possible to disgrace, McClellan," wrote Secretary of the Navy Gideon Welles in his diary on September 1. He noted that Treasury Secretary Salmon P. Chase "deliberately believed McClellan ought to be shot, and should, were he President, be brought to summary punishment."[62]

McClellan had sensed for weeks the mounting Cabinet plot against him. "I am satisfied the dolts in Washington are bent on my destruction," Little Mac complained to his wife. "The more I hear of their wickedness the more am I surprised that such a wretched set are permitted to *live* much less to occupy the positions they do."[63]

Anxiety rocked the Cabinet as it awaited the president's arrival on September 2. Washington and the country faced imminent danger. The army was in shambles. "The army has no head," recorded Navy Secretary Welles. Pope, without consultation or advice, was falling back, retreating within Washington's entrenchments. "No one seems to have had any knowledge of his movements, or plans, if he had any," wrote Welles. The next Confederate move portended invasion of the North — unimaginable only a few short weeks ago. No previous Cabinet gathering during the war faced such a foreboding future.

As the members quietly discussed the petition to dismiss McClellan, Welles noted that the Cabinet agreed Pope had been a failure, but there was "a belief and admission on all hands that he ha[d] not been seconded and sustained as he should have been by McClellan." Welles concluded, "Personal jealousies and professional rivalries, the bane and curse of all armies, have entered deeply into ours."[64]

The president soon appeared. Lincoln apologized for his tardiness. He explained he had been at the War Department seeking the latest intelligence. Then the unthinkable occurred.

The Commander in Chief announced that he had placed McClellan in command of all troops within the fortifications of Washington.

The Cabinet was shocked.

"This seemed to me equivalent to making [McClellan] Commander-in-Chief," recorded Treasury Secretary Salmon Chase. "I could not but feel that giving the command to him was equivalent to giving Washington to the rebels."[65]

The president attempted to explain. Practicing pragmatism rather than politics, and ignoring for the moment McClellan's machinations and foibles, Lincoln expressed his belief that McClellan could defend the capital better than any other man. He cited McClellan's advantages. He knew the whole ground about Washington; he helped layout the defenses; his specialty is to defend — *he can be trusted* to act on the defensive. Organization was another skill. In the wake of the Manassas debacle, the army about Washington was demoralized, polarized, and disorganized.

Lincoln believed McClellan could lift morale, unite factions, and bring order out of chaos. "Though deficient in the positive qualities which are necessary for an energetic command," Lincoln determined McClellan's "organizing powers could be made temporarily available till the troops were rallied."[66]

"It would prove a national calamity," retorted Secretary Chase.[67]

Since Lincoln had made his decision independent of his cabinet, much discussion ensued. "There was a more disturbed and desponding feeling than I ever witnessed in council," observed Secretary Welles. The president said "it distressed him exceedingly, to find himself differing on such a point," but he could identify no one who could perform the momentary mission of defending the capital better than McClellan.[68] The decision was final.

"A terrible and thankless task" was how Gen. McClellan labeled his new assignment. Still smarting from embarrassment, and still scornful of the president, McClellan assumed his new job "reluctantly." "I only consent to take it for my country's sake and with the humble hope that God has called me to it."[69]

Lincoln, seeking his own Divine guidance, prepared to receive a delegation representing God.

CHAPTER 3

Slavery's Shackles

We have got, North as well as South, to unlearn this silly, unchristian nonsense. It is our destiny, in the world's progress, to show that an educated and humane people can rise superior to prejudices.

— *Harper's Weekly,* June 28, 1862

Not since the commencement of the war did the future of the Union appear more doubtful. Robert E. Lee had marched a portion of his Confederate army nearly to the Mason-Dixon Line, preparing to invade Pennsylvania. Secession's tidal wave had reached a crest not previously achieved — or imagined. Invasion of the North's second most populous state seemed imminent.

Considering the Confederate Stars and Bars were about to be planted upon Pennsylvania's soil, it did not seem the opportune time to discuss the eradication of slavery from Southern soil. Yet the ecumenical Christian ministers arrived in Washington on September 11 determined to present an "emancipation memorial" to President Lincoln.

They waited two days before Lincoln could meet with them at the White House. Despite his multitude of worries on multiple military fronts, the president greeted the clergy with courtesy and attention. The ministers acknowledged their timing was inauspicious, "in view of recent disasters which make the authority of the

Government over the Slave States less extensive and influential than before." But the pastors believed these reverses were "tokens of divine displeasure," requiring the president and the country to immediately emancipate four million slaves as "repentance for the sin of oppression."[70]

The president listened patiently. A recorder for the clergy kept notes, closely documenting Lincoln's words. "The subject presented in the memorial is one upon which I have thought much for weeks past, and I may even say for months," Lincoln opened. "I am approached with the most opposite opinions and advice, and that by religious men, who are equally certain that they represent the Divine will."

Regarding Divine intervention, Lincoln expressed a wish. "I hope it will not be irreverent for me to say that if it is probable that God would reveal his will to others, on a point so connected with my duty, it might be supposed he would reveal it directly to me." The discussion lasted for more than one hour, with frank interchange of questions and replies. "What good would a proclamation of emancipation from me do, especially as we are now situated?" the pragmatic Lincoln asked. "I do not want to issue a document that the whole world will see must necessarily be inoperative. . . . Would my word free the slaves, when I cannot even enforce the Constitution in the Rebel States?"[71]

The ministers did not relent. Emancipation would withdraw slaves from the Rebels, leaving them without laborers. Emancipation would secure the sympathy of Europe and the civilized world. "No other step would be so potent to prevent foreign intervention." Emancipation would "send a thrill through the entire North, firing every patriotic heart, giving the people a glorious principle for which to suffer and to fight."[72]

The president, returning to his lawyer instincts, rejoined throughout the discourse. "I admit that slavery is the root of the rebellion . . . I will also concede that emancipation would help us in Europe . . . I grant, further, that it would help somewhat at the North, though not so much, I fear, as you and those you represent imagine. . . . It would weaken the Rebels by drawing off their laborers, which is of great importance."

Lincoln refused to yield, however, on the ministers' immediate demand for emancipation. "Understand, I raise no objection against it on legal or constitutional grounds; for, as commander-in-chief of the army and navy, in time of war I suppose I have a right to take any measure which may best subdue the enemy." Timing, not philosophy, was the president's issue. First he must vanquish the Confederate invaders. "I think you should admit," Lincoln counseled the ministers, "that we already have an important principle to rally and unite the people, in the fact that constitutional government is at stake."[73]

The Chicago clergy prepared for departure with no affirmative from the president. They did have reason for hope, however. "I have not decided against a proclamation of liberty to the slaves," concluded Lincoln, "but hold the matter under advisement; and I can assure you that the subject is on my mind, by day and night, more than any other. Whatever shall appear to be God's will, I will do."[74]

The church's representatives were not the only powers exerting influence on the president's emancipation dilemma. Newspaper editors had been thundering their own positions — the most vociferous volumes echoing from New York. Journals that embraced the Democratic Party decried emancipation as radical, diabolical, and even unconstitutional. They denounced any proposition that the war's purpose was to end slavery. Republican papers countered that abolition had matured as a just and righteous cause, with the war offering the best opportunity for slavery's eradication.

Leading the Republican editors' chorus was Horace Greeley, oracle and tycoon of the *New York Tribune.* Greeley's paper was the largest in the country, boasting a circulation of 200,000 subscribers. His influence was so weighty that Ralph Waldo Emerson crowned him "the right spiritual father of this region," who did "everyone's thinking and theory for them, for two dollars a year."[75]

Three weeks prior to the ministers' meeting in Washington, Greeley became enraged. Tired of Lincoln's perceived procrastination on emancipation, he stammered into a tirade. Entitling his August 19 piece "The Prayer of the Twenty Millions," Greeley pontificated on behalf of the Northern population. Lincoln loyalists were "sorely disappointed and deeply pained by the policy you seem to be pursuing with regard to the slaves of the Rebels," Greeley wrote in his 2,200 word diatribe. "We complain that the Union cause has suffered, and is now suffering immensely, from the mistaken deference to Rebel Slavery. . . .

"On the face of this wide earth, Mr. President, there is not one disinterested, determined, intelligent champion of the Union cause who does not feel that all attempts to put down the Rebellion and at the same time uphold its inciting cause are preposterous and futile." Greeley summarized his feelings with certainty. "Every hour of deference to Slavery is an hour of added and deepened peril to the Union."[76]

Stung by the censure of his friend, and aware of his vast influence, Lincoln had to respond — and quickly. Three days after Greeley's newspaper challenge, Lincoln crafted his own letter for the *Tribune* on August 22. "As to the policy 'I seem to be pursuing,' as you say, I have not meant to leave any one in doubt," proffered the president. "My paramount object in this struggle is to save the Union, and is not either to save or destroy slavery. If I could save the Union without freeing any slave, I would do it; and if I could save it by freeing all the slaves, I would do it; and if I could do it by freeing some and leaving others alone, I would also do that." The president emphasized his theme: "What I do about slavery and the colored race, I do because I believe it helps to save this Union."[77]

SLAVERY HAD DOMINATED Abraham Lincoln's political life for years.

Famous for his oration from the Illinois capital in 1858 — *A house divided against itself cannot stand. I believe this government cannot endure permanently half-slave and half-free* — his antebellum debates on the subject had gained him national notoriety.[78]

Lincoln rose rapidly in the nascent Republican Party, catapulted into the presidency in the divisive election of 1860. Southerners considered Lincoln and the Republicans hazardous to their slave-labor economy and caste-system culture — so dangerous,

"Am I not a Man and a brother?" Abolitionist pressures to end slavery intensified on President Lincoln during the summer of 1862. *(Library of Congress)*

in fact, that they severed their states from the Union. Declaring independence from assumed abolitionist despots who threatened their lives and their property, the South created its own nation — the Confederate States of America.

Southern hyperbole branded Lincoln an abolitionist. He was not. Lincoln, indeed, railed against the extension of slavery into new states or U.S. territories, but he vowed not to interfere with slavery where it existed. The president reinforced his conservative position at his 1861 inauguration. But months of bloody, inconclusive civil war had modified Lincoln's views. To win the war, he determined emancipation had become a military necessity. Victory may be delayed on the battlefield, but Lincoln understood that ending slavery would wreck the Southern economy, deprive the South of labor, destroy Southern wealth — and eventually collapse the Confederacy.

Freedom presented its own problems, however. Freedom did not erase racism. Lincoln grappled with a distressing question. What were the social consequences of widespread emancipation?

Prejudice prevailed, North and South, against persons of African descent. "Our weakness, in our present national childhood, is not to be able to tolerate negroes, except as slaves," exclaimed the editor of *Harper's Weekly*, a popular Northern journal. "We can't bear them. We don't want them in our houses. We won't meet them in public assemblages, or concede to them any rights whatsoever, except the bare right of living and working for us, sometimes for wages, generally without."[79]

Examples of prejudice abounded, even for freedmen living in the North. Black waiters in New York City were "in a state of perturbation" during the first week of September, horrified to learn that saloon and eating-house owners resolved "to turn them out of their situations and fill their places with white men." In Philadelphia, the country's second largest city, the railway system postponed a resolution allowing blacks within the passenger cars, resulting in the stoppage of a city train because the passengers "refused to ride with a negro who had entered the vehicle." In celebrated Independence Square, birthplace of the Declaration of Independence and the Constitution, a black man was assaulted "by a large number of boys and driven into the street" for reasons unknown. Even in the nation's capital, U.S. soldiers from the 61st Pennsylvania Infantry preyed on the corner of Seventh and M Streets, assaulting "such colored men as came in their way, having [as] pretext . . . difficulty with a negro peddler." When police and the provost guard arrived to break up the thugs, residents in the neighborhood were induced to "close their doors and windows for the time."[80]

The prospect of racial amalgamation horrified many Northerners as much as it did the South. In the capital of Pennsylvania, white and black boys playing on street corners were "practically carrying out the Abolition doctrine of perfect equality between the races." "We wonder that parents do not interpose to correct an evil so demoralizing to the rising generation," grumbled the *Harrisburg Patriot and Union*. "The juvenile admixture of blacks and whites of which we now complain may hereafter increase them to such a degree as to disgrace the community and deteriorate the race!" The paper concluded with this salvo: "Let it not be forgotten that ours is a Government, of white people, and that all inter-mixture with inferior races degrades our own, producing a motley rabble unfit for self-government."[81]

President Lincoln's postmaster general represented this widely accepted proposition with respect to the races. "The rebellion is waged not so much in the interest of slavery as from the innate horror with which the whites regard the black race, and their determination not to be placed on equality with them," Postmaster Montgomery Blair of Maryland argued. "This feeling is not confined to the Southern States. The Constitutional Convention of the State of Illinois, following the example of Indiana, prohibits negro immigration within the borders of the State. The white people of the United States will not live side by side with black men as their equals."[82]

Labor fears also fueled racism in the North. Irish and German immigrants, most of them newly arrived or first generation Americans, believed abolition would increase competition for their jobs and lower their wages. When a group of nearly 100 runaway slaves arrived in Philadelphia in the spring of 1862, enticed by employment opportunities at the arsenal and naval yards, a correspondent for the *New York Herald* recorded the reaction. "Here, now, we have a practical demonstration of the effect of the efforts of the insane abolitionists to free the negroes." The writer then identified the effect. "As these blacks are willing to work cheaper than white men, our white laborers will, as a matter of course, be thrown out of employment. . . . Pennsylvania being a border state, we will get more than our share and may expect to suffer more than others."[83]

The Democratic Party appealed to the laboring classes frightened by the presence of blacks. Most Democrats favored "letting these negroes remain in the South and earn(ing) their living on the plantations where they have been reared." "We do not want them here," exclaimed Democrats, "to throw our white laboring population out of employment, to steal from our farmers and to fill our Poor Houses and Prisons. We have as many colored people here as we need."[84]

White leaders perceived two futures for race relations if slavery were abolished — permanent apartheid, or amalgamation of the two races. Abraham Lincoln adopted a third option: "colonization."

Colonization espoused the voluntary removal of people of African descent from America and returning them to Africa. The American Colonization Society, established in 1816, had created the nation of Liberia on the African continent and had populated the new country with several thousand African-American descendants. Lincoln had embraced this doctrine as a reasonable way of dealing with the institution of slavery, influenced to this position by his "ideal of a great man," U.S. Congressman and Senator Henry Clay of Kentucky. In his eulogy to Clay in Springfield in 1852, Lincoln declared: "This suggestion of the possible redemption of the African race and the African continent was made 25 years ago. Every succeeding year has added to the hope of its realization. May it indeed be realized!"[85]

Ten years later, amidst the rumblings of emancipation and the depths of civil war, President Lincoln continued to believe that colonization was the answer to the racial conundrum. The president invited a delegation of free black men to the White House in mid-August 1862, after Congress had appropriated $100,000 for the purpose of colonization. Lincoln sought their support for a scheme he believed more humane and less harmful than the racism of America.

He opened his gathering with questions: Why should the people of the black race be colonized, and where? Why should they leave this country? The president, in substance, then responded to his own queries. "Your race [is] suffering, in my judgment, the greatest wrong inflicted on any people. But even when you cease to be slaves, you are yet far removed from being placed on an equality with the white race. . . . The aspiration of men is to enjoy equality with the best when free, but on this broad continent not a single man of your race is made the equal of a single man of ours." Lincoln abjectly concluded: "I repeat, without the institution of slavery and the colored race as a basis, the war could not have an existence. It is better for us both, therefore, to be separated."

The pragmatic Lincoln had no earthly idea how to remove more than four million human beings from the North American continent. But he wanted to adopt the experiment. "The practical thing I want to ascertain is whether I can get a number of able-bodied men, with their wives and children, who are willing to go." Lincoln first requested 100 "tolerably intelligent men" with their families, but he would be satisfied with 50, even as few as 25. "I want you to let me know whether this can be done or not."[86]

Less than a month later, on September 11, the president issued a contract to establish a colony of American blacks, not in Africa, but in northwestern Panama. Central America had been substituted for Africa to reduce ocean vessel time and to take advantage of coal fields, harbors, and the prospect of future transportation routes across the isthmus. Sen. Samuel Pomeroy of Kansas, a like-minded champion of colonization, agreed to personally escort the expedition. He rushed to New York with the president's endorsement to obtain a ship for the venture, expecting to sail in October with more than 500 voluntary "colonists" aboard.[87] The president's plan did not generate a good public response. "We think the future historian of the period in which we live will be somewhat embarrassed to decide which was the more insane — the conspiracy of [Confederate President] Jeff Davis to divide the Union, or the efforts of the loyal Government to . . . get rid of the negroes as speedily as possible, and at whatever cost."[88]

RELOCATION COSTS concerned the president, but even more troubling was the escalating price of the war itself. By the summer of 1862, the war siphoned $2 million per day from the U.S. Treasury. The country had become a debtor nation, with more accumulated debt than at any time in its history. To reduce future debt burdens, and hopefully shorten the war, Lincoln conceived an audacious plan — the government would purchase slaves in the Border States. By compensating slave owners, then emancipating the enslaved, Lincoln believed he could sever these states from the economic noose of slave labor and strengthen their ties with the Union. He theorized this would isolate and hasten the demise of the rebellion, constricting the Confederacy to the Deep South, and ultimately strangling it.

The president summoned Congressional members from Maryland, Kentucky, Missouri, Delaware, and loyalists from Virginia and Tennessee to the White House on July 12 to pitch his plan.

It had been on the table since March, but had generated little interest. Employing his persuasion, Lincoln claimed his compensated-emancipation plan as "one of the most potent and swift means of ending" the war. "Let the States which are in rebellion see definitely and certainly that in no event will the States you represent ever join their proposed confederacy, and they cannot much longer maintain the contest." Then Lincoln preached practical economics. "How much better for you as seller, and the nation as buyer, to sell out and buy out that without which the war could never have been."

The meeting ended with the president requesting that the representatives present his plan to their respective states, with this reminder: "I do not speak of emancipation at once, but of a decision at once to emancipate gradually."[89]

Lincoln anxiously awaited their response. How could they resist such a prudent offer? By the president's estimates, less than half a day's cost of the war would pay for all the slaves in Delaware at $400 per slave. Only 87 days of war would, at the same price, pay for all of the slaves in Delaware, Maryland, Kentucky, Missouri, and the District of Columbia.[90] The president had warned the members to give his plan careful consideration. "If the war continues long," he predicted, "the [slave] institution in your States will be extinguished by mere friction and abrasion — by the mere incidents of the war. It will be gone, and you will have nothing valuable in lieu of it."[91]

The response deeply disappointed the president. Twenty out of 28 Border State congressional members refused to pursue the idea. They cited numerous reasons. First, it proposed "a radical change of our social system." Championing states rights, "it seemed like an interference, by this government, with a question which peculiarly and exclusively belonged to our respective States." Many doubted "the constitutional power of this government to make appropriations" to purchase slaves. All thought "our finances were in no condition to bear the immense outlay" from the Treasury. They did not feel justified in adopting a measure that would add a "vast amount to our public debt, at a moment when the Treasury was reeling under the enormous expenditures of the war."

On slavery, the members were adamant. "The right to hold slaves is a right appertaining to all the States of this Union. They have the right to cherish or abolish the institution as their tastes or their interests may prompt, and no one is authorized to question the right, or limit its enjoyment."[92]

Not all agreed with this majority expression. Sen. J. B. Henderson of Missouri complained bitterly about the intransigence. "The Border States, so far, are the chief sufferers by this war," he argued. "Our states are the battlefields. Our people, divided among themselves, maddened by the struggle and blinded by the smoke of battle, invited upon our soil contending armies — the one to destroy the Government, the other to maintain it. The consequence to us is plain. The shock of the contest upturns society and desolates the land."

But the senator saved his ire for his fellow congressional members who placed selfish interest above the public's interest. "In this period of the nation's distress, I know of no human institution too sacred for discussion; no material interest belonging to the citizen that he should not willingly place upon the altar of his country, if demanded by the public good. The man who cannot now sacrifice party and put aside selfish considerations is more than half disloyal."[93]

As the plan for compensation failed, the idea of *confiscation* soared. Since slaves legally were defined as property, seizure of slaves from rebellious slave owners was considered a justifiable act of war. Confiscation of slaves as property not only shattered the investment of slave owners, but it destabilized market values for slaves, reducing Southern wealth dramatically. In addition to this attack on personal capital, confiscation of slaves removed the principal source of labor from the Southern economy, thus making its agricultural basis unstable. Confiscation, in short, threatened to ruin the South's primary means of generating wealth.

Confiscation came in three forms: seizure, capture, or extrication. Seizure occurred when U.S. troops precipitated the action, such as collecting and removing the enslaved from a known Rebel sympathizer. Capture happened when Union troops occupied an area previously held by Rebel forces. Extrication occurred when slaves seeking freedom initiated the move — literally deporting themselves from their places of bondage — then migrating to safe shelters behind Federal lines, whereupon the U.S. government guaranteed they would not be returned to captivity (hence confiscation).

Congress adopted two Confiscation Acts to legitimize these practices. Neither applied only to slave property, but "any property of whatsoever kind or description" belonging to Rebels "aiding, abetting, or promoting such insurrection or resistance" to the United States.

In the first act (August 1861), confiscation did not equate to freedom. The law still defined the slave as property — but ownership shifted from the slave holder to the government of the United States. This was a peculiar position indeed, creating a new term in the English language — "contraband" — meaning an escaped slave shielded by the Union army, now owned by and protected by the United States government.

The second act (July 1862) defined any former slave under U.S. control as "captives of war" and forfeited Rebel property, but it granted these former slaves the dignity of freedom — they "shall be forever free of their servitude, and not again held as slaves."[94]

Neither Confiscation Act freed enslaved persons throughout the South. Both applied only to former slaves ensconced behind Union lines or under Federal control. Thus, most slaves remained in bondage. In addition, President Lincoln did not urge aggressive enforcement of the numerous property seizure provisions in the Second Confiscation Act. He desired his armies to win battlefield victories and not be distracted by property roundups. Lincoln's lackluster enforcement led to editor Horace Greeley's volcanic eruption in "The Prayer of the Twenty Millions."

Yet, the president realized momentum, slowly and steadily, was building toward emancipation. "It is known, probably, to nine out of ten slaves in the South that every Slave State now contains a safe refuge whither fugitives can fly for emancipation, and where no overseer or blood hound can follow them," observed *Harper's Weekly*. "Neither the rifle or the stake can expel from the mind of the slave the knowledge that freedom is near him, and that he can obtain it when he chooses to make the effort."[95]

Thousands did make the effort — and not just in the Deep South.

Harpers Ferry, Virginia, served as a magnet for slaves seeking freedom. Located at the confluence of the Potomac and Shenandoah rivers, and at the northern mouth of the fertile Shenandoah Valley, an estimated 5,000 contrabands had collected at the Ferry during the hot, dry summer of 1862. This nearly doubled the community's population during the antebellum period.

"Poor bedraggled, foot-sore wretches" suddenly would appear in front of Federal pickets "in the gray of the morning, having walked ten or fifteen miles during the night — frequently a woman, carrying a baby, and with little children clinging to her skirts," recalled the regimental historian of the 22nd New York State Militia. "The men carried their few possessions in a big bundle, tied to a stick, and the women usually 'toted' a roll of bedding. . . . How they lived was a mystery," he marveled. "They crowded the empty houses, and overran the camp, washing clothes, selling pastry, berries and similar articles, and doing odd jobs." He witnessed "nearly every mess, and many of the men, had a servant who was glad to do anything for something to eat, or for a small quantity of loose change."[96]

Many contrabands received their first paying job once they were safely under U.S. protection. The Second Compensation Act permitted employment by the government, and average pay for the contraband was $7 per month. Work ranged from constructing fortifications, building roads, assisting the quartermaster with supplies, to cooking and washing.

NEARLY 1,000 MILES SOUTH of Virginia at New Orleans, something improbable was occurring. Union Maj. Gen. Benjamin F. Butler was uniforming and drilling a black regiment.

"A free Colored Regiment formerly in Rebel service is being organized," U.S. Treasury agent George S. Denison reported back to Treasury Secretary Chase on August 26. The regiment previously was known as the "Native Guards" and was enrolled in the Louisiana state militia during the war's first weeks for the protection of New Orleans. Denison expressed admiration at the composition of the troops. "The free negroes of Louisiana, are certainly superior, as a class, to the Creoles. . . . They are intelligent, energetic and industrious, as is evident from the fact . . . that they own one seventh of the real estate in this city. This is their own work, for they commenced with nothing, of course."[97]

By the end of the first week of September, Gen. Butler's first black regiment had received arms; a second had been enlisted and was drilling; and a third was about to be organized, "but the General has arms for no more." Denison noted that Butler had managed this controversial action with shrewdness. "By accepting a regiment which had already been in Confederate Service, he left no room for complaint (by the Rebels) that the Government was arming the negroes." Denison admitted, however, that nobody inquired whether any recruit had been a slave. "As a consequence the boldest and finest fugitives have enlisted, while the whole organization is known as the 'Free Colored Brigade.'" Denison predicted "without doubt it will be a success."[98]

Despite Butler's efforts, his example generally proved an exception. Strong sentiment within the army and throughout the Northern population was opposed to arming blacks, primarily out of racial prejudice.

The proposal was too radical, even for some Republican politicians. Sen. Ten Eyck of New Jersey doubted whether his fellow citizens would fight side by side with black soldiers. This prompted a *Harper's Weekly* response: "That is to say, their prejudice against the colored race is dearer to them than the Union."[99] A Philadelphia petition to the president voiced support for black troops, but not for altruistic reasons. "The lives of white men can and ought to be spared by the employment of negroes as soldiers," the petition read. "Employ black men as soldiers, and thus spare the lives of a proportionate number of white men."[100]

Racial prejudice remained entrenched, but 18 months of civil war had modified — and even moderated — views on slave emancipation. "If Mr. Lincoln had commanded our generals to seize the property of Southern men in May, 1861," reflected *Harper's Weekly*, "three-fourths of the North would have protested against the act as needless and barbarous. If [the president] had authorized generals to enlist negroes, at least as large a majority of the

Northern people would have opposed him. . . . History teaches us very plainly that revolutions are steadily progressive, and that a Government, to be safe and strong, must never be in advance of the people."[101]

The people of Lincoln's nation were advancing — not in overcoming prejudice, but in accepting emancipation. "It is gradually becoming plain to the blindest eyes that the country can be saved only by the heroic effort of all her children," prophesized *Harper's Weekly*. "The authorities are willing, but the people are the Government. The authorities must be stimulated and supported by public opinion."[102]

Abraham Lincoln had an innate sense of gauging the public's perspective. As he met with the Chicago ministers at the White House on September 13, the president never disclosed he already had prepared a draft emancipation proclamation two months earlier. But he didn't issue it because it was not yet the right time.

"It is my earnest desire to know the will of Providence in this matter. And if I can learn what it is I will do it!" the president reminded the ministers. "These are not, however, the days of miracles, and I suppose it will be granted that I am not to expect direct revelation."[103]

A miracle, perhaps, was close. Providence, perhaps, would grant Mr. Lincoln revelation through the resolve of the people.

CHAPTER 4

Patriots' Passion

The nation which is here struggling for its very existence calls forth from the heart of every patriot a will and a determination to do or die in her holy cause.

—John Summerfield Berry, August 27, 1862,
Former Speaker Maryland House of Delgates

The people of Boston sensed the emergency.

The first Sunday of September brought bad news to the Puritan City. The U.S. Army had been defeated near the nation's capital. Three days of ferocious fighting had produced thousands of casualties. The wounded needed urgent help. The government imperatively needed lint, used by surgeons to staunch the flow of blood.

"To the Loyal Women and Children of the United States," commenced the plea from the Surgeon General of the United States. "The supply of lint in the market is nearly exhausted. The brave men wounded in the defense of their country will soon be in want of it. I appeal to you to come to our aid in supplying us with this necessary article."

The second paragraph personalized the plea. "There is scarcely a woman or child who cannot scrape lint, and there is no way in which their assistance can be more usefully given than in furnishing us the means to dress the wounds of those who fall in the defense of their right and their homes."[104]

Boston mobilized. "Sunday was one of the most stirring and exciting days our city has ever experienced," witnessed the *Boston Post*. "For a Sunday it was without precedent." Preachers from every church in the city appealed to their congregations for an immediate supply of lint and linen of all kinds, as well as stocks of brandy and whiskey as medications for the wounded. Services were brief on Sunday, September 2, consisting of "an earnest, fervent, eloquent prayer followed by an equally sincere exhortation for the congregations to at once repair to their homes to furnish the called for supplies."

Scenes at home were frantic. Throughout hundreds, perhaps thousands of households, "closets, drawers, barrels, bags, whole attics, were hunted and ransacked for supplies of linen of various sorts and ages, of old sheets, drawers, shirts, etc, etc; while cellars, sideboards, and similar localities were set upon and made to disgorge whiskey, brandy and wines in quantities without limit."

Packages and parcels were then delivered or forwarded to receiving stations throughout the city. "Our streets never presented, on a holiday, greater throngs or a more intense feeling." The volume was so great in Ward 4 that Tremont Temple ceased services and "transformed into the greatest workshop ever seen in Boston."

"Not less than one thousand women were busily, earnestly at work in the manufacture of bandages and lints. Innumerable sheets, garments, towels and other articles and fabrics were torn into strips, sewed together and then rolled up in the best manner. Upstairs and down, in the gallery, upon the platform, in the aisles, in the doorways, on the stairways from top to bottom, were these ministering angels." The writer concluded, "It was a glorious, a beautiful and a rare spectacle."

Husbands, sons, and brothers also lent their hands for the lint. The men busily cut and tore the fabrics before handing them to the women for sewing and rolling. Boys and girls kept the seamstresses supplied with needles and yards of thread. This makeshift manufacturing, operated with the precision of a New England factory, produced "bandages by the thousands [and] lint by the cartload."[105] The difference, however, was that the women were in charge, proving a favorite philosophy of the time that "in women, there is at once a subtle delicacy of tact, and a plain soundness of judgment, which are rarely combined to an equal degree in men."[106]

On the first floor of the Tremont Temple developed the packing and shipping department. Here the area merchants became involved. They furnished 2,000 boxes and cases of various sizes for shipping on that Sunday morning. As each case filled, volunteers moved it to the sidewalk, where more volunteers filled waiting wagons. Teamsters then conveyed the cargo to the Worcester Depot, ready for transport via the evening train to New York and thence to Washington. By 5 p.m. that first Sunday of September, 1,800 boxes and cases had filled nine freight cars. Two hours later the train departed, escorted by the mayor, members of the council, police to protect the cargo, and the city's best surgeons. The next night, the shipment arrived at the nation's capital.[107]

During this remarkable day, the citizens of Boston also collected $6,000 to aid soldiers' relief societies. This was quite impressive considering the private in the army made $13 per month!

This outpouring of assistance was not limited to Boston. Caring people from other major northeastern cities, such as New York, Philadelphia, and Baltimore also acted upon the Surgeon General's plea, and they mirrored the Bostonian response. More than 400 pounds of lint arrived from Philadelphia alone.[108]

Scandal then marred this patriotic lint-gathering performance. A writer in the *Boston Post* pronounced "lint a humbug. . . . Every ounce of lint sent to the army does mischief. It's only use is to cover up the blunders of bad surgery." The informant continued, "It is seldom used by the best surgeons here. In the army it is crowded into wounds by men who know no other way to stop hemorrhage, and there it remains until it becomes filled with filth and maggots." As an exclamation to this appalling disclosure, the observer graphically reported: "[Lint] retains the discharges till they putrefy, and produces intolerable stench. The termination of its work is the death of the patient."[109]

A tornado of dejection swept across the North. All of that effort, for naught? And perhaps killing soldiers rather than assisting them? The charge appeared in countless newspapers, supported by a nameless army surgeon, effectively shredding enthusiasm and depressing a dedicated population. How could this happen? "Why cannot this matter be settled at once?" demanded a letter writer to the editor of the *Philadelphia Inquirer*.[110] The drama eventually subsided when the army reassured citizens that its lint was useful, explaining it an acceptable method of treating wounds as practiced in Europe. It soon became known that the surgeon intended no scandalous disruption. He was presenting alternative methods in an evolving world of enhanced medical treatments.

CONVALESCING FROM A Civil War wound was difficult. The size and weight of a .58 caliber bullet often crushed bones upon penetration, requiring amputation of limbs. Liquor like whiskey and brandy helped reduce the spread of gangrene, and the constant replacement of bandages helped decrease germ fermentation. Surgeons knew this instinctively, as Louis Pasteur had not yet discovered his germ theory. Surgeries using anesthetics often occurred in primitive field hospitals near the battlefields, and this saved countless lives. The transport of thousands of wounded soldiers often proved a tougher challenge.

Wounded from the three-day battle at Manassas (during the last days of August) reached Philadelphia on September 3. The first 275 soldiers arrived by train just before noon, and were taken to the Central Military Hospital at Broad and Cherry streets. Another 1,400 arrived at 4 p.m., and before the day ended, 2,500 injured U.S. soldiers had arrived in the City of Brotherly Love. Makeshift ambulances provided by the city's fire companies carried the wounded to their designated destinations.[111] "Our hospitals are full; our churches are being occupied by the brave and suffering soldiers," reported the *Philadelphia Inquirer*. "Everywhere, unchronicled, our fair women are dressing their wounds, soothing their pains, and taking to them such supplies and such delicacies as they so much require."

The city did not have the food, supplies, or hospital accommodations to handle this sudden spurt in its population. That same day, policemen went from house to house "to tell the sad story" and call the people to action. "At once husbands' wardrobes were ransacked and spoiled; preserves and jellies, meant for social discussion at peaceful winter tables, were given up to the last jar. . . . Hundreds of our ladies went forth themselves to succor and nurse the brave defenders of their country." This was nearly revolutionary, as Victorian mores frowned upon women nursing strange, injured men. Yet even the newspaper expressed its desire to forgo culture during this emergency. "Their example should be electric and contagious."

The paper pleaded for more. "Mothers, as you think of your sons; sisters, as you love your brothers; wives, as you picture to your fancies your husbands in like suffering and sorrow — leave your comfort, your social pleasures, and join the increasing army of noble women now volunteering." The *Inquirer* finished with patriotic ardor. "Let every woman in Philadelphia have it to say when Peace returns to bless us — 'I did what I could for the poor, naked, starving, bleeding heroes who came thronging back from the terrible fields where our country was fighting for her life.'"[112]

The women of Philadelphia helped organize and manage the Penn Relief Association for sick and wounded soldiers, collecting donations of clothing, hospital supplies, and money. The city's matrons also established a book drive for the patients. Energetic ecumenical responses came from the Presbyterian Board, the Old School Baptist Publication Society, the Protestant Episcopal Methodist Book Society, the American Tract Society and the Christian Commission. Bibles were furnished by the Philadelphia Bible Society. The *Inquirer* noted that "the supply of literature is never equal to the demand."[113]

One of the largest private donations of the war came from the citizens of San Francisco. Though California was far from the battlefields, and few Californians were fighting in the war, Californians nonetheless staunchly supported President Lincoln and the Union. A gold shipment arrived in New York via steamship that included $100,000 in gold as a contribution to the National Sanitary Fund, which was used to improve soldiers' health and well being.[114] This equated to 334 full-time jobs, considering the average American salary of $300 per year.

Women humanitarians saved thousands of lives, volunteering generous care in hospitals both North and South. (*Harper's Weekly*)

Volunteerism and philanthropy inspired the people of the North in September 1862. They appreciated the service of U.S. soldiers. They witnessed the personal scars of war, and acknowledged the soldiers' personal sacrifices. They grieved with family and friends at graveyard ceremonies, or worse, watched when a letter arrived, but the remains of the loved one never returned home. The war predicted to last three months had now entered its 18th. But instead of quitting, Northerners remained resolute in their actions.

MANUFACTURING, ESPECIALLY, reflected the U.S. determination to conquer the Confederates. Factories operated at unparalleled capacity. With so many men absent from home and fighting in the ranks, thousands of women began working outside the home for the first time. Women and young girls cut and rolled gun powder cartridges at the Pittsburgh Arsenal, an extremely volatile and hazardous job. Under contracts with the Philadelphia Arsenal, 175 women busily worked covering canteens with cloth. In fact, more than 12,000 women were employed by the Philadelphia Arsenal and its branches at needle-work — "the majority, if not all, of whom are the wives and relatives of soldiers."

But competition from the nation's largest city, New York, threatened the Philadelphia workforce. Manufacturers in Gotham offered to furnish goods at the minimum price, forcing a reduction of wages in Philly. Pants, which previously paid 42 cents per pair (as of the first day of September) brought only 27 cents. Jackets formerly bringing $1.12 per piece dropped to just 90 cents. "This

The Northern war effort brought tens of thousands of women into factories. Here women produce gunpowder cartridges at a U.S. arsenal. *(Harper's Weekly)*

reduction in rates makes a perceptible decrease in the incomes of nearly five thousand women who do the sewing," wrote the *Philadelphia Inquirer*.[115] Though contributing to the war effort, these working women had discovered the theory of competitive capitalism.

In shipyards and foundries, American ingenuity and perspiration created war machines never before envisioned. At the Fort Pitt Foundry in Pennsylvania, workers fashioned molten iron into guns weighing nearly 50,000 pounds apiece. They were engineering a larger gun, capable of hurling a 1,000 pound shell up to four miles. In the New York City harbor, Captain John Ericsson commenced development of the *Dictator*, "a monster iron-clad vessel" with armor thicker than two ordinary iron-clad ships. "The ball that can penetrate nearly fifteen feet of solid matter . . . can hardly be molded in the South. It would require all the balls in Rebeldom to make it."[116]

One weapon of war the U.S. government could not manufacture was manpower. Over 600,000 men had volunteered for service in the Federal army, but they were not enough to squash the stubborn Confederacy. This was not because they were inferior fighters. The U.S. pursued a strategy of advancing upon and occupying Southern territory from Mississippi to Maryland. This required hundreds of thousands of men, spread over 1,500 miles, where individual armies on occasion concentrated for combat, but never enough to completely vanquish the Confederates. Fierce fighting could produce casualties never before seen in American armies, with individual regiments sometimes losing more than half their men in combat. Battlefield survival did not guarantee escape from death in the camps, where contagious disease ravaged the ranks. By the summer of 1862, Mr. Lincoln's armies were too small to end the rebellion, and everyone knew it.

To remedy this deficiency, the governors of the loyal states petitioned the president to call for another 300,000 volunteers. Additionally, in July the Congress authorized the president to conduct a draft — something never required or attempted for the United States Army.[117]

For a democratic society with freedoms based upon the Bill of Rights, the draft, for many, seemed an infringement upon personal liberties. But Northerners understood. Without more men, the war might be lost. Without more soldiers, the South might succeed. Without more warriors, tens of thousands will have died or been maimed in vain. Hoping to avert the draft — and the embarrassment of failing to uphold an American ethos of volunteerism — Northern states and cities utilized a combination of peer-pressure patriotism and old-fashioned capitalism to spur recruitments during the late summer of 1862.

War meeting before the Washington Capitol during the summer of 1862. In the largest plea for troops in the first century of U.S. history, President Lincoln called for 600,000 additional volunteers to defeat the surging Confederacy. (*Harper's Weekly*)

New York hosted one of its famed mass meetings to encourage enlistment. "The streets are almost entirely deserted this afternoon, the business community having all migrated up to Union Square, to swell the mighty multitude assembled there in response to the president's request for additional men," a correspondent reported. The Stars and Stripes was prominently waved from the New York Stock Exchange, from all of the newspaper offices, from vessels in the port, and from building after building. Artillery salvos from the Battery, Washington Square, and Union Park "served to excite the enthusiasm of the people." Speeches from political leaders and military veterans rushed blood to the heart and men to the recruiting tables. They came with "a calm determination to submit to any and every sacrifice that may be necessary to enable the Government to suppress the Rebellion."[118]

"Philadelphia must not be backward in sending her sons a similar response," demanded the *Philadelphia Inquirer*. "It is time the preliminary arrangements for a mammoth gathering in this city were in progress."[119] War meetings like this occurred in other metropolitan cities, including one at the U.S. Capitol, attended by President Lincoln. "It was a large and most enthusiastic gathering, and the feeling in favor of the thorough prosecution of the war was unanimous."[120]

Confederate newspapers dismissed these demonstrations as grandstanding. "Whenever there is a prodigious show *for effect* to be made of Yankee enthusiasm," growled a Petersburg, Virginia editor, "it always begins with a 'monster public meeting.'" The Southern writer satirized the New York gathering. "It is the easiest thing in the world to collect together at a short call in that bloated city, whose streets are now thronged with an idle and excitable multitude . . . many thousands around speakers' stands to listen to the oratorical clap-trap of the most unprincipled demagogues that can be found in the whole world."

The writer theorized the meeting actually was a Wall Street conspiracy, prompted not by patriotism, but by protection of its war investments. "[Lincoln] has grabbed so much money out of the Wall Street bags, that unless the millionaire gamblers of that swindling thoroughfare continue to shell out and shout out for the war, they will lose every dollar that has been wrenched from them, and hence the late Monster Meeting."[121]

Not all in New York embraced the War Meeting, or the additional call for troops. "We regret to see the clamor which comes from every quarter for a general uprising of our population," wrote the *New York World*. "It is occasioned by an unmanly fright, and is calculated to do infinite damage in withdrawing men from useful and productive occupations, to spend their time in trying to be poor soldiers." The *World* concluded: "This frantic calling for more soldiers is a sign of real weakness of heart. . . . If we cannot conquer the South with one million men, it is quite clear that with two million we shall only conquer ourselves by exhausting the nation's resources."[122]

Tens of thousands of men disagreed, however, and began rushing to area recruitment stations. Cash, as well as patriotism, prompted their eager response. The Congress authorized bonuses, or enlistment "bounties," ranging from $25 to $100 (equivalent to a wage for one-third of a year). States, counties, and municipalities offered bonuses on top of the Federal enticement, resulting in total bounties often surpassing one full year of average pay. Workers had never seen so many dollars paid in advance, and the temptation proved difficult to resist. To the credit of many recruits, they didn't pocket the money, but offered it to their families for investments or safe keeping.

One further enticement was the length of service. You could enlist in a veteran regiment for three years, or you could muster in with a new regiment with a nine-month term. Either permitted you to avoid the coming draft, and either allowed you to help your state in meeting its volunteer quotas.

Men flocked to the Army. They came not only from the metropolitan areas, but also from the rural North. Around Hagerstown, Md., located over 70 miles west of Baltimore, Washington County led the state in furnishing troops. More than a quarter of the county's voting population (all men) had committed to service by September. In nearby Franklin County, just north of the Mason-Dixon Line in Pennsylvania, companies from Chambersburg, Waynesboro, and Greencastle assembled and were "escorted to the Depot by hundreds of their fellow citizens, their whole route a complete ovation."[123]

No one could have predicted in mid-August 1862, that in less than one month, they would be returning to defend their *own* homes.

CHAPTER 5

Political Poison

Political schemers and visionaries have already tested their endurance to the utmost limit, and some conclusion will have to be reached, and soon, or there will be another upheaval which will bury every traitor out of sight in the new revolution that must come.

—*Baltimore American and Commercial Advertiser,*
September 11, 1862

Abraham Lincoln was relieved.

Thousands of new recruits streamed into Washington during September's first weeks. They came from New York and Pennsylvania and Ohio, the country's most populous states. New England responded with fresh regiments from Massachusetts, Vermont, Connecticut, Maine, and New Hampshire. Tiny Rhode Island answered the call, along with the Chesapeake colonies of Maryland and Delaware.

The Midwest presented its best. Indiana, Wisconsin, Michigan, and Illinois sent eager volunteers to join the U.S. armies operating in Kentucky, Tennessee, and Mississippi. The president needed the new soldiers immediately. Lincoln required every recruit to help stop the Confederate armies surging toward United States territory.

"Fresh legions of the best material are coming into the field," marveled a correspondent from the nation's capital. Observing the old army was "wearied, thinned, and disorganized," he desired to "weave the fresh muscle on the iron framework that [had] been tried on a hundred battlefields." A Baltimore observer noticed the new recruits were "men of education, whose standing and character are calculated to strengthen the morale and elevate the tone of the army."[124]

Men of education, indeed, but not educated as soldiers. These raw recruits had been in the army for less than three weeks. They were afforded no time for drilling. No time for practicing formations and maneuvers. No time for learning the nine-steps to load and fire a single rifle-musket. The enemy was at the gates!

Harpers Ferry, Virginia, typified the situation. New recruits from New York arrived during September's first week to boost the U.S. garrison commanding the entrance into the Shenandoah Valley. Four embryonic regiments, totaling almost 4,000 men, trickled in over several days to the headquarters of Col. Dixon S. Miles.

The 42-year veteran of the U.S. Army was unimpressed. The 115th and 126th regiments had been in the army but six days. The 111th Infantry had worn its blue uniforms for only one week. The 125th Regiment arrived just three days after mustering. Miles protested that his command was becoming nothing more than "a fortified camp of instruction." The grizzled colonel fumed in a letter to his department commander in Baltimore: "The general states he has sent me two strong regiments. I have received but one, and the men belonging to it never had a gun in their hands until the boxes were opened and muskets issued to them yesterday; nor does an officer of the command . . . know how to drill or anything about the drill."[125]

This lack of military training and discipline did not dampen the martial determination of Lincoln's volunteers. "The men are all in the highest spirits and anxious to have their courage put to the test; though there seems to be a general regret that they are not better drilled," reported a writer embedded with the Franklin County troops. Recently christened as part of the 126th Pennsylvania Infantry, theirs was the first nine-months regiment to arrive in Washington from the Quaker State.

Most of the men had never been to the nation's capital, and they were awed by the Capitol, the White House, the imposing department buildings, and the Smithsonian. "There is something very attractive in all the features of the soldier's life," reflected the novice. "A meal never tastes so sweetly as after a day's fasting. One never sleeps so soundly as after an eight miles march. Water never proves more grateful than when drank out of some gurgling little stream."[126] The writer had not yet witnessed a Confederate bullet or shell. His wait would not be long.

Enthusiasm for enlistment even brought a few women into the ranks — not as women, however, but disguised as men. They joined because of their own patriotic fervor or to accompany their loved ones. Regardless of motive, how they fooled the examining doctors became the subject of much speculation. Even more mysterious was how they maintained their disguise in a camp full of 1,000 men.

Most of the female interlopers failed to hide their true identities. As example, two soldiers in the 116th Pennsylvania were picked up in Washington for failing to exhibit the proper passes. When the provost commenced examination, he discovered "their faces and general appearance excited suspicion that they were not of the right gender to serve in the ranks." The provost called upon a woman to investigate, and she reported her discovery of two females. "The two girls were then given clothing suitable for their sex, and were ordered to be sent to Philadelphia, from whence they came. They did not seem at all pleased at the results of their venture, but desired to be sent to their regiment."[127]

Innocent of war's horrors, inspired by patriotism, and committed to terminating the rebellion, more than half a million men answered President Lincoln's 1862 summer calls for volunteers. Something more, however, stimulated this outpouring. The country was war weary. It fervently believed, and earnestly prayed, that this mass infusion of Northern manhood and muscle would conquer the Rebels and end the nation's fratricide. Upscale New Yorkers reflected this tone. "There is a sad undertone to fashionable life," lamented a Gotham dweller. "The absence of young men is particularly felt . . . and the presence of an occasional officer, coming to the [hotel spa] to recuperate his wasted health, does not atone for the dearth of beaux."[128]

Depression permeated the national consciousness during the early weeks of September. "Our Ship of State is now in a heavy sea," characterized orator and parson, William G. Brownlow. "At no period since the Rebellion broke out, has so deep a depression fallen upon the hearts of loyal citizens."[129]

"The dowager wall flowers talk about war and its concomitants more than about bonnets and modes," observed a New York socialite. "The skeleton [soldier] stalks into the parlor, and the fabric of fashionable life seems borne aloft on the points of the bayonet. You cannot help thinking, amid the brilliant pleasures of hotel life, of the camps and battlefields of Virginia."[130]

AS CONFEDERATE ARMIES postured menacingly near the banks of the Potomac and Ohio rivers, concerned citizens asked: "How did we come to this?" Washington, Baltimore, Harrisburg, Philadelphia, Cincinnati, Memphis, Nashville, Louisville, and New Orleans all were threatened "by an enemy that shows prodigious activity, talents and strength. Indeed, they have us now where they had us *thirteen months ago!*"[131] Where had the country gone wrong?

Critics had plenty of answers. The primary venom was spewed at Lincoln and his Republican cohorts. "Our rulers seemed to have had no adequate conception of the task before them," complained the editor of Chambersburg's *Valley Spirit*. "This rebellion was to be crushed out in a few weeks or months at most. It was to be a mere breakfast-task some told us, and he who dared to differ from these absurd notions, was put down as a 'sympathizer with treason.' We have all since been convinced of [that] fatal error by sad experience."[132]

Underestimating the resolve of the Confederacy proved a constant theme. "First and from the beginning, we have undervalued the forces, valor and energy of the Rebels," opined the *Philadelphia Inquirer*. "They have fought with greater bravery, more skill, and far more perseverance than the public here gave them credit for possessing." But the *Inquirer* also identified a lack of resolve in the North. "We have been content to let the war go on, with lukewarm desires and vague hopes, to sail upon the current rather than stern." The editor's answer: "Every man and woman in the country must be made to understand and feel [our] condition thoroughly and keenly; its reality, grave import, its humiliation; until the North rises like a strong man armed and refreshed."[133]

The *Inquirer* posed its own solution to the country's woes. "We must never again cease to go on without enlistments. . . . Numbers, steadily supplying losses; numbers, steadily increasing our army; numbers, steadily enlarging the difference between us and the Rebels; numbers, leaving nothing to the hazard of 'artillery duels' or 'fair stand up fights'; numbers, to overpower, crush down, and tramp out the bale fires of Secession."[134]

The national self-examination continued with Congress as the most tempting target. With the Republicans commanding majorities in both chambers, and Lincoln the Republican in the White House, people contended the country was controlled "in a great measure by men of one idea — miserable charlatans, abstractionists and theorists, devoid of common sense and lacking in everything necessary to constitute practical statesmanship."[135]

The argument here was distraction; that the Republicans were using the war to end slavery, rather than focusing solely upon ending the war. "It must be realized at last that this is a white man's war and that the negro must take his chances without exercising controlling influence. He cannot help us essentially, and we ought to be ashamed to depend upon him."[136]

Allowing the issue of slavery to become a distraction infuriated many. "President Lincoln was induced to step aside from the plain path of his duty and tinker at the slavery question," wrote the *Valley Spirit*. "We want the whole power and resources of the loyal portion of the country thrown into this struggle, in order to suppress this unholy, terrible and damning rebellion at once."[137] Another paper was more direct: "Let there be a truce to the political discussions respecting the status of the enslaved class now more than ever. . . . If only the Government and the people shall rightly address themselves to the military tasks of the hour."[138]

Another problem was the newspaper editors themselves. Newspapers commonly aligned with either the Democrats or Republicans, with their virulent words persecuting the opposition and bellowing the party line. No middle ground existed; no negotiation ever conceived; no surrender of party principle was possible. Hardened positions segregated sentiments and divided communities, sometimes resulting in fisticuffs and public brawls. Editors inflamed an already passionate population, making consensus nearly impossible.

Favorite targets of the newspapers included government officials, but also the army's generals, who themselves adopted public and unabashed political positions. Gen. George B. McClellan, commander of Lincoln's largest and most famous army, admired and flaunted his Democratic positions; he often was hoisted up as the most likely challenger to President Lincoln in the 1864 election. "Certain public journalists have deemed it their province to assail our commanders, and weaken public confidence in their ability," recognized the *Philadelphia Inquirer*. "Deceived by these assaults, and induced by the plausible style in which many of them were worded, the public has been betrayed."

The *Inquirer* believed that every noteworthy general had "their acknowledged admirers or recognized villifiers," and that leading public officials were "recipients of abuse and detraction, which could not fail to shake the faith of the people in their integrity and wisdom."[139] A few moderate papers recognized the venomous influence of extremist editors, and they begged for a moderating tone. "Let there be an end also of the vain glorious and fatal deceptions which have been practiced . . . by the arrogant guides of public opinion."[140]

Partisan politicians, especially in Washington, received their own warning from the *Valley Spirit*: "We want that miserable tribe of fanatical and one-idea men who occupy seats in the present Congress turned out, and their places filled by men of sense. . . . Men who have the ability to comprehend the magnitude of the crises through which we are passing, and the patriotism to adopt the means to the end, regardless of sectional prejudices or partisan bigotry. We want no more trifling whilst the nation is trembling upon the brink of ruin."[141]

Outspoken politics sometimes landed men in prison, especially those who objected to Lincoln administration policies, and especially members of the Democratic party. At the birthplace of the American Constitution, Independence Square in Philadelphia, Pennsylvania's leading Democrats announced they were holding a massive rally on Saturday night, August 23, to fire up the base for the upcoming 1862 fall elections. This was dangerous for the Democrats. Two weeks earlier, the Secretary of War had ordered the arrest of any person engaged in speech or writing that discouraged volunteer enlistments or, in any way, "gave aid or comfort to the enemy" or "for any other disloyal practice against the United States." The writ of *habeas corpus* was suspended for anyone charged with these crimes.[142]

This controversial assault on freedom of speech and freedom of assembly worried the *Philadelphia Inquirer*. The paper anticipated trouble, and it cautioned the Lincoln administration and its executors (police and provost marshals) to exercise restraint at the Democrats' rally. "The spirit which has assailed the proposed meeting is the spirit that breeds turbulence and riots, and this is no time to incite either," warned the editor.

"There is another strong reason why there should be no attempt at this time to interfere with the customary rights of political parties. Such interference cannot fail to have the strongest influence in deterring enlistments." The *Inquirer* reasoned that "sons of Democratic fathers may very well say, why should I volunteer, and leave my father at the mercy of men who, in my absence, will seek to deprive him of his civic rights?" With the First Amendment at stake, the paper challenged the Lincoln administration's intentions. "This whole affair of attempting to deny the free and indefeasible right to assemble in public meeting is pregnant with evil consequences."[143]

Notwithstanding these calls for calm, one speaker, Charles Ingersoll, was arrested for "uttering treasonable language." The affidavit against Ingersoll charged him with making remarks like: "the whole object of the war, hitherto, was to free the [negro]. . . . A more corrupt Government than that which now governs us never was in the United States, and has been seldom seen in any European part of the world. . . . That anything half as corrupt as this Government of the United States never was imagined until Mr. Lincoln came into power," and, "I want to know whether any Government that ever exercised so much power has with [700,000 soldiers] in the field ever accomplished results so insignificant."[144] Ingersoll was jailed and then escorted to Washington by the provost marshal.

Ingersoll's arrest raised indignation across the country, forcing such heated rhetoric and criticism that the secretary of war was compelled to release him on September 1. Ingersoll, however, was but one example of the suspension of the First Amendment. The two editors of the Harrisburg, Pa., *Patriot and Union*, a paper loyal to Democrats, were incarcerated in the notorious Old Capitol Prison in Washington after two of their "printer boys" issued a prank handbill announcing a recruiter was in town to enlist African-American units. The editor of the *Maryland News Sheet* in Baltimore was seized and confined in Fort McHenry (the site that inspired the *Star Spangled Banner*), where dozens of other political prisoners were held. Eighteen "secession gentlemen" attending a party near Baltimore were imprisoned simply for engaging in a social gathering. "It would be well for all such socials hereafter," satirized the Baltimore correspondent for the *Philadelphia Inquirer*, "to have mixed up with them a slight sprinkling or salvo of loyal neighbors to evade suspicion."[145]

A judge in Dauphin County, Pennsylvania, calling the grand jury into the fall session, reinforced the War Department's stringent regulations. "If a man rails or writes against the Government, and against entering the army, we naturally and properly infer that the intention is to prevent the hearer or reader from entering the army." With wide legal construction, the judge stated, "the law does not require that any one should be actually dissuaded; it is sufficient that the act is *attempted*." The judge warned newspaper editors that they were responsible "not only for what they write themselves and publish to the world, but also for injurious or treasonable communications extracted from the columns of other papers." He proclaimed that editors had no right "to promulgate and spread abroad the injurious writings of other editors; they dare not disseminate treason at second hand."[146]

On top of these restrictions on speech and assembly, Lincoln's War Department also issued restrictions on travel. Concerned that males between the ages of 18 and 45 who were required to enroll in their home jurisdictions for a possible draft might travel or even leave the country to avoid registration, the government clamped rigid restrictions upon railroad, stage, and boat travel. The order initially created havoc, effectively shutting down or slowing all means of transport in the North as zealous provost marshals and police checked men's passports.

In Chicago, 30 men were arrested with railroad tickets to Detroit, under assumption they were fleeing to Canada. When two passenger vessels left the Windy City's port, a tug was dispatched to chase them down and take into custody any male who was "unable to give satisfactory reasons for their departure." The next day a tug, boasting a six-pound cannon on deck, was stationed at the mouth of the harbor to "overhaul every passenger boat and vessel that passes out." The *Chicago Times* accepted the reality. "Our citizens may as well bring their minds to a realization of the fact that Chicago is virtually *under martial law*."

The *Times* discovered that some men had, indeed, attempted escape from the required enrollment. "This running away from duty has been practiced in most instances by wealthy men, while the poor men have been left to become the victims of the draft. In future there will be no more sneaking, no more running away, no matter what may be the wealth of the individual."[147] The War Department finally rescinded travel restrictions on September 7, but not before much resentment had brewed throughout the Northern population. "We cannot disguise from ourselves the perception that their enforcement was attended with serious detriment to the cause of the Union in the loyal States."[148]

Many citizens questioned the Constitutional basis of these actions by Lincoln's government. Basic freedoms seemed no longer free. Why had suppression of the South produced suppression in the North? "The discrimination between loyalty as a virtue and treason as a crime has been confused by a policy, which, in its execution, has apparently confounded the innocent with the guilty."[149] The controversies generated strengthening opposition for the Democratic party. The Democrats had an issue other than restoring "the Union as it was." A perceived usurpation of power and dictatorial despotism in Washington became a clarion call to oust the Republicans during the forthcoming fall elections.

THROUGHOUT THE NORTH during the first weeks of September, Democrats and Republicans met in state conventions to prepare their platforms and select their candidates. It was not a presidential election year. But every seat in the U.S. House of Representatives was up for challenge, and key governorships and state legislatures were subject to the franchise.

The timing could not have been worse for the Republicans. With Confederate armies surging and U.S. forces reeling, it appeared Lincoln and his party had lost control of the war. Generals appeared in chaos and confusion, and Union armies were defeated, disorganized, and demoralized. Battlefield setbacks did not bode well for President Lincoln and his political legions. Despite the military disappointments, the Republicans vowed to fight with determination, guaranteeing the Union's restoration, while at the same time siphoning slave labor and slave value out of the Southern economy.

Democrats rejected any incursion into slavery, defining the war as a war for reunion, not for freedom. They argued that each state had the constitutional right to deal with slavery "at its own time and in its own mode, irrespective of the views of the Federal Administration." Democrats equated freedom to equality, sending a shiver through white society. "The evident intent of the Republican Party is to place the negro on a footing of equality with the white man," contended the Delaware Democratic platform. The aim of the "Black Republican Abolition Disunion Party" was "to degrade the white race to a level with the negroes, at the bidding of false philanthropists and fanatical men."[150]

"The Constitution is in danger, too, from the mischievous doctrines that are every day promulgating in louder and louder tones," warned the Democrats. "Already you hear it claimed that after the Rebellion is over, we will want a stronger Government than that which our fathers gave us. You hear it asserted, and sometimes in high places, too, that the Constitution may be suspended during the Rebellion, and that the civil power is subordinate to the military. . . . Bulwarks which the Constitution has provided for personal liberty and the freedom of the press have been swept away. . . . It is no wonder, then, that the arrests which have been made in the loyal States . . . without the privilege of habeas corpus, should have filled the minds of friends of constitutional liberty with anxiety and alarm."[151]

The two parties agreed on one matter: the Union must be reunited. But the heated rhetoric and differing visions between the political partisans made it appear that Lincoln's North was hopelessly divided and permanently torn asunder. This rupture was symbolized by Mrs. Lazarus Shorb, a widow in Gettysburg, who had five of her six sons fighting in the Union army. Her sons were Democrats, but because of their political sentiments, she was denounced as a secessionist.[152]

The Confederacy noted with glee that the United States was suffering from its own brand of disunion. "By sowing dissensions, [we] assist the Rebels," explained the *Philadelphia Inquirer*. "This is the inevitable result, and the originators and promulgators should be punished with the same severity as is awarded those sympathizers with treason."[153]

"Lincoln wants three hundred thousand more men, and it is considered a life and death business with him," observed one Confederate newspaper. "The people, worn down by the disasters, losses, and troubles of the war, are very slow and reluctant in giving themselves up to Southern malaria and gunpowder." The Rebel journal then portended a good outcome for the Confederacy's future: "They do not rush forward to the cry of 'To Arms!' with the alacrity and enthusiasm they did twelve months ago."[154]

The Europeans noticed the unease, and even unruliness, in their former colonists in the North. "If we look attentively — as all Europe is looking — at the America war, we shall discover an extraordinary contrast between proceedings and results," wrote the *London Times*. "The end . . . is no nearer than at first; and indeed, may be considered as more remote than ever."[155]

Perhaps the monarchies could lend Mr. Lincoln some direction.

CHAPTER 6

Nominal Neutrality

When your enemy is eating himself up, keep off, he is doing your work for you gratis.

—*Napoleon Bonaparte*

Her Majesty was emphatic.

Queen Victoria intended no involvement by Great Britain in America's great fratricide.

"Civil War, which has been for some time raging in America, has unfortunately continued in unabated intensity," the Queen observed in a speech proroguing Parliament in the summer of 1862. "The evils with which it has been attended have not been confined to the American continent; but her Majesty, having from the outset determined to take no part in the contest, has seen no reason to depart from the neutrality which she has steadily adhered to."[156]

Evils? What evils evoked, or provoked, England from across the Atlantic?

Cotton.

The English had become dependent upon American cotton. The industrial revolution had transformed England into the largest manufacturer of textiles in the world. Cotton fiber, extracted from white-blossomed, white-boll, short-staple cotton plants grown in the South, harvested by slaves, and imported from America, fueled the British manufacturing engine. "White gold" from the American South provided more than three-fourths of the cotton used in the English textile industries. And nearly one-quarter of the English population worked in jobs associated with the British textile business. Half of England's export trade was in cotton textiles. About a tenth of English wealth was invested in the cotton business.[157]

Then the cotton stopped.

When war erupted in America in the spring of 1861, President Lincoln commenced a blockade of the Confederate coastline to prevent any trade from entering or leaving the Rebel states. By the war's second year, the U.S. Navy had strangled most Southern ports, ensuring that almost no Confederate cotton escaped through the blockade. Before the war, the South provided 75 percent of the world's cotton. Now the North had sealed the globe's cotton gusher.

At the war's outset Southern leaders had, oddly enough, restricted cotton exports on their own, hoping to create an artificial shortage that would bring Great Britain, and even France, to economic prostration. "Cotton Diplomacy" would force the Europeans to cast its economic lot with the Confederacy. The South would enlist Europe's military muscle by extorting Europe's economies — through the weapon of cotton.

The Confederacy believed its "King Cotton" doctrine infallible. "Would any sane nation make war on cotton?" pondered South Carolina Sen. James Henry Hammond three years before the outbreak of the Civil War. "Without firing a gun, without drawing a sword, should they make war on us we could bring the whole world to our feet." Hammond's boasting continued in the halls of the U.S. Senate. "What would happen if no cotton were furnished for three years? I will not stop to depict what everyone can imagine, but this is certain: England would topple headlong and carry the whole civilized world with her, save the South." Hammond then issued this warning: "No, you dare not make war on cotton. No power on earth dares to make war upon it. Cotton is king."[158]

"King Cotton Bound." England's dependence upon King Cotton threatened its neutrality with the United States. *(Punch)*

King Cotton assaulted Queen Victoria. Economic depression attacked the English textile industry during the American Civil War. By September 1862, mass unemployment had swept through the manufacturing districts of Yorkshire and Lancashire and the "Cottonopolis" of Manchester. Work was reduced to two days per week, or eventually vanished. The spinning machines stopped. The steam engines ceased. The looms shut down. Many factories stalled, then were silenced. Tens of thousands lost their jobs.

Misery and poverty abounded. "I found a poor woman with three children, whose husband had three days' [partial] work," reported a *London Times* correspondent while investigating the depression in the manufacturing districts. "All their furniture was gone, but a table and two chairs, and all five slept in one bed. . . . All their clothes had been pawned." Nearby the reporter found another family of six struggling to survive on about one shilling per day, less than one-seventh the factory wages. He discovered a sick mother of two girls, who had been factory employees and could afford no health care, stretched on a bed, "worn to a bone — a very skeleton, in fact, her body covered with putrid sores, with not a rag on her — literally naked, but for the coarse sheet which was spread over her."

He ventured across a family of 11, where no one had worked for 28 weeks. He encountered another family of five, where the father, as a supervisor, once made 39 shillings each week, but he had not worked in more than 12 months. With his resources completely exhausted, "he was compelled to apply for relief," and was now receiving from various charitable sources about nine shillings per week. "Even among a somewhat better class," the writer observed, "the suffering is hardly less extreme." In the textile town of Preston, the *Times* estimated "23,000 persons receiving parochial and charitable relief," or nearly one-quarter of the local population "steeped to the lips in misery." "Sad were the tales to which I had to listen of the gradual descent from comfort to utter destitution."[159]

BRITISH POLITICIANS COULD NOT ignore the sufferings of their people. Many blamed the United States. The emotional thermometer in the Parliament sometimes erupted into open indignation of the North. Lincoln's war policy, they claimed, had caused this economic disaster. The Union blockade, they bellowed, had stifled their textile industry. The Yankee war had stolen their prosperity. How could England remain neutral, they asked, when neutrality harmed the English people?

The question eventually boiled into debates in the British Parliament. Those favoring the Confederacy introduced a resolution in the House of Commons recognizing the South as a separate, independent nation, and offering mediation between the two warring countries. Confederate contenders argued that the South "had long maintained itself as a separate and established Government," proved by the Rebels "determination and ability to support their independence." Proponents believed restoration of the Union was impossible, and pleaded that the unprecedented bloodshed end "for the sake of humanity." They proposed a negotiated peace, with England the mediator.

Opponents argued otherwise. Though surprised by its resilience on the battlefields, they refused to accept the Confederacy had established its permanence. They believed mediation would fail because of the intransigence of the combatants. "What Government would go between these two powerful and furious foes, both confident in the right of their cause, both sanguine of success, neither prepared to submit to dictation." They disclaimed any intervention, believing it "would rather aggravate and prolong [the war], and possibly drag us into it." They cited Ireland as an example of how external meddling would offend the British. "If any disturbance arose in Ireland, if a contest were going on there, and if another power stepped in saying to us, 'Let Irishmen alone, and let them govern themselves,' should we be prepared to submit to dictation in such a matter?"

Opponents of the intervention resolution seized the moment to explain the probable reaction in the North. "If we wished to find President Lincoln his three hundred thousand men, we had only to send out by the next mail the statement that England, in concert with other Powers, threatened intervention if she did not put a stop to the war."

With respect to the proposition that intervention would end the suffering of the masses in the textile industry, the retort was convincing. "We could keep the working population of Lancashire in luxury for less than the price it would cost us to interfere. . . . [Should] we break all the rules of international law, on the grounds of mere interest, because we could not get a certain commodity[?]"

The British Prime Minister, Lord Palmerston, then entered the debate. "There can be but one wish on the part of any man in this country with respect to this war," he commenced, "and that is, that it should end." The British political sage, who had served in public office for more than 50 years, including stints as foreign minister and secretary of war, acknowledged that in Parliament "the war had been enacted by the champions of either side."

Palmerston then expressed disappointment that the debate had occurred, as it publicly challenged the government's position of neutrality. Palmerston dismissed recognition, stating that the "contest [had] not yet assumed a character to justify this country in assuming that the independence of the South [was] fully established." He also rejected intervention on behalf of the English destitute. "We all know the privations and suffering which a large portion of the people now are undergoing in consequence of this unfortunate war; but . . . any attempt to put an end to the war by active and violent interference would only produce still greater privations."[160]

The resolution was withdrawn following Palmerston's logical monologue, but the discussion would continue. Three weeks later, in the House of Lords, the representatives of the aristocrats examined the same questions. This time, however, the debate occurred in a different context. Word had arrived that the Federal army had failed in its attempt to seize the Confederate capital, thus boosting the Rebel claim to permanent independence. This resulted, some argued, in firm evidence that the Confederacy could stand alone in the world of nations.

The Lords worried that France would lead while England dallied, stepping forward with other European powers to negotiate a successful truce. The result: Lincoln's million-man army would turn to the *north*. "In two months Canada might be assaulted and Great Britain be without the least support on that continent." Lord John Russell, previous prime minister and present Foreign Secretary, dampened the ardor on this occasion, and again a motion was withdrawn without a vote.[161]

These dalliances by the English into intervention attracted considerable attention in the Northern press. Editors, regardless of political affiliation, scorned any idea of conciliation through external interference. They refrained that we would settle this matter ourselves. Some U.S. journals roared that any unwelcome intervention meant war with the United States. All understood that mediation, or even worse, Confederate recognition, was harmful to Northern interests.

Great Britain's selfish interest in a permanently divided America also was acknowledged. The British recognized that America was the fastest growing industrial country in the world, thus the greatest threat to the Empire — the strongest nation on the planet. If the United States separated into two countries, this growing challenge to British domination might subside, and possibly evaporate. A *divided states of America* offered handsome appeal to the Mother Country.

"America, while shaking her sword at us, is, at the same time, opening her own veins," observed the *London Times*, an ardent advocate of intervention. "The old school of diplomacy would ask, why should we interfere with our tourniquets and bandages? Perhaps it may be answered . . . that [their] own population are suffering, and that by putting an end to that war we shall be putting an end to our own distress."[162]

This humanitarian appeal landed with a thud in the North. "If the English people desire a plausible pretext for intervention, they can hardly find it in the distress that is said to exist in their manufacturing districts," recoiled the *Philadelphia Inquirer*. "The civilized world would certainly regard as monstrous the doctrine that because England, or France, or any other country, has obtained its chief supply of raw cotton from the United States, it may aid, even by mediation, the rebellious citizens of this Republic in their treasonable endeavors to destroy it, in order to revive a commerce which the Rebellion has interrupted." The *Inquirer* left no room for discussion. "If every cotton manufacturer in Europe should fail, and every cotton spinner starve . . . that fact would not . . . warrant any European power in interposing between this Government and its disloyal subjects."[163]

Then the *Inquirer* delivered an intriguing revelation concerning the cotton conundrum. The British were exporting cotton!

The paper proudly revealed, using reports from the British cotton market as its source, that England had been exporting cotton for months at the rate of 14,000 bales per week. The *Inquirer* also exposed that British speculators were withholding most of the cotton stocked in the country, rather than releasing it to the textile mills. "Hence it appears that it is not any actual deficiency of raw cotton in England, but only the avarice of English merchants, unrestrained by a wise, economical providence of the British Ministry, to which the operatives in the manufacturing districts must attribute their want of work and the consequent distress they suffer."[164]

Abraham Lincoln's secretary of state had a solution for the suffering: invite the textile workers to emigrate to the United States. In the aftermath of the intervention debate in the House of Commons, and the assertion that the American war was causing economic distress, Secretary of State William Seward prepared an employment circular for the British people. "At no former period of our history have our agricultural, manufacturing or mining interests been more prosperous than at this juncture," began the open letter from Seward, and published in the *Liverpool Post*. "Nowhere else can the industrious laboring man and artisan expect so liberal a recompense for his services as in the United States. You are authorized and directed to make these truths known in any quarter which may lead to the migration of such persons to this country."[165]

Since the outset of the war, diplomacy between Lincoln's government and Great Britain had been sensitive, and sometimes perilous. Secretary Seward worked tirelessly to keep the English out of the fray. Both countries irritated each other.

The U.S. barely avoided an international rupture eight months into the war when it seized, upon the open seas, two Confederate diplomats bound for England and France in the English vessel *Trent*. The U.S. blockade infuriated British merchants, and the prowess of the Federal Navy threatened England's domination of the oceans. Meanwhile the British — despite the Queen's initial dictum of neutrality during the war's first month — exported English weapons to the Confederacy; refused port access to American warships for refueling; enabled British entrepreneurs to construct Confederate warships in English harbors; and hosted blockade runners in Bermuda as they attempted penetrations of the Southern coast.

This blockade running particularly alienated Secretary of the Navy Gideon Welles. "We are insulted, wronged, and badly treated by the British authorities, especially at Nassau," complained Welles in his diary. "I am for no rash means, but I am clearly and decidedly for maintaining our rights."

The secretary unloaded his frustration. "Almost all the aid which the Rebels have received in arms, munitions, and articles of contraband have gone to them through the professedly neutral British port of Nassau. From [there] the Rebels have derived constant encouragement and support, from the commencement of hostilities." Welles fumed more with every word. "Our officers and people are treated with superciliousness and contempt by the authorities and inhabitants [of Bermuda], and scarcely a favor or courtesy is extended to them while they are showered upon the Rebels. It is there that vessels are prepared to run the blockade and violate our laws, by the connivance and with the knowledge of the Colonial, and, I apprehend, the parent, [British] Government."[166]

INDIGNATION OVER ENGLISH impartiality increased in volume over construction of the "No. 290." At the beginning of September, word reached the U.S. that the privateer ironclad steamer built in a British dockyard could steam up to 18 knots and was a large and powerful vessel that matched the best ship in the Royal Navy. "For all practical purposes invulnerable," boasted the London correspondent of the Dublin *Evening Mail*. "Will prove to any vessel she may encounter as formidable."

The U.S. knew about the No. 290, and had assigned a warship to maintain reconnaissance. The Rebel privateer escaped to open seas, however, where it rendezvoused with another English merchant ship carrying a cargo of massive armaments. "It needs no extraordinary powers of discernment to discover what excitement must be caused at the other side of the Atlantic by the arrival of the 'No. 290.'"[167] Soon christened the *CSS Alabama*, it preyed on Northern commerce and became the most feared vessel on the seas.

The Northern press urged a response that matched strength with strength. "Let every iron foundry in the country, and every shipyard, be kept employed to its fullest capacity in the construction of the most approved kind of iron-clad ships," championed *Harper's Weekly*. "Until the war ends, let us never stop building. One hundred impregnable vessels would not be too much to defend so long a coast line as ours." The editor counseled: "There is no guarantee that is absolutely reliable against foreign intervention but the certainty of being able to repel it."[168]

Distrust between the two nations even extended to the Irish. Millions of Irish had migrated to America in the decades prior to the Civil War, most to escape famine, others to avoid British rule. Tens of thousands of Irishmen served in the U.S. Army. Conspiracy theorists in England believed one purpose of the war was to weaken British control of the Emerald Isle. "It is an Irish War, because it is every day reducing the power of England, destroying her trade, filling her cities with paupers and threatening her with irreparable ruin," proclaimed a Catholic priest in Cincinnati. "We have captured already her best iron-built mercantile navy, and she dare not declare war. The capture of Canada will soon follow — it must follow as a necessity, and England can do nothing."[169]

The British were leery of enthusiastic receptions granted to Brig. Gen. Michael Corcoran during his Irish enlistment tour from Boston to New York to Philadelphia to Baltimore. "This appointment of General . . . it is well known, was made in response to the wild cries of the Irish, and was designed as a special mark of honor to one known as a noisy and determined enemy of England. Happily Gen. Corcoran is impotent to do us harm. A few thousand like him would speedily jeopardize the British hold on Ireland."[170]

Dueling editorials hurled vitriolic language and insults back and forth across the Atlantic, increasing animus between the two countries. The *London Times* served as the chief agitator in Britain. The journal cheered Confederate victories that rescued the Southern capital and brought the Rebel army surging to the outskirts of Washington during September's first week. "The Federal Government is brought to the verge of ruin," trumpeted the *Times*. "That word may be used when the Executive Government of the North is no longer safe in its capital."[171]

More invective came forth on the perceived condition of Lincoln's country:

> "The central power is weakened."
>
> "The war itself is splitting the North into factions."
>
> "The probability of breaking up the Union between the Northern States themselves."

> "[The] Republican Party, through its official press, all but disowns and repudiates the Government it created."
>
> "President Lincoln will have to struggle against the legitimate effects of the war — a violent reaction against his own army and arbitrary acts."[172]

The *Times* reached a new level when it advocated for Confederate states rights: "We ought to give our whole moral weight to our own English [Southern] kin, who have so gallantly striven so long for their liberties against a mongrel race of plunderers and oppressors."[173]

"The most expert intellectual acrobat now performing before the public is the *London Times*," observed the *Philadelphia Inquirer*. "There is sort of tumbling or twisting, genuflection or manipulation, in which it is not an adept. In treating the American question, facts under its nimble treatment cease to be facts, and ignorance is tricked out in the guise of knowledge."[174]

"John Bull has written himself down an ass," wrote *Harper's Weekly* of England's most famous political caricature.

> If he had boldly stated what he felt, that he was delighted with the prospect of the destruction of this Government — that we had always been hateful to him, and that now he would gratify his spite — if he had once recognized the rebellion and sent men and ships to help the traitors, his course would have at least been frank and manly.
>
> But to whine and snivel and sneer — to do all that he could to harm us, short of actual hostilities — to eat all his words and swallow all his principles — to let 'I want to' be forever held in check by 'I don't exactly like to' — this is the mean and contemptible course he has preferred to pursue.

Then *Harper's Weekly* pinched an English nerve. "The reason of British hate lies deeper than the want of cotton. It is a political and social sympathy." The editor explained the kindred relationship between the aristocracy of the Mother Country and the oligarchy of the Confederacy. "The British system is only a modification of feudalism. It is a system of special privilege, not of equal rights. And although ameliorated by the greater civilization of modern times, it is feudal and despotic still, and stretches out its hand muffled in cotton to grasp the hand of its ghastly kinsman, the hideous hag of Southern slavery. John Bull is ashamed of the relative — but he involuntarily owns the kinship."[175]

Finally, someone explained it. Republicans and Northern abolitionists were having difficulty with English incongruity. Why were the British — who had imperiously abolished slavery three decades previous to the Civil War — supporting a system and society dependent upon slavery? Were the English more interested in the demise of American democracy than the subjugation of Southern slavery? Was it "a morbid dread of the Democratic polity, and a keen desire for its ignominious overthrow," that spurred English clamor for the Confederacy?

"The success of the Rebels is a blow at democratic institutions, and therefore, to be desired," surmised the *Philadelphia Inquirer*. "This is the veritable English argument, lurking in the hearts of such journals as the *Times*, and this is the secret virus which infects all their discourse."[176]

Some Englishmen rejected the infection of this virus. "England had indeed much to answer for in the prolongation of this war, by deviating from the proud position she once occupied as the friend of the oppressed," wrote the *London Star*. "For without her leaning in favor of the South, this war would long since have ended."[177]

Yet England did lean, exasperating the Lincoln administration and the people of the North. As news of U.S. reverses reached the British Isles in September, momentum built in the Ministry and Parliament for some form of intervention. With Lincoln's armies reeling, Washington threatened, panic striking major Northern cities, and the Union in political and constitutional chaos, perhaps now was the opportune time to intercede.

"Great Britain is ready to avail herself of any pretext and any safe opportunity to ruin this country," predicted *Harper's Weekly*. "For the sake of destroying a commercial rival and at the same time demonstrating the failure of democratic institutions . . . we must hereafter regard England as our enemy, lying in wait for us, and seeking to destroy us whenever opportunity offers."[178]

The wait would not be long.

The most dangerous enemy, however, was not across the Atlantic, but across the Potomac.

CHAPTER 7

Divorce Decree

It is useless to disguise the scope of the contest. Their system must be annihilated or ours must.

—*Harper's Weekly,* August 30, 1862

America's ugly Civil War turned uglier during the summer of 1862.

Thousands of dead and wounded piled upon bloody battlefields, but the war extended its tentacles beyond the soldiers' butchery and into the front yards of Southern civilians.

It began with an order — an order with a harsh tone that threatened severe consequences.

Any citizen living near a wagon road or railroad in Northern Virginia would pay a penalty if guerrillas attacked or damaged any of these supply routes. Punishment also waited civilians if telegraph lines were hindered. Innocence or involvement was immaterial. All residents "living within five miles of the spot shall be turned out en masse to repair the damage." Additionally, they must pay all expenses for the soldiers compelled to round them up and guard them.

"If any soldier or legitimate follower of the army be fired upon from any house," the same order directed, houses were to be razed and all inhabitants seized. "If the shooting occurred in an uninhabited area, all citizens within five miles of the incident would be accountable and made to pay an indemnity."[179]

A second order demanded loyalty or relocation. It required either forced allegiance or forced migration. It affected all men living in occupied Confederate territory in Northern Virginia. Adult male citizens were required to take an oath swearing allegiance to the United States; otherwise, they would be escorted south beyond the limits of the U.S. Army. If they attempted to return to their homes and families, they would be "considered spies and subjected to the extreme rigor of military law."

Once removed from their abodes, the inhabitant became isolated. Communication "with any person whatever, living within the lines of the enemy," was prohibited. Any person carrying or writing letters or messages would be treated as a spy.[180]

A third order created fear in Southern minds. It sounded innocent and reasonable — no U.S. soldier operating in Northern Virginia would provide protection of homes or any private property. "The soldiers were called into the field to do battle against the enemy, and it is not expected that their force and energy shall be wasted in protecting the private property of those most hostile to the Government."[181]

Southerners interpreted this, however, with frightful implications. They believed this potentially opened their homes, businesses and farms to plundering, ransacking — and most feared of all, slave insurrection.

"The *war* has actually begun," proclaimed the *Philadelphia Inquirer*, embracing the new definition of war inclusive upon the Southern populace. The president had just instructed his generals — in compliance with a new law passed by the Congress — to seize personal and real property throughout the Rebel states (including slaves), and to employ newly freed slaves as laborers for military or naval purposes. "Heretofore the contest with the Rebellion has been a one-sided conflict," complained the *Inquirer*. "It is only the Rebels who have been waging *war*. We, although we have periled hundreds of thousands of lives, and spent hundreds of millions of dollars, we have *not* been making *war*."

The resolute editor reinforced the change in U.S. policy. "The brawny fists of our Northern freemen have been muffled in boxer's gloves, our swords have been but the fencer's foils, and our cartridges have been but blanks. . . . We have been models of fraternal forbearance, patterns of courtesy, and paragons of chivalry. . . . In our honest and confiding natures we have treated the Rebellion as an outbreak of a big mob that could be dispersed by the reading of the riot act."

The newspaper made a final review of the past 16 months of national strife. "We have treated these Rebel conspirators and traitors as mistaken and deluded men, who could be convinced by reason and won back by kindness." Those "deceptive theories" were now played out, and the new policy would "begin to make war."[182]

A guaranteed enforcer of this attitude was U. S. Maj. Gen. John Pope. Pope authored the stringent orders that transformed home front into warfront for the citizens of Northern Virginia. President Lincoln had selected Pope to command the newly organized Army of Virginia in July, assigning him the mission of advancing against the Confederate capital at Richmond. But capturing Richmond was not Pope's only cause. He now had legal license to push the war into Virginia households. Pope accepted his assignments with boastful bombast. "I have come from the West, where we have always seen the backs of our enemies — from an army whose business it has been to seek the adversary, and to beat him, when he was found — whose policy has been attack and not defense." Pope concluded his announcement with certitude. "Let us look before us and not behind. Success and glory are in the advance. Disaster and shame lurk in the rear."[183]

The *Philadelphia Inquirer* strongly endorsed Pope's fresh approach. "It has the true ring of the Union metal, and is the only tone that befits the cause. . . . This is the only orthodox text for addressing a Union Army — this is the true catholic doctrine of our American Pope."[184]

Confederate authorities recoiled at this U.S. expansion of the war. "The military authorities of the United States, not content with the unjust and aggressive warfare hitherto waged with savage cruelty against an unoffending people," responded the Confederate government, "have now determined to violate all the rules and usages of war, and to convert the hostilities, hitherto waged against armed forces, into a campaign of robbery and murder against innocent citizens and peaceful tillers of the soil."[185]

"Under no excess of provocation could our noble-hearted defenders be driven to wreak vengeance on unarmed men, on women or on children," boomed President Jefferson Davis before the Confederate States Senate. "The exasperation of failure has aroused the worst passions of our enemies; a large portion of their people, even their clergymen, now engages in urging an excited populace to the extreme of ferocity, and nothing remains but to vindicate our rights and to maintain our existence."[186]

Davis ordered Gen. Robert E. Lee to send a letter of protest to the general commanding the U.S. Army in Washington. Lee outlined Confederate grievances to the new U.S. war policy. Concerning private property, a general order "directs the military commanders of the United States to take property of our people for the convenience and use of [their] army, without compensation." Pope's directives order "the murder of our peaceful citizens as spies, if found quietly tilling their farms in his rear, *even outside of his lines*." Lee complained Pope's army had "seized innocent and peaceful inhabitants, to be held as hostages to the end that they may be murdered in cold blood, if any of [Pope's] soldiers are killed by some unknown persons, whom he designates as 'bushwhackers.'"

Lee then delivered these instructions from President Davis. Gen. Pope and his commissioned officers will be recognized as "robbers and murderers, and not that of public enemies entitled, if captured, to be treated as prisoners of war." The Confederate chieftain concluded, "We shall reluctantly be forced to the last resort of accepting the war on the terms chosen by our enemies, until the voice of an outraged humanity shall compel a respect for the recognized usages of war."[187]

The U.S. Army General in Chief in Washington responded upon receipt of Lee's missive. "As these papers are crouched in language exceedingly insulting to the Government of the United

States, I must respectfully decline to receive them. They are returned herewith."[188]

WHAT HAD BROUGHT "brother against brother" to such vitriolic villainy?

The Confederates abhorred the Second Confiscation Act adopted by the U.S. Congress. The law, entitled "An Act to suppress Insurrection, to punish Treason and Rebellion, to seize and confiscate the Property of Rebels, and for other Purposes," infuriated the South. Especially enraging were the sections that seized and condemned private property, including slaves, now deemed "captives of war . . . forever free of their servitude, and not again held as slaves."[189]

Southerners reacted with scorn. "The Abolitionists have at last succeeded in usurping complete control of the Government at Washington, and in imparting to the war the unholy zeal of fanaticism," clamored the *Richmond Examiner*. "Universal emancipation in the South, and the utter overthrow of all property, is now the declared policy of the desperate and demented leaders of the war." The editor declared the legislation "violent and barbarous . . . intended to envenom the war, to insult and torture the South . . . and to keep the Government in the hands of fanatics and crusaders of abolitionism."

Southerners also believed the Second Confiscation Act intended to incite slave insurrection. "'Rebellion' is to be punished by a warfare of savages, and the devilish, skulking revenge that pillages, burns and assassinates, is to follow in the bloody footsteps of the invading armies."[190] President Davis concurred. "Two, at least, of the generals of the United States are engaged, unchecked by their Government, in inciting servile insurrection, and in arming and training slaves for warfare against their masters, citizens of the Confederacy."[191]

The South had suspected a Northern war on Southern culture — pursued through abolitionists and slave insurrection — for more than three decades. They now surmised it as reality. In the Southern mind, the Second Confiscation Act of 1862 confirmed and legalized the fanaticism and violence of abolitionist John Brown's attack at Harpers Ferry, a painful memory for Southerners.[192]

President Lincoln's proclamation to enforce the provisions of the Second Confiscation Act was interpreted by Southerners as a "proclamation of rapine, murder, and devastation" that were "in harmony with the leaders of the war spirit of the North, and with the ravings of the mob." The *Richmond Enquirer* believed that Lincoln had surrendered himself "to the most violent of the most rabid class." The paper asked: will Lincoln recede? Can he? If not, the *Enquirer* made a prediction: "We will show Lincoln that if he failed at his wicked attempt when employing the means of civilized war, he shall be doubly unsuccessful and doubly punished when taking counsel of the fiends of the bottomless pit."[193]

"The Secessionists at the South, at this hour get hold of this Abolition stuff, and reproduce it in their newspapers and speeches, falsely magnify it, charge it on the whole North, and thus succeed in arraying the Southern people in solid phalanx against what they term the 'Abolition Lincolns,'" observed the *Valley Spirit*, speaking in concert with Northern Democratic newspapers. "The Abolition policy of Congress does more to embitter the feelings of the Southerners towards the North than all the military expeditions that could be fitted out."[194]

The new U.S. law validated, in Confederate opinion, explanations for the Union's inevitable rupture. The Second Confiscation Act confirmed pronouncements in various "Declaration of Causes," adopted by several Southern states at secession's outset. Texas, when rationalizing its departure in 1861, cited the principal reason it severed its bonds from the U.S. "[Abolitionists] have invaded Southern soil and murdered unoffending citizens, and through the press and their leading men and a fanatical pulpit have bestowed praise upon the actors and assassins in these crimes." Mississippi held a similar belief. Abolitionists had "enlisted its press, its pulpit and its schools against us, until the whole popular mind of the North is excited and inflamed with prejudice." Mississippi summarized the feelings of the offended South with one line in its "Declaration of Causes": "There was no choice left to us but submission to the mandates of abolition, or a dissolution of the Union."[195]

The Northern press discounted the slave rebellion theory. "Has there been any solitary instance of Rebel life taken except upon the battlefield?" inquired *Harper's Weekly*. "None; none at all."

The editor explained the North's rationale:

> Nor does anyone ask for an inhuman or savage policy now. All that is asked is that we understand that we are at war, and that we use every lawful means of warfare. Having found that tufts of grass and twigs lightly thrown will not drive the enemy away, let us try stones. Having been forced to rely upon war, let us show those who have invoked it that we are more terrible in its use than they; that if they hit, we shall hit harder; that if we bleed, they shall bleed more copiously; that if we suffer, they shall endure anguish.
>
> The severity that drives an enemy to despair is wanton cruelty.[196]

The South would accept no explanation for a harsher policy of war. They especially railed at the orders of Gen. Pope that promulgated the new Northern tactics. "There is no atrocity of modern times comparable to the Yankee policy of deporting and imprisoning the whole population of a country."[197]

The *Richmond Examiner* demanded a ruthless policy in response. "No formality, no official circumlocution, is necessary for this retaliation. Let every Confederate soldier constitute himself an avenger of the brigandage warfare of the North." The mean and unforgiving spirit of this new mode of war was then enunciated. "Let there be no quarter on the battlefield for Federal assassins; let there be no prisoner taken; let the blood of the bayonets of our troops attest to a savage foe the spirit of retaliation and the fury of awakened vengeance."

The *Examiner* hoped that both sides would come to their senses, but if not, it warned: "If, however, it should steep the land in blood and make of this war the most infernal of civil conflicts, on the head of our enemy be the crime of these horrors."[198]

Few expected such a bloodbath, but the orders remained offensive to the South. Pope's directives "surpass in barbarity anything ever yet proclaimed by the Federals in a Virginia latitude," determined the *Richmond Dispatch*. "They sweep away from every citizen who refuses to convert himself into a slave, every vestige of his possessions on the face of the earth. They despoil him of property, home and liberty, leaving him no possibility of redress except by *proving his loyalty* to the despotic power which inflicts upon him the most intolerable wrongs."

The *Dispatch* then commented on Pope's genetics. "It is a striking illustration of the degrading influence of Puritan association, that this man Pope, a Kentuckian, with good Virginia blood in his veins, should become so degraded by his affiliation with Yankees as to surpass them all in his atrocious schemes of plunder and oppression."

Something had to be done. Pope could not be tolerated. His miscreant behavior could not go unchallenged. "The Confederate Government and people must meet this inhuman tool of tyranny in the same spirit which he has evoked," the *Dispatch* demanded. "It will not do to fight monsters with gloves on. Men of Pope's caliber construe forbearance into fear. It is high time that they should be disabused of that delusion by the most summary vengeance."[199]

THE CONFEDERATES, INDEED, concocted a retaliatory response for Gen. Pope and his compeers. First, Pope and his commissioned officers (from lieutenants through generals) were "hereby expressly and especially declared to be *not* entitled to be considered as soldiers," but rather as common criminals. Second, any officer of Pope's command captured by the Confederates would not be eligible for prisoner exchange, but instead "held in close confinement" and as a bargaining chip to protect civilians from harm. "In the event of the murder of any unarmed citizen or inhabitant of this Confederacy . . . it shall be the duty of the commanding General . . . to cause immediately to be hung, out of the commissioned officers [prisoners] a number equal to the number of our own citizens thus murdered by the enemy."[200]

Confederate President Jefferson Davis. (*Frank Leslie's Illustrated Newspaper*)

The Southern press approved of holding Pope and his officers accountable. Furious that Pope had come into genteel Virginia with the "impetuosity of a madman," the Richmond journals shouted for Pope's demise. "Let our cool and astute and energetic leaders, and their brave troops, catch him and put him in a straight jacket."[201]

Confederate authorities anticipated these retaliatory measures would check or prevent commissioned officers from following Pope's orders, granting them the "power to avoid guilty action by refusing service under a Government which seeks their aid in the perpetration of such infamous barbarities."

The Confederacy acknowledged it intended retribution only against commissioned officers, and not U. S. enlisted men, "who may be unwilling instruments of the savage cruelty of their commanders."[202]

Jefferson Davis seemed satisfied with his government's response. "*But stern and exemplary punishment can and must be meted out to the murderers and felons*, who, disgracing the profession of arms, seek to make of public war the occasion for the commission of the most monstrous crimes."[203]

Northern newspapers decried this decree of Southern retaliation. "The Rebel leaders have vainly thought that it was for them to give laws to the Government of these United States," replied the *Philadelphia Inquirer*. "They talk in great blustering tones. If at any time the Government attempts to assert its own legitimate power, they talk big of retaliation. . . . Jefferson Davis does not like retaliation when it pinches on his dear rebellious minions."[204]

With respect to the imprisonment and possible hanging of U.S. officers, "simply atrocious" was how the paper labeled the Confederate order. "We trust that our Government and our people will read in these shameful orders the real character of those men with whom we have to deal . . . count carefully the cost before any concession is made to the infamous threats of an arrogant and unscrupulous enemy." The writer concluded with grit. "We must learn to dare to do right, to dare to maintain the dignity of our Government in the face of even the most ferocious threats or the most atrocious barbarities of the Rebel leaders."[205]

The South refused to relent. In fact, it demonstrated its resolve for retaliation when Confederate Gen. Stonewall Jackson captured 28 of Pope's officers in the Battle of Slaughter Mountain. They were escorted to the Confederate capital in irons and "consigned to close confinement with deserters and other persons to whom infamy attaches."[206]

Tension mounted as both sides awaited the next move. "They have noble men of ours now, and they are thrust into cells and treated like the worst criminals," observed *Harper's Weekly*. "If we subsist our troops upon the enemy, and shoot spies and secret foes, they will hang our men, their prisoners." Many Northerners championed the capture of an equivalent number of Jackson's officers, believing their "brave comrades in felons' cells" would inflame Gen. Pope to take retaliatory action. "Retribution of this kind should come with a trenchant sweep," argued the *Philadelphia Inquirer*. "There should be no cooling of the hot pursuit until Gen. Pope has in his power such hostages from the officers of the enemy as will terrify Davis for his infamous purpose."[207]

Gen. Pope became the devil incarnate for the South during the summer of 1862. He symbolized the diabolical and distrustful Yankee who intended to destroy the Southern economy, seize Southern property, incite Southern slaves, and collapse Southern culture. Confederates used Pope to personalize — in one visible individual — their enemy.

"If pompous and pretentious proclamations could make a soldier, Julius Caesar would be a baby in the hands of General Pope," opined the *Richmond Dispatch*. "The man is simply a compound of vulgar self-conceit, impudence and brutality, and will be exploded in due time, like all the military humbugs that have preceded him. The tyranny he threatens to practice upon peaceful citizens will inflame instead of intimidate."[208]

Despite the Confederate indignation and rancor, Pope did not yield. One reason for his intransigence was the Confederate authorization of guerrilla warfare during the summer of 1862. Pope defined guerrillas as "evil disposed persons in the rear of our armies." Civilians by day and attackers by night, Pope considered guerrillas as "lawless bands of individuals not forming a part of the organized forces of the enemy." Without uniforms, and under the "pretext of peaceful citizens," Pope considered them very dangerous — operating in his rear, with intention to "attack and murder straggling soldiers, molest trains of supplies, destroy railroads, telegraph lines, and bridges, and commit outrages disgraceful to a civilized people and revolting to humanity." [209]

This explained Pope's incentive for his threats against civilians. He considered guerrilla warfare barbaric, and in his war against guerrillas, his inspiration was more than vengeance, it was also self-defense.

"Ever since the war began some of the Richmond papers have been urging every man who could load and fire a musket or wield a pike to hang on the flank of our armies and pick off our soldiers one by one," recalled the *Philadelphia Inquirer*. "They even chuckled with fiendish mirth as they computed the number that might be cut off in a march of a hundred miles by this sneaking butchery." The editor argued the North had every right to reject the Confederacy's official endorsement of guerrilla warfare as a new military strategy of the South, a "shameful and horrible system which all modern civilization has branded as barbarous."[210]

THREATS OF THE WAR degenerating into barbarism were not confined to Virginia. More than 1,000 miles distant in Louisiana, tempers were erupting.

Confederate guerrillas were ranging along the Mississippi, dodging to and from the river from hideaways in woods and swamps, and attacking U.S. commerce between Union-occupied New Orleans and Baton Rouge and Vicksburg. Guerrillas destroyed the U.S. gunboat *Sumter* that had grounded near the town of Bayou Sara, inviting a vengeful Federal gunboat barrage that wiped out most of the village. The U.S. gunboat *Essex* prowled the river "with a determination to demolish any place along the banks which had been used to protect guerrilla bands" that fired upon steamboats and other U.S. craft. Despite Federal efforts, guerrilla attacks on lower Mississippi shipping became "bolder and bolder every day," prompting supply constriction, exorbitant inflation, and food shortages in New Orleans.

Confederate attempts to retake the Louisiana capital of Baton Rouge intensified the tension and rage. When U.S. forces holding the town established a defensive perimeter along the Mississippi, they burned numerous buildings to clear a line of fire for their gunboats and the marines occupying the position. This enraged the Confederate commander in the sector, Maj. Gen. John C. Breckinridge. Breckinridge — a former vice president of the United States and a Democratic candidate against Lincoln in the 1860 election — accused the U.S. forces at Baton Rouge of wantonly burning houses; destroying private property without compensation; seizing and imprisoning unarmed citizens; and arming slaves "to be employed against us."

"The above acts are regarded as in violation of the usages of civilized warfare," Breckinridge informed the chief officer at Baton Rouge. "In future, upon any departure from these usages, [my commander] will 'raise the black flag, and neither give nor ask quarter.'"[211]

The black flag! No quarter! Such merciless language from *military men* had little previous parallel during the Civil War. All knew the meaning: no mercy for the vanquished; no surrender for the loser; only death for those defeated.

The tension subsided a bit at Baton Rouge when the U.S. commander, Col. Halbert E. Paine, responded to Breckinridge. He explained the general had received erroneous information. Buildings had been burned, but with discretion for defensive purposes; government property had been destroyed, but private property had not; citizens had not been seized; and slaves were not being armed. Following his denials, Paine reminded Breckinridge that "the most barbarous system of guerrilla warfare is authorized by your officers and practiced by your men in this department." Paine argued this, too, could legitimize the black flag; but he vowed: "I shall never raise the black flag which all civilized nations abhor."[212]

Meanwhile, as a message to the Confederates operating in the Baton Rouge sector, U.S. Maj. Gen. Benjamin F. Butler ordered a famed statue of George Washington removed from the Louisiana capital and transferred to New Orleans. Reports circulated that Butler was "unwilling to suffer the marble image of the Father of his Country to remain among savage guerrillas and thieving Rebels." Some suggested it be transported to New York "as a gift for the adornment of Central Park." Others concurred "it is of no possible use to Secessionists."[213]

Back in Richmond, where another grand statue of Washington overlooked Virginia's capitol grounds, the drumbeat for retaliation thumped louder. "The people of the South in this war are willing to endure every privation, to give their blood, their wealth, their lives to the cause," broadcast the *Richmond Examiner*. "But it is hard for them to submit tamely to the atrocities and insults of a base, vindictive enemy, when submission, without an effort at retaliation, surrenders their honor, displays to the world a weak and dastardly spirit, and outrages the memory of the dead." The *Examiner* proclaimed the response. "The mind of the South is made up as to the necessity of retaliation — the atonement of blood for blood. . . . Surrounded as we are by mourning families, wounded brothers and sons, desolated fields and firesides, it is no time for rose water philanthropy and womanly tenderness."[214]

Precisely. Northerners agreed, except the words applied to the Rebels. The U.S. must not equivocate. The war must become a complete war against the entirety of the South. "We must conquer and subdue them utterly or they will absolutely overcome us," determined the opinion writer of *Harper's Weekly*. "And there is but one thing that can help it . . . the resolution of the North that they shall be exterminated, if extermination is necessary to our success."

The language of conquest poured forth. "We shall disintegrate their society. We shall make the foundations of their social system quiver and shake beneath their feet. We shall fill the sky with blackness over them and the air with terror around them. . . . The death and horror and desolation in which they would engulf us all shall yawn for them."[215]

Southerners had their own target."The city of Washington itself must be annihilated. There can be no peace until that nest of Yankees and traitors is exterminated."[216]

No longer were things civil in America's Civil War.

"The fate of Carthage must be that of Washington," bellowed the *Richmond Whig*, as August melted into September, 1862. "Let Stonewall [Jackson] have one lick at it, and we shall have no more trouble from that quarter."[217]

Stonewall, indeed, was on his way toward Washington.

CHAPTER 8

Rebel Roulette

Thousands at the North, who heretofore silently submitted to the popular cry, will now speak out and demand peace, since all their armies have been defeated, and no force intervenes between our victorious armies and the northern cities.

—*Richmond Enquirer,* September 11, 1862

Stonewall Jackson menacingly advanced toward Washington on September 1.

The direction was ominous. The Confederate army was victorious. The Union army was in retreat. And no Rebel triggered more fear in a U.S. soldier than Stonewall Jackson.

The Federals knew their opponent well. Gen. Jackson's stature and prowess were legendary by the summer of 1862. Jackson had earned initial fame as the Southern commander who stood "like a stone wall" during the war's opening battle, helping to carry the day for the Confederates. During the war's second year, his exploits became fabled, as he outwitted and outmaneuvered hapless Union generals with bigger armies and boastful commanders.

Jackson's tactics employed deception and the rapid strike. He would disappear, move with stealth and speed, and then suddenly reappear at some vulnerable point in the U.S. flank or rear. His infantry moved fast — its motions mostly mysterious — earning his soldiers the sobriquet "foot cavalry." As Jackson's reputation grew to mythic proportions, his warriors accomplished feats that seemed superhuman.[218]

No one wearing a United States uniform, it appeared, could conquer Stonewall Jackson — not even the bombastic John Pope.

Jackson rumors and Jackson fears intensified during the last weeks of August. Stonewall secretly circumvented Pope's army, ending up in his rear. About 30 miles from Washington, he promptly and efficiently destroyed Pope's supply base and cargo trains at Manassas Junction, with the smoke visible from the Union capital.

Satisfied, but not finished with his mission, Stonewall then set a trap, luring the frantic Pope into battle near Manassas. Pope's arrogance became exuberant, and then delusional, as he believed *he* had bagged the Mighty Stonewall. This fantasy produced poor decisions by Pope — including ignoring evidence that Robert E. Lee and the rest of his army had united with Stonewall — more than doubling Confederate strength. The Rebels then pounced on Pope, branding him with ignominy, while forcing the U.S. Army into a rapid retreat into the defenses of Washington.[219]

The turnabout was remarkable. Eight weeks earlier, Union forces were within sight of the spires of Richmond, threatening capture of the Confederate capital. Two months later, through the leadership of Lee and the assist of Stonewall Jackson, the Rebels had shifted the war to the outskirts of Washington.

"A column from a Yankee journal shows that the greatest panic prevailed in the Yankee capital," reported the *Richmond Enquirer*. "Old Abraham doubtless has his Scotch cap at hand, ready to make his exit."[220]

Following a summer of success, what was the Rebel denouement? What should the Confederates — flushed with victories and bolstered in confidence — do next?

"We cannot afford to be idle," Gen. Lee apprised President Jefferson Davis.[221]

Lee did not wish to lose his momentum. His string of victories was contagious. His soldiers felt confident, even unconquerable.

Confederate Maj. Gen. Thomas J. "Stonewall" Jackson was the most feared general in the North by September, 1862. *(Frank Leslie's Illustrated Newspaper)*

Under Lee's leadership, the Army of Northern Virginia had suffered no meaningful defeats. The triumvirate generals of Lee, Jackson, and James Longstreet had no equal in the U.S. Army. "Marse Robert's" Confederates seemed unstoppable, unless they stopped themselves.

The effect of Confederate victories produced a contagion in the Union army. Demoralization rampaged through the ranks; disorganization rattled the brass; and dereliction poisoned the trust in Federal generals.

Lee knew the moment was ripe. But what was right for the moment?

"I propose to enter Pennsylvania . . ."[222]

Lee's words rocked Richmond. His proposition to President Davis altered the course of the Confederacy. The Southern army would launch an invasion into Northern territory. This had not been attempted — not even seriously considered. Was it a gamble worth taking?

"I am aware that the movement is attended with much risk, yet I do not consider success impossible, and shall endeavor to guard it from loss." Lee was determined and convincing. Davis assented. The war would go north of the Potomac.[223]

Gen. Lee knew the dangers, but he envisioned unparalleled results. If he could defeat the Northern army on U.S. soil, the ramifications could be stunning. Lee kept abreast of matters other than military. He was an avid reader of Northern newspapers. Journals from New York, Philadelphia, Baltimore, and Washington — smuggled into the South — provided him with excellent sources of intelligence on the psyche of the North.

The papers revealed the precarious situation of the Lincoln Administration in September 1862. Lee knew the Republicans were under assault for incompetence and mismanagement of the war. He read about Northern political fractures over confiscation of Southern property. He saw long columns describing the fractious debate over freeing slaves and arming blacks. Lee knew that Democrats voiced angry objection to strict martial law that stifled their opposition and silenced their newspapers. Lee sensed the Northern phobia of the impending draft.

It appeared Lincoln and his Republicans were teetering on political collapse. With the fall elections of 1862 only weeks away, Lee realized combat victories upon U.S. territory could alter the political landscape in the North, evolving into a U.S. Congress more favorable to the Confederacy.

Opportunity also availed itself on the diplomatic front. The debate in the British parliament the previous month over English recognition of the Confederacy — or perhaps mediation of the American conflict — appeared in newspapers both North and South. The British were impressed by Lee's salvation of Richmond, but not impressed enough to intervene in the war. English newspapers, regardless of the political stalemate in parliament, berated the North and influenced their populace against the U.S. They urged that the Confederacy be acknowledged in the world of nations. But British leaders, in particular, remained unconvinced the South had established enough military might to sanction Confederate independence. Victories by Lee on Northern soil could perhaps alter their position.

Confederate General Robert E. Lee led the invasion of the North. *(Currier & Ives)*

Lee also faced practical reasons for an invasion that transcended politics and diplomacy. He recognized: "the two grand armies of the United States that have been operating in Virginia, though now united, are much weakened and demoralized."[224]

These armies still existed, however, hunkered down behind the defenses of Washington. Here they licked their wounds. Incessant campaigning had cost the Federals fighting in Virginia more than 34,000 casualties — the bloodiest three months of the war for the North. Lee knew they eventually would recover. Not only were the Yankees weary, but they were wandering without direction. Pope had been disgraced. Gen. George B. McClellan's machinations had exhausted President Lincoln's patience, producing "Mac's" temporary removal. The Federals appeared leaderless and lost. Chaos infected their command. Now was the time for Lee to exploit the Union's vacuum in military leadership.

Another issue confronting Lee was U.S. reinforcements. Lincoln had called for 600,000 volunteers to bolster the Union ranks. If not enough men volunteered, they would be drafted. Lee understood he could never equal the enemy's numbers, but numbers did not equate to trained soldiers. "Their new levies, of which I understand 60,000 men have already been posted in Washington, are not yet organized, and will take some time to prepare for the field."[225] Sixty thousand! That was more new soldiers than Lee had veterans in his entire army. It seemed imperative that Lee strike before the raw recruits received training and discipline, improving his odds for a more even match on the battlefield.

"Of the 600,000 new Yankee levies, not one from East of Ohio knows how to load a gun or ride a horse," surmised the *Richmond Whig*. "Six or eight months will be necessary for them to learn those indispensable qualifications for war." The paper recalled recent history: Gen. McClellan had spent seven months preparing his Union Army of the Potomac for the field. The *Whig* boasted that "every Southern man and boy can ride and shoot, and have only to learn one or two words of command, and a few simple movements, to be as good soldiers as 20 years' drilling could make [the Yankees]." The editor deemed premature disposition of the fresh U.S. soldiers would make them "food for panics."

The *Whig* called for immediate action. "If the war is pushed — pushed at once, and into the enemy's country — the new levies of the Yankees will avail them nothing; but, on the contrary, being little better than a rabble rout, will prove an invaluable aid to our advancing columns."

As an assist to Gen. Lee, the *Whig* called upon the Confederate Congress to pass a new conscription law. "To meet this new array [of Federals] is the first duty of the Congress," the paper announced as the legislature returned to session in August. Men between ages 18 and 45 should be drafted. The editor knew this would produce no immediate boost in battle-ready soldiers, but he believed the martial abilities of Southerners would adapt them quickly for the army.

The Confederate Congress needed to do something. Prior to ending its previous session, it had "damaged its reputation by voting itself an annual salary and then deserting its post." The *Whig* editor deemed this conduct "unworthy of the times and the Southern people." He anticipated redemption with a focus upon conscription. "We must even venture to hope that the members, for a moment oblivious of self, will be inspired by the gravity of the crises, and address themselves, like men, to the mighty responsibilities which rest upon them."[226]

The Rebel Congress could govern a draft, but it could not grow crops. Lee's army needed food. But there was little food in war-ravaged Northern Virginia. "This unfortunate portion of the State has been desolated," reported the *Richmond Examiner*. "At the end of 18 months is has been reduced to a condition nearly resembling that of Middle Germany after the Thirty Years War." The journal predicted "it will take 100 full years to restore the country to the condition in which the war found it."[227] Lee knew this situation, and realized the region could not sustain his army. Temptation came into view just across the Potomac, where Maryland's crops and herds looked enticing.

Maryland had an allure for the Confederates beyond food. "If it is ever desired to give material aid to Maryland and afford her an opportunity of throwing off the oppression to which she is now subject, this would seem the most favorable," Lee advised President Davis.[228]

THE CONFEDERACY HAD coveted Maryland since the outbreak of secession. From the outset, the secessionists had hoped the Mason-Dixon Line would be the northern border of the new nation, not the Potomac. Maryland was a slave state, sharing the sisterhood of the South's culture and economy. Baltimore was the South's largest city, and the fourth largest metropolis in the country. Maryland's position astride the Chesapeake Bay, along with its array of railroads, made it crucial to Southern trade and commerce. The fact that Maryland surrounded much of Washington, D.C., enhanced its desirability for the South.

Abraham Lincoln knew these facts as well. When war erupted in the spring of 1861, and rioters in Baltimore killed Massachusetts volunteers en route to the capital, Lincoln seized the state. Baltimore was the first Southern city occupied by the Federal army. Annapolis was the first Southern capital patrolled by U.S. troops. Maryland was the first state with martial law imposed.

Maryland's legislators were placed under house arrest to guarantee no votes for secession. Bayonets ensured Maryland stayed in the Union.

"The state, overwhelmed by the power of the foe, sank into the stolid quietude of helpless, though not hopeless, subjection," observed the *Richmond Whig*. "To free [Maryland's people] from their shackles and avenge their wrongs was expressed as the universal determination."

The "liberation" of Maryland never looked so favorable. The *Whig* predicted how the oppressed would respond. "If their experience of despotism has produced its proper effect . . . and kindled the fire of resistance, instead of emasculating their spirit, they will hasten to seize the prize within their grasp. The pride, the self-respect, and the sympathies of Maryland link her with the cause of the South."

Benefits of an incursion into Maryland reached beyond the cause. "If the feeling of the people be what it has been represented, they will rush to arms," anticipated the *Whig*. "We have every right to expect that her people will not only be prepared to fight in the cause, but that they will cheerfully contribute all in their power to the support of the army."[229]

Lee needed men. His army required supplies. Was Maryland Lee's invitation for both?

"I am more fully persuaded of the benefit that will result from an expedition into Maryland," Lee wrote President Davis on September 4. "I shall proceed to make the movement at once, unless you should signify your disapprobation."[230]

Lee did not wait for permission. Confederate soldiers began splashing across the Potomac at White's Ford and Point of Rocks on the 4th, planting the Rebel flag upon Maryland's soil. Alert Union lookouts immediately spied the river crossings from their observatory atop Sugarloaf Mountain. They signaled their sightings, via flag codes, to Washington. Invasion of the North!

Confederates cherished the moment. "Every regiment singing and as happy as if going to a ball," recalled Virginia Capt. Samuel Buck. Buck rode his horse across the Potomac, then turned to see hundreds of men wading the shallow ford, brass bands playing and joyous men singing, *Maryland, My Maryland*:[231]

Dear Mother! Burst the tyrant's chain,
Maryland!
Virginia should not call in vain,
Maryland!
She meets her sisters on the plain –
"Sic simper!" 'tis the proud refrain
That baffles minions back again,
Maryland!
Arise in majesty again,
Maryland! My Maryland!

I hear the distant thunder-hum,
Maryland!
The Old Line's bugle, fife, and drum,
Maryland!
She is not dead, nor deaf, nor dumb –
Huzza! she spurns the Northern scum!
She breathes! she burns! she'll come! she'll come!
Maryland! My Maryland![232]

"The war has assumed a new phase," declared the *Richmond Enquirer*. "The tables have been turned, and the Confederate army is now an army of invasion."[233]

SOME IN THE SOUTH viewed the Confederate offensive as an opportunity for vengeance. They abhorred the U.S. armies for endless occupations that destroyed their crops and farms and plantations. They detested Federal orders that made war upon civilians. They bristled at the sanctioned theft of private property by Union forces. They scorned the Yankees for offering protection for their slaves. They were terrified by Northern laws that, in their judgment, encouraged slave insurrection. They were angry that their homeland had been invaded. They sought retribution.

"Let us now prove that we have learnt something from the bitter lessons of experience, and show our enemy that we are just beginning the war so far as his participation in its calamities is concerned," warned the *Richmond Dispatch*. "Let us prepare not only to meet the new legions he is raising, but to push the tide of battle at once into his own country."

The editor explained two outcomes from an invasion. Northerners, who thus far had escaped the devastation of war, would feel its hard hand first hand. This, in turn, would compel the enemy to seek peace. "If the North sees that we are no longer intoxicated with the fumes of [military] victory, that it only makes us more energetic and determined for the future, it will begin to turn its thoughts to peace, and recoil from the horrors which are impending over its own head."

The *Dispatch* called for action. "Let our commanders push promptly into the enemy's country; let cavalry expeditions make raids into their territory, and seize and bring off their prominent citizens, to be held as hostages for the security of those of our own people who now languish in Federal prisons. Now, now is the time for the Congress and for the Army to strike a decisive blow for our salvation."[234]

The Southern Congress enjoined in debate within days of the Confederate invasion into the North. Such a move was counter to all previous Confederate war policy. This had been a war of defense. Defense of states' rights, defense of secession, slavery; culture, and defense of house and home. An offensive strategy of invasion into the enemy's territory had the appearance of making the Confederacy the aggressor — and the transgressor. Was invasion acceptable?

The debate commenced with a resolution: "Resolved, That Congress has heard with profound satisfaction of the triumphant crossing of the Potomac by our victorious army . . . [and now] to achieve new triumphs to relieve oppressed Maryland and advance our standard into the *territory* of the enemy."

James Lyons of Virginia immediately objected. He moved to strike out the words "advance our standard into the *territory* of the enemy." Lyons posed this question to his fellow members within the Confederate House of Representatives: "Do you believe that we could safely go into the heart of the North?"

The inquiry brought a response, and a rebuke, from South Carolina's William Miles. "The whole country had literally rung with the cry for the onward movement; the press had been loud in . . . denunciations of our officers for not pursuing an aggressive policy." Miles presented this question: "What are the wishes and desires of the people, and what is the determination of the people?"

He answered his own question. "It is the determination of the people of the Confederate States to retaliate, to free themselves, to drive their oppressors back into their own territory, and let our swords gleam and our banners float over their soil; make them bleed, and strike the dagger to their hearts."

Miles came to a crescendo. "We do not propose a war of conquest; but we do propose a war of invasion."

Alabama's William Russell Smith rose with a retort. "The opinion of the people is not always wise; the voice of the people is not always the right voice; the people are very often wrong."

Following a brief discourse on the evils of too much democracy, Smith turned from political philosophy and focused upon military practicality. "It is a question yet as to whether we shall be able to hold Maryland. We have never been invited to enter Maryland and we do not know how we shall be received." He then evoked an ancient verse. "It was an old saying that 'whom the gods would destroy they first made mad.'" Finally, he warned: "No war of invasion had ever been successful except it was for the purpose of colonizing the country which they invaded." Smith concluded that if the invasion policy continued, "we might look for the second day which tried men's souls."

South Carolina's Lewis Ayer, Jr. defended the position of the people. "It is the desire of the people that the war should be carried into the enemy's country. Mirabean, the French philosopher, said that the only way to conduct a successful revolution was 'to dare, to dare again, and still to dare!'" Ayer was emphatic. "Now is the time to make the enemy suffer — to make them bleed, and feel the iron heel of war. I believe we can do it — at least I am willing to make the experiment. We have battled long on our own territory, and now is the time to cease . . . go into the enemy's country."

When the time came to vote on the resolution, the Confederate House defeated the motion to remove the words "advance our standard into the *territory* of the enemy." It concurred instead with Gen. Lee and President Davis. The South had adopted a new policy sanctioning invasion.[235]

The House Committee on Foreign Affairs formalized the resolution with a short treatise on the conduct of the war. "The expediency of conducting the war in which we are engaged with all possible activity, and of carrying that war into the enemy's country . . . is believed to be now universally admitted by all enlightened men. . . . It is evident that we must rely alone upon our own energies for success."[236]

Reliance *upon our own energies* for success? Not only did invasion mark a new phase of the war, but it emboldened a shift in the attitude of the Confederacy in its European policy. From the war's outset, the South believed its independence depended upon intervention from England and France. Now flush with their own military victories, and combined with an aggressive policy of invasion, Southerners became convinced they could achieve their independence on their own.

Hope of foreign intervention had lulled the South "into remissions of preparation and relaxation of effort by a fatal delusion," explained the *Richmond Enquirer*. "If we shall succeed in eradicating from the public mind every seed of this fatal hallucination, and in bringing Government and people to rely upon the power of their own armies for independence and peace, we shall have performed substantial service."[237]

Returning to its affairs with the United States, the Confederate States House Committee on Foreign Affairs adopted a harsh doctrine of retribution. "The enemy will never be willing to desist from the unjust and ferocious war which they are now waging until the evils and inconveniences thereof shall have been brought home fully to themselves."

The committee endorsed vengeance. "When our valiant and disciplined armies . . . shall have once found their way to the heart of the enemy's country, and have inflicted a just retaliation upon those who have so ruthlessly ravaged our territories, pillaged our towns, and desolated our homes, it is to be reasonably expected that even they will at last be able to discern the rank injustice and brutal cruelty which they have compelled us to experience." For the perpetration of these crimes, the committee advocated "adequate punishment."

Robert E. Lee expected to engage — and hoped to defeat — the U.S. Army in combat on Union soil. He did not, however, intend to commit war on civilians — certainly not in Maryland. "This army is about to engage in most important operations," Lee informed his army on the eve of the invasion. "Any excesses committed will exasperate the people, lead to disastrous results, and enlist the populace on the side to the Federal forces in hostility to our own." Lee instructed his quartermasters and commissaries to make "all arrangements for purchase of supplies," and to issue requisitions to commanders, "thereby removing all excuse for depredations."[238]

What a contrast to John Pope's declarations, where depredation was the norm. Lee intended to prove, through the discipline of his army, that the Confederacy abhorred war against civilians. In Maryland, Lee viewed his army as one of liberation, not oppression. Marylanders were not his enemy. Maryland had been occupied and forced into subjugation by the Lincoln government. Lee came to remove the Union bayonets that enforced martial law in Maryland. He reasoned that his well-behaved and respectful army would encourage Marylanders to cast their allegiance with the Confederacy. As his army crossed the Potomac on September 5, Lee reminded President Davis he was entering Maryland "with a view of affording the people of that State an opportunity of liberating themselves."[239]

President Davis prepared his own proclamation to the people of Maryland, instructing Lee to deliver it, and to make known "the motives and purposes of your presence among them at the head of an invading army."

First, Davis declared that "the Confederate Government is waging this war solely for self-defense." His second sentence explained the South had "no design of conquest, or any other purpose than to secure peace and the abandonment by the United States of their pretensions to govern a people who have never been their subjects, and who prefer self-government to a union with them."

Davis then justified the invasion. "We are driven to protect our own country by transferring the seat of war to that of an enemy, who pursues us with a relentless and, apparently, aimless hostility." The president appealed to a common bond of loss. "Our fields have been laid to waste, our people killed, many homes made desolate, and rapine and murder have ravaged our frontiers." He warned that "the sacred right of self-defense demands that, if such a war is to continue, its consequences shall fall on those who persist in their refusal to make peace."

The Confederate president then made an intriguing peace offer, based upon the premise of states' rights applied equally to Northern states. "If [the people] are unable to prevail on the Government of the United States to conclude a general peace, their own State government, in the exercise of its sovereignty, can secure immunity from the desolating effects of warfare on the soil of the State by a separate treaty of peace."[240]

The test had come. Would the Northern states retain their bonds to the Union? Or would pleas for peace, compelled by invading Confederate armies, further divide the "united" states?

Gen. Lee sensed history was about to change. "The present position of affairs, in my opinion, places it in the power of the Government of the Confederate States to propose with propriety to that of the United States the recognition of our independence."

As the Confederate chieftain gazed upon his invading army, resting now in western Maryland near the town of Frederick — less than 25 miles from the Pennsylvania border — he continued his letter to President Davis. "Such a proposition, coming from us at this time, could in no way be regarded as suing for peace; but, being made when it is in our power to inflict injury upon our adversary, would show conclusively to the world that our sole object is the establishment of our independence and the attainment of an honorable peace."

Lee knew he was in a position to control the destiny of the Confederacy, and to influence the future of the United States. "The rejection of this offer would prove to the country that the responsibility of the continuance of the war does not rest upon us, but that the power in the United States elects to prosecute it for purposes of their own."

Lee was aware his actions could affect the 1862 fall elections — only weeks away. "The proposal of peace would enable the people of the United States to determine at their coming elections whether they will support those who favor a prolongation of the war, or those who wish to bring it to a termination."[241]

The future of the United States appeared, at this moment, in the hands of Robert E. Lee.

CHAPTER 9

Five Fronts

The present is full of danger and terror. Wherever we look we find the prospect one of gloom.

—*Baltimore American and Commercial Advertiser,* September 5, 1862

Not only were the Rebels crossing the Potomac. They were approaching the Ohio River. The Confederacy captured its first Union capital on September 3 — in Abraham Lincoln's birth state.

Frankfort was a coveted prize for the Confederates. The South had claimed Kentucky as one of its slave sisters from the outset of the war. The Bluegrass State had refused to adopt secession, however, despite the efforts of a pro-Southern governor. It declared official neutrality, instead, much to the disappointment of the fledgling Confederacy. Unlike in Maryland, where Federal cannon and bayonets patrolled and controlled the state, Kentucky remained in the Union by choice. This satisfied Abraham Lincoln, Kentucky's native-born president: "I hope to have God on my side, but I must have Kentucky."[242]

Dissatisfied with Kentucky's pro-Union legislature, Southern sympathizers created their own provisional government in the fall of 1861, and the state was admitted into the Confederacy. The pro-Confederate government was largely symbolic until Rebel soldiers paraded the Confederate battle flag down the streets of Frankfort on September 3. The central star (and the last of the 13 stars) represented Kentucky.[243]

Kentucky's strategic position between the Ohio River and the Tennessee state line, along with its fertile fields, navigable rivers, and multiple railroads, made it a tempting target for both sides. Neutrality became meaningless during the war's first summer, and Union and Confederate armies ventured into and out of the state at will.

Something was different, however, about the Rebel incursion in the summer of 1862. Two Confederate armies were racing north, driving directly at two of the most important cities on the Ohio River: Louisville and Cincinnati. The Rebels moved with extraordinary speed. No U.S. army was nearby to hinder them. Northern governors in both Indiana and Ohio began to tremble. If not stopped, the Confederates could invade the Midwest.

"The Rebel movement towards the Ohio should not be regarded as a mere raid," warned the *Philadelphia Inquirer*. "The use of that word is a euphemism with which we have allowed ourselves of late to be too much self-deceived and self-beguiled. It is doubtless a deliberate massed movement: part of a plan comprehending the East as well as the West."

Impressed by the Confederates' coordination between advancing armies in Kentucky and Maryland, the editor attempted to formulate the Rebel strategy. "This step is intended to remove the line of warfare to the Ohio in the West, and the Potomac in the East, as preparatory to making those streams the respective bases of offensive operations northward."

This appeared dubious for the U.S. "Let us comprehend the full magnitude of the danger so imminent. . . . We are no alarmists, but it is better to be even alarmists than indifferentists."[244]

People felt the panic. Uprooted and in flight, the Kentucky legislature abandoned Frankfort and scurried to Louisville. The public archives were removed from Frankfort, along with $1 million in treasure from the capital and nearby Lexington. Cotton bales, in storage at Louisville, were transported rapidly across the Ohio to the Indiana shore. The panic caused an instantaneous price rise in the commodity. The Confederates disrupted traffic on the Louisville and Nashville Railroad, as well as the Louisville and Frankfort Railroad, and reports arrived that bridges were being burned. The nearest U.S. army with any experience and strength began rushing north from Nashville, trying to outrace the Rebels to Louisville.

Louisville's mayor recognized the danger and issued an unprecedented proclamation. "All citizens who are able to bear arms who fail or refuse to report themselves for enrollment, for the protection of their homes and firesides, will be looked upon as a common enemy."[245]

"The situation in Kentucky has grown suddenly into one of great importance," reported the *Cincinnati Gazette*. "Within three days the Rebels have successfully invaded the Central portion of the State," and within four days, they could be wading the Ohio River.[246]

The *Cincinnati Commercial* sounded a stronger alarm. "The people of Cincinnati must prepare to defend themselves. There is no mistake about it this time. We are very seriously menaced."

The editor of the *Commercial* assessed the situation. "There is no question the Rebels exhibit the audacity which distinguishes a high order of generalship. They move without transportation, and have now entered a country in which they will have no difficulty in supporting themselves as they march." Then came this warning: "We may be sure they will make no delays, as they know their opportunity is passing away rapidly. . . . It is pretty certain they will strike in this direction. We should act as if no doubt existed that they were advancing directly upon this city."[247]

As the first week of September reached its midpoint, reports worsened. The Confederate army of Maj. Gen. Edmund Kirby Smith continued pushing north toward Cincinnati. Smith's Rebels had departed Knoxville on August 14, and in three weeks, had marched nearly 250 miles. It was an extraordinary achievement, unmatched by any Federal army. A small U.S. force attempted to block Smith at Richmond, Kentucky, but he pushed them aside — earning one of the most lopsided victories in Confederate history — on the same day Robert E. Lee was thrashing the Union army at Manassas 30 miles from Washington. Stunning Union authorities with his speed and audacity, Smith captured Lexington, then Frankfort, opening the way for Cincinnati.[248]

Meanwhile, further to the west along a parallel route, Maj. Gen. Braxton Bragg's Confederate army marched nearly as far, driving from Chattanooga near the Georgia border toward Louisville. Never before had two Southern armies marched so far in such a short time in such a coordinated fashion. These aggressive offensives were breathless in scope. The Federal forces were stunned, surprised, and suffering from an anemic response.

"The Rebels are substantially in possession of the whole Blue Grass region, reported the *Cincinnati Commercial*. "The Union people are fugitives, flying for safety in every direction. The roads are represented to be thronged with men, women, and children, escaping in vehicles of every description, and many farmers are driving their most valuable stock towards the Ohio River to preserve it from the enemy."

With no army to defend his city, the editor of the *Cincinnati Gazette* pleaded with his fellow citizens. "The first duty is for every man who has a gun to put it in order for service. No matter what may be the description of the weapon, it should be made ready for use."

The *Gazette* sensed the urgency. "In view of the tremendous interests at stake our preparations should be on the most extensive scale, and as there is but little time for preparation, we cannot afford to postpone action a single hour. This morning, with the rising sun, our citizens should go to work [building defenses]."[249]

The Federal government responded as well. Union gun boats began steaming to Cincinnati, patrolling above and below the Queen City. Maj. Gen. Lew Wallace arrived to take control, imposing martial law and organizing militia and local residents for Cincinnati's defense. A pontoon bridge hastily was constructed across the Ohio, connecting Cincinnati with Covington on the Kentucky bank of the river. Dirt began flying and piling along approaches to both Cincinnati and Covington as Gen. Wallace impressed 3,000 citizens to construct earthwork defenses to fend off the Confederates.

Rumors filled the streets and households. Where were the Rebels now? How many were coming? 16,000? 20,000? Perhaps 25,000? From what direction would they attack?[250]

"We cannot give any idea of the exaggerated reports which are flying from mouth to mouth," recorded a correspondent with the *New York World*. "Reports that the Rebels are within five miles, that they have driven in our pickets, and a hundred more appalling . . . destitute of foundation. The worst feature of all is that these reports are believed by the commanders, in some cases, and by the men in many."

The *World* reporter marveled that Cincinnati had transformed into "one vast barracks." He described the street scenes. "Soldiers on every hand; soldiers lying on sidewalks, lounging on doorsteps, drilling and marching; soldiers on guard, cannon and caissons moving hither and thither; all is war."

The city's society had been reorganized in less than a week to meet the impending threat. "The young men and old, the high and the low, are all side by side, ready, if need be, to die at the call of their country. The fair maidens and the stout matrons — some with smiles, others with suppressed blushes, and some weeping violently — are bidding adieu to their brothers, husbands, and lovers, as if, indeed, it were a real and not an imaginary foe against which they are arrayed."[251]

Imaginary foe? Not on September 10. That Wednesday morning at 6 a.m., "every church and fire-bell in the city was tolled as a signal for the gathering of the reserve forces, and at the same hour 3,000 extra laborers were detailed from among the citizens to proceed at once to the entrenchments."

Word had arrived at Gen. Wallace's headquarters that the Confederates were advancing from two directions. Intelligence estimated the Rebels would encounter U.S. outposts by noon. They were coming!

At 8 a.m., all ward and other militia organizations throughout the city were ordered to report to their rendezvous points. Thousands assembled, with each man armed with his own weapon. Some carried flintlock muskets of the Revolutionary War period; others came with rifles and shotguns. Nearly 10,000 militia-

Troops rushing past the Cincinnati Market House en route to defend the city against the Confederate advance. (*Harper's Weekly*)

men assembled, "each anxious to lend a hand towards the punishment of the mendacious foe who were coming forth to rob them of their homes, their families and birthrights."

By 9 a.m., the city troops were marched across the pontoon bridge spanning the Ohio, and stationed behind the earthworks and rifle pits at Covington, "where a good shot is worth more than two thoroughly disciplined soldiers who have never tried the range and accuracy of their pieces." Gen. Wallace personally superintended the deployments, wheeling regiments, cavalry, and artillery into positions.

Near 10 a.m., movements ceased, and "everything was in readiness for action." Then there was silence. "Now followed a long period of entire calm . . . where before all was noise and confusion, there was naught but a perfect calm, and a quiet but earnest look of expectation sat upon every face."

Hours passed. Nothing happened. No enemy appeared.

"The troops, beginning to weary of long waiting in vain, began to grow clamorous for the fight to commence. The men were impatient, the officers anxious, [and some] who had at first been somewhat nervous, began now to grow decidedly sleepy."

The Confederates did not appear, and by evening, the troops were dismissed back to their quarters, their adrenaline emptied, but their powder pouches full. When the correspondent for the *Philadelphia Inquirer* remarked to Gen. Wallace that the day's work had accomplished nothing, the general replied, "Three days of that kind of drill were almost equal to a battle and a victory."[252]

September 11 remained tense. Reports arrived that skirmishing had occurred only six miles from Cincinnati. It rained throughout the day. It poured so hard, in fact, that the Ohio River raised, the current dislodging river steamers, breaking them loose from their moorings and threatening to smash the pontoon bridge — the umbilical cord to the Kentucky defenses. Some relief occurred when word circulated that 45,000 experienced U.S. soldiers were arriving from Nashville, via Louisville, and were expected soon. Even before their arrival, spirits rose when 10,000 militia volunteers, "with squirrel guns, came in from the country today."[253]

Two days later, it ended. Ohio's governor sent the militiamen back home. "After a long period of most painful apprehension and suspense, the people of this portion of the Union are beginning to breathe more freely," wrote the correspondent of the *Philadelphia Inquirer*. "A few days ago a battle on the Kentucky side of the Ohio River was looked upon as almost unavoidable, and the result was by no means certain." Then the observer commended the patriotism and unity of Cincinnati's residents. "The promptness and courage of the citizens alone saved Cincinnati from becoming a conquered city."[254]

The Confederates, indeed, had retired. Gen. Smith did not intend an attack upon fortified positions. He did not have time to conduct a siege. He could not contend with the armament and prowess of Union gunboats. Smith could retrograde into Bluegrass Country, survive off the land, gather food and supplies, and dare the Yankees to come after him. He was leaving Cincinnati, but he was not departing Kentucky.

The Confederates had scared Cincinnati. They had frightened Louisville. They had captured Kentucky's state capital. Midwest states along the Ohio River had been shaken. The North appeared surprised and incoherent. The cities were safe, at least for the moment, and so were the state borders. But two Rebel armies lurked in Kentucky, where they remained a menace. They could not be ignored, and President Lincoln knew it.

FIVE HUNDRED MILES to the east, at the biggest port city along Maryland's Chesapeake Bay, Baltimore anxiously watched the approach of Robert E. Lee's Confederate army.

During the first week of September, Lee had settled his invasion force around the western Maryland town of Frederick, less than 50 miles west of Baltimore — a three days' march. News of the Confederate invasion "caused a deep and strong excitement in the city," and people assembled in throngs on Baltimore streets "anxiously looking for news . . . everywhere the important event was discussed with reference to its probable or possible effect upon our city."[255]

Baltimore presented an inviting target for the Confederates. The fourth largest city in the United States in 1860, its population had a divided allegiance. Most of the city's prominent residents heralded secession, but their voices had been stifled, and many had been arrested and imprisoned during the war's first year. Lincoln's inaugural army occupied the city during the war's first weeks, and ruled it with an iron fist, planting cannon on its highest point at Federal Hill, pointing toward the heart of the downtown.

Still, Marylanders resisted. One week before the Confederate invasion, Federal authorities seized "a treasonable bed quilt" from a house on Hoffman Street. "It is made of silk, and in the center is a large Confederate flag, with a white cross in the center of the blue ground. In the cross was embroidered, 'Jefferson Davis, President of the Confederacy.'" Other portions of the flag displayed names of Confederate cabinet officers and prominent Rebel generals. Southern sentiment remained strong in Baltimore.[256]

Maryland officers and Maryland men served in Lee's Confederate army, but Maryland women who remained behind in their "occupied" state refused to hide their sympathies for the South. According to a traveler who ventured North to record "Personal Observations in Yankee Lands," Maryland women were "the only noble spirits" who had not been "crushed into a servile and cowardly submission to the [Lincoln] despotism." Impressed with their opposition, he witnessed Maryland ladies "everywhere and always intensely Southern, and [they] dared express it, even in the face of Yankee officers."[257]

One form of Rebel expression was Southern women in Baltimore appearing daily in secession colors (red, white, and blue), parading up and down the streets before being hauled off to Fort McHenry for interrogation. Before the war, Baltimore had earned the notorious nickname of "headquarters of mobocracy." The Federal occupiers had ended the city's corruption and gang rule, but Baltimoreans resented being "but galley slaves of the Abolition Administration."[258]

The city's Southern proclivities made its possession even more important to the Lincoln administration. Located 40 miles due north of the U.S. capital, Baltimore was crucial to the protection and sustenance of Washington. Into Baltimore ran the arteries of railroads providing the principal source of soldiers and supplies coming from the North. The city could not fall into Rebel hands.

Baltimore's Unionists scorned the secession sympathizers and welcomed the rule of U.S. troops over the city. "The Union sentiment we have endeavored to foster has kept roofs over our heads [and] has prevented our streets from being torn up by shot and shell, our people from being scattered abroad in destitution," reflected the *American and Commercial Advertiser.* "With the elements of danger accumulated in and around us, the Government has not yet had occasion to crush us."

With Lee's Confederates on the western horizon, Baltimoreans predicted his course. "It requires no interpreter of their purposes. . . . Ever since the war began and the embargo [coastal blockade] made effective, they have had their eager eye upon the supplies to be secured in this city. This has been *avowed*."

Now Baltimore's loyalists pleaded for U.S. protection. "What are our chances of rescue, so far as can be seen?" Baltimore had virtually no defenses. The Federals present were an occupying force, not a force for defense. It was too late to rendezvous the state militia — the Confederates already were here. "We have so far relied almost wholly upon the forces and generalship concentrated about Washington for our defense. . . . These began to fail us when the Rebels drove back our troops [following Manassas], and they seem to have been failing us ever since."

With Lee also posing a threat to Washington, Baltimore's Unionists suspected little help from the Yankee army. The tone turned dark. "Whilst Baltimore has at present abundant materials provided *for its swift destruction*, it has but little of consequence for its defense." Pleas then circulated for people to help fortify every approach to the city and "to sacrifice life and property, if necessary."

The editor of the *American and Commercial Advertiser* warned, "This is no time for trifling — we must all be up and doing, and be prepared to heartily sustain the Government . . . [for] the preservation of the public peace and the supremacy of the flag against the horde of despicable traitors threatening our borders."

The paper delivered a stern message to Confederate sympathizers within the city. "Let us remind any Secession sympathizer, right here, that a portion of the formidable New Orleans mortar fleet is quietly at anchor near the heart of the city, as an adjunct of the terrible batteries [on Federal Hill] — [all] ready to rain destruction upon hostile occupants from so many points, if they were once to obtain a foothold here."

Nothing more could be done now. Baltimoreans could only await "the most eventful week in the history of our beautiful city, perhaps in our own lives."[259]

WASHINGTON WAS THE MOST heavily fortified city on earth in September, 1862.

Military engineers had begun studying the topography surrounding the capital city and penciling forts on maps following the Federal defeat at First Manassas during the war's first summer. Now after months of construction, an extensive line of earthworks ringed the city, covering approaches from every direction. Nearly 50 forts, boasting almost 500 cannon, protected the U.S. capital. These forts occupied the highest elevations, ensuring the best observation points of the enemy, and enabling artillery and infantry to sweep all approaches to the city.[260]

Assembled behind these fortifications were 150,000 Union soldiers — the largest concentration of armed men anywhere on earth. Most of them were veterans of two Union armies, but new levies numbering several thousand a day were arriving in response to Lincoln's call for volunteers. Robert E. Lee, himself a trained West Point engineer, knew what he faced from the imposing exteriors of the forts, and from within.

Faced with a Confederate invasion, Washington did not tremble like other Northern cities. As Cincinnati worked itself into a frenzy on the Ohio, and Baltimore quivered on the Chesapeake, Washington remained calm on the Potomac.

"Today all seems more tranquil," observed the *Philadelphia Inquirer* correspondent from his station within the capital. "If [Stonewall] Jackson is coming, people do not seem to care. People are flocking in, by heavy trains, as though there was nothing the matter. On the streets there is no panic, no excitement; those who give the matter a second thought, say, 'well, they are not coming here first, anyhow.'" The agent writing for the Associated Press concurred. "Affairs are hourly assuming a more cheerful aspect."[261]

The protection offered by the massive fortifications explained much of the ease. "Great activity is displayed in the forts in and around this place. Gleaming bayonets may be seen glistening from the ramparts. Heavy guns are in position, and veteran troops command them. When the hour comes for action, they will, no doubt, give a good account of themselves."[262]

It was so relaxed in the U.S. capital that its two theaters played before crowded houses, and "two thirds of the audience wore shoulder-straps." Officers dined at the city's best restaurants, and Union Gen. Ambrose Burnside and his staff "enjoyed a fine dinner up to a late hour at Willard's [hotel]."[263]

Even the rumor incubator ceased operation. "No one seems bold enough to manufacture and circulate an exciting rumor to disturb the general monotony."[264]

The biggest irritant for the moment was not the Rebels or rumors, but the lack of rain. Hot, dry weather for weeks had baked the Washington region. Anytime anyone or any animal moved, it generated a dust storm. The network of roads leading into the capital could be discerned by the clouds of dust that hovered over them. The dust could give away Confederate movements as well, but for the time being, the Rebels were resting at Frederick, just about 50 miles distant. Anyone coming into Washington "looked like dusty millers. We want a rain, most terribly."[265]

The drought worried the Union high command. The Potomac River flowed at its lowest stage in recorded history, making it passable and accessible for Confederate crossings at numerous locations. Throughout the Chesapeake watershed, rivers and streams that might have presented obstacles to the Southern intruders now trickled, thirsty for water. The Federals could not count upon these normally natural barriers to halt, or even slow, Lee's invasion.

President Lincoln, however, expected one man to terminate the Confederate invasion — Maj. Gen. George Brinton McClellan. Though his cabinet distrusted the arrogant and insubordinate McClellan after he failed to take Richmond during the summer of 1862, Lincoln decided he was worthy of reclamation. "The fact is that late [disasters] in the field in front of Washington have brought more than one high personage to their senses, and made them realize that the time for conducting the war on a pettifogging, partisan basis has passed." Lincoln first assigned McClellan to defend the capital; then he expanded McClellan's mission to rid the Rebels from Northern soil.[266]

The announcement of McClellan's return to command electrified the troops in Washington. "They have faith in him, and no one else, whatever may be the opinion of the politicians," witnessed a Baltimore correspondent. "Their recent experience, and the apparent design of the Government to set him aside, has increased their faith, and what was before enthusiasm has now become almost devotion and man-worship."[267]

Tasked with defending Washington, organizing a disorganized army, and tracking down Lee and defeating him, McClellan commenced moving a portion of his reconstituted Army of the Potomac north and west toward Frederick on Saturday evening, September 6. "The night was clear and moonlight, and as the troops marched along 14th Street windows were thrown open. The pavements were filled with people, and as the veterans marched in solid column through the dusty streets — and their flags, proudly floating in the air, though riddled with balls and tattered by the iron hail through which these brave soldiers bore them — cheer after cheer greeted them as on they went."[268] Washington, at last, had broken its stillness.

INVASION ALONE could not secure Southern independence. The Confederacy also needed salt.

Salt shortages were becoming severe in the South. Not only was salt necessary as a food preservative, but saltpeter was an essential component of gunpowder. The Confederacy could not survive without salt.

During the war's first summer, the U.S. had occupied one of the upper South's largest salt-producing regions: the Kanawha River valley in southwestern Virginia. Salt had been extracted from a 10-mile stretch along the river, dating back to the first decade of the 19th century. Nearly 3,000 people, including up to 1,500 slaves, worked in the salt industry by mid-century, producing over 1.2 million bushels of salt in a good year.

The Confederates had lost the salt region near Charleston simply because it did not have the military manpower to retain that section of remote Virginia. But opportunity called in September 1862, after a division of U.S. troops was extracted from the Kanawha Valley to meet the emergency near Washington. Union troop strength was reduced by more than half, opening the door for an active Rebel front.

The Southerners wasted no time. "Clear the valley of the Kanawha," ordered the Confederate Secretary of War to his commander in western Virginia, Maj. Gen. William W. Loring. Loring hurriedly collected forage and transportation to carry him through the "sterile district of 100 miles between me and the enemy."[269] He then conducted a masterful coordination of Confederate cavalry and infantry during a week of aggressive movements through western Virginia's rugged mountain passes and deep river canyons. Alarm sounded in Wheeling, home to the Unionist government of Virginia. "The news of these movements having spread rapidly throughout our city, our population was in a commotion almost equal to any which has agitated it since the commencement [of the war]."[270]

The Rebel expedition out-marched and out-flanked the stunned Federals holding the Kanawha Valley. When Washington learned of the Confederate incursion, it understood its gravity and wired the commanding officer occupying the Charleston district on September 8: "It is reported that the enemy is likely to compel you to fall back to the Ohio River."[271]

Another threat to Ohio! Union Col. J.A.J. Lightburn determined, however, to make a stand at Charleston. With his contingent of Ohio and Union-supporting Virginia troops, he attempted to stop the Rebel thrust on September 13. But he was overwhelmed by Loring's 5,000 men, and compelled to make a nighttime escape. Before departure, he torched Charleston, destroying much of the town. The Union force did not stop until it reached Point Pleasant, 55 miles from Charleston at the confluence of the Ohio and Kanawha rivers.

Lightburn expected the Confederates to pursue, and he found Point Pleasant "untenable without some [earth]works, which I shall proceed to erect as speedily as possible."[272]

Meanwhile, Confederate cavalry *crossed the Ohio River* at Ravenswood on September 4 and penetrated some 20 miles into the Buckeye State.[273] For the first time, an organized Confederate army unit planted the Rebel flag on Ohio soil. The raid lasted only a day, but it further alarmed Washington that a second avenue of invasion, in addition to Cincinnati, was contemplated by the Confederates.

Loring's success was remarkable. He had seized the salt works, including 700 barrels already processed. "[I] only lack labor to supply the whole Confederacy. The Negroes, by whom they were formerly worked, have been carried off by the enemy." He held the Kanawha Valley, "with its magnificent crop of growing corn and its salt." He expected "many recruits will be added to my command here if I hold the country long enough." He recommended he remain in the Kanawha Valley to ensure no "fresh invasions from the enemy."[274]

Not only did the Confederate exploits along the Kanawha River threaten another invasion route into Ohio, but it also embarrassed the Lincoln administration's support for a pro-Union government for the proposed State of West Virginia. Representatives from western Virginia had voted unanimously against Virginia's secession, and since the war's outset, a "loyalist government" had been operating out of Wheeling.

The September invasion had cleared the central and southern portions of western Virginia of all U.S. forces, and it undermined the pro-Union initiative. After Loring seized Charleston, he declared in a bold proclamation, "The army of the Confederate States has come among you to expel the enemy, to rescue the people from the despotism of the counterfeit State government imposed on you by Northern bayonets, and to restore the country once more to its natural allegiance to [Virginia]." Loring also issued this warning. "Those who persist in adhering to the cause of the public enemy and the pretended State government he has erected at Wheeling will be dealt with as their obstinate treachery deserves."[275]

THE LINCOLN GOVERNMENT encountered a "western" problem more insidious than in western Virginia. "There is no longer any doubt that we are on the eve of a terrible Indian war," came the grave news from Minnesota. "All the Indian tribes have formed a league for the purpose of waging war on the frontier settlements of the whites. . . . They know that the Regular United States troops, which used to be stationed in the forts along the border, have all been called away; and they have got the impression that most of the men in the white settlements have also gone to the Southern war."[276]

Trouble had been brewing with the Santee Sioux or Dakota of western Minnesota for nearly a decade. Treaties signed ten years before the Civil War had forced the Dakota to cede large tracts of land in exchange for money and goods, and had confined the tribes to live on a 20-mile wide reservation centered along the upper Minnesota River. Corruption in the U.S. Bureau of Indian Affairs and by local government agents pilfered the promised compensation and annuity payments, and whites settled on Indian lands in violation of treaty stipulations.

Food shortages and crop failure, along with a reduction in hunting areas for wild game, brought near starvation to the Dakota by August 1862. Bands attempted to negotiate with the U.S. for food, but when a corrupt agent demanded up-front payment and no credit, the Dakota rebelled.

Vicious attacks occurred, starting with the government trading post at Lower Sioux Agency in Renville County, then proceeding to the villages of New Ulm and Henderson, and then to Fort Ridgely. Led by veteran chief Little Crow, homes were burned and citizens killed, and "the great Indian panic" began to rage. The warriors were all armed with rifles, "and every man was a dead shot."

Frantic reports arrived that the Indians intended to lay waste to all the country in south-central Minnesota. Frantic people ran for their lives. "This terrible state of affairs kindled one of the greatest panics that mortal eyes ever be held. Men, women and children came into [Carver County] screaming with fright — some barefoot, some shirtless, some with little or no clothing at all; some with guns, but more without. . . . The whole people from the Minnesota River to Crow River became one vast area of excitement." [277]

The Dakota progress stopped, temporarily, at Fort Ridgely. Here hundreds of refugees sought safety, but they knew danger lurked nearby, as during the nights they could see the light from burning buildings and grain stacks in all directions. With the Indian war only one week old, nearly 800 Dakota attacked Fort Ridgely, besieging the garrison for seven days. With the aid of artillery, the post withstood the attacks until finally 1,400 Minnesota militiamen arrived to push the Dakota away.

As September opened, a detachment left the fort to bury dead settlers. About 16 miles from the fort, nearly 400 Dakota ambushed the sortie at Birch Coulee on September 2, killing the soldiers' horses first, and then surrounding and fighting them for 31 hours. When relief finally arrived on the next day, 13 soldiers were dead and 47 wounded (along with 90 dead horses). Nearly 40 percent of the U.S. force became casualties.

No one could calculate the civilian deaths. Reports arrived in Washington estimating the toll from dozens to hundreds. Newspapers published stories that denigrated the Dakota as savage and exaggerated the panic of the populace. The governor informed the legislature that an estimated 500 people had perished within the opening days of the conflict, and that "the theater of depredations" extended on a front of 200 miles and included an area of 20,000 square miles.[278]

No one doubted a war was underway — yet *another* war front for President Lincoln's government. This war, though, was not in the Confederacy.

Nor was the Civil War confined to the Confederacy. It had exploded beyond its previous boundary along the Potomac River. Robert E. Lee had marched into Maryland, bringing the war for the first time into the United States.

Lee's Rebel army had invaded the North.

And further north he intended to go.

CHAPTER 10

Invader Intrigue

Mystery magnifies danger, as a fog the sun.

—*Baltimore American and Commercial Advertiser*,
September 9, 1862

The guessing began almost immediately.

Where were the Confederates going? What were Gen. Lee's intentions? What would be the first Rebel target? How far into the United States would the invaders advance?

Lee's movement offered no answers. His abrupt halt, in fact, at Fredericktown, simply stirred suspicions.

The western Maryland town of Frederick offered the Confederates ideal advantages. From this position at Frederick, within a couple of days marching distance from Washington and Baltimore, Lee threatened both cities simultaneously. The Federals froze behind the capital's defenses — watching and waiting for Lee to telegraph his punch. Lee knew his maneuvers would force a reaction, and he knew he controlled the timing and location of the U.S. response.

From Frederick, Lee could march into Pennsylvania in a single day. The nearest Pennsylvania town on his map: Gettysburg. Gettysburg had strategic attraction. Its array of roads radiated toward all points of Pennsylvania, and it offered the most direct route to the state capital at Harrisburg. U.S. military authorities, trying to foreshadow Lee's direction, could look at their own maps and identify Gettysburg as a likely Confederate destination.

Lee also had the option of moving west from Frederick. The National Road, an advanced macadam highway running the length of Maryland, wound westward over two mountain ridges and into the rich pasture land of the Cumberland Valley. Once ensconced in the valley, Lee could move north toward Harrisburg, offering him the advantage of mountains protecting his eastward flank from the trolling Yankees coming out of Washington. This foothold also connected Lee with his base of supplies in Virginia's Shenandoah Valley, so necessary for the Confederates to sustain their invasion.

North, east, or west — all presented good alternatives for the Confederate commander. South was not an option. Lee had no intention of returning to the Confederacy until he had achieved war-changing — and possibly war-ending — goals north of the Potomac.

Even the Confederates wondered where they would be spending *their* Thanksgiving Day.

President Jefferson Davis selected September 18, 1862 as Confederate Thanksgiving Day. "It is my privilege to invite you once more to His footstool, not now in the garb of fasting and sorrow, but with joy and gladness, to render thanks for the great mercies received at His hand."

Davis explained his reasoning for a reverent day of glad tidings and thanks. "A few months since, our enemies poured forth their invasion legions upon our soil. They laid waste our fields, polluted our altars, and violated the sanctity of our homes. Around our capital they gathered their forces, and with boastful threats, claimed it as already their prize. The brave troops which rallied to its defense have extinguished these vain hopes."

The president concluded with solemnity. "In such circumstances it is meet and right that, as a people, we should bow down in adoring thankfulness to that gracious God who has been our bulwark and defense, and offer unto Him the tribute of thanksgiving and praise."[279]

Davis invited his congregation of Southerners to meet in their respective houses of public worship on September 18, not only to give thanks for past victories, but to ask God "to conduct our country safely through the perils which surround us, to the final attainment of the blessings of peace and security."

On the same day Davis issued his Thanksgiving proclamation from Richmond, Gen. Lee's Army of Northern Virginia began wading across the Potomac. Appropriately, they came upon Maryland's shore near the village of Poolesville after splashing through 400 yards of knee-high water at White's Ford.

"I imagine that to the ancient Israelite the crossing of the river Jordan was not fraught with more interest than was the crossing of the Potomac to the conquering Southron," described a soldier correspondent for the *Savannah Republican*. "The first sight of its broad surface was hailed by a shout from the whole column that made the hills echo for miles around, and told how rejoiced was their hearts."

Preparatory to sinking into the water, the writer witnessed a novel site. "The army, officers and all, bared their legs and waded over. While every variety, color and style of coat could be seen, there was perfect uniformity in the lower dress!"

The Georgian was pleased with the reception on the Maryland shore. Many persons "hailed our approach with demonstrations of unfeigned joy." Many young men were present, and in addition to their welcome, they showed relief. They had "already been enrolled by Lincoln's officers, and were to have been drafted on the 16th of this month."

Once across the river, the excited Confederates gazed at the Maryland landscape. "The country so far is unsurpassed in beauty. The distant mountains, the blue fringed hills, and the vast green fields, stretching out like an ocean on side, presenting a prospect, in my notion, unparalleled in beauty. It is a modern Eden."[280]

Confederate cavalry commander Maj. Gen. J.E.B. Stuart was among the first Rebel generals to step onto Maryland soil. Stuart rode into Poolesville, where "he was received with exultant demonstrations of favor, nearly all the population turning out to welcome him." This disgusted local Unionists, who were horrified at the spectacle. "Ever since the war commenced, Poolesville has been little more than a Rebel general-delivery post office."

The U.S. sympathizers also suspected the local secessionists had been tipped off about the invasion. "The farmers hereabout, who have been saving their crops, and whose harvests and farms have been guarded by Union soldiers, flocked to Poolesville with wagons and all manner of vehicles, negro slaves, and working men, carrying forage, food, clothing, articles of necessity and luxury for man and beast, and offering them to the Rebel soldiers."[281]

The provisions were welcomed by the ranks. "This was not half-starved Virginia — we can get here all we want," remarked one joyous Rebel. When asked why they were entering Maryland, another observed, "They might as well die in Maryland as in Virginia, for they were dying there by inches, and had to come for something to eat."[282]

New garments also proved popular, as the Rebels discarded their tattered uniforms. "Their sympathizers and emissaries must have smuggled new clothing through, and supplied them immediately on landing [in Maryland]." One observer witnessed abandoned clothing "in piles, and it appeared as though they had worn it for months without washing. Certainly there were several [train] carloads of it."[283]

As Maryland Southerners beamed and Maryland Northerners stared, Montgomery County well represented the sectional strife in Maryland. Jammed between Confederate Virginia and the symbolic line of freedom in the North, the Mason-Dixon Line, the sentiments of Marylanders were sharply divided. Until Lee's invasion, the occupying Union army inhibited shouts of Southern sympathy. With the Yankees now entrenched in Washington, Marylanders with Confederate leanings felt safe in expressing their affection for the Southern cause.

"Many people in Maryland are not to be trusted as regards [U.S.] loyalty. Any one might be well convinced were he to see the manner in which many of the old farmers of Maryland pilot through the State the satellites of Jeff. Davis & Co."[284]

Now was the turn of the Unionists to mind their words, whence surrounded by thousands of Rebels. "There are avowed

Lincolnites in the neighborhood, whom we leave to the quiet enjoyment of their opinions," observed the correspondent of the *Savannah Republican*. "We are determined to show our superiority over the Federals in every respect, by not imitating their nefarious example."

The writer commented on Gen. Lee's strict orders that private property "is to be scrupulously respected. We are not allowed to burn a rail or pull a roasting ear [of corn]. How different was the conduct of the vandals towards our people!"[285]

Unlike private property, the Chesapeake and Ohio Canal company did not receive the favorable treatment. As the principal conveyer of coal to the U.S. capital, the Confederates considered it an enemy transport route, and they inflicted damage up and down the canal along a stretch of 12 miles. The canal presented "a scene of the desolation which sufficiently attests the malignity of the Rebels." The Confederates breeched the canal in five places, spewing its water into the paralleling Potomac. They destroyed lock gates, and from adjoining heights, large boulders were dislodged and thrown into the basin. The canal basin became perfectly dry in many places, and where water remained it was less than a foot deep. Trees were chopped down and placed across the canal to further impede its use. "It will take considerable time to repair the damage."[286]

NO SIMILAR DESTRUCTION was occurring in Frederick where the Confederates nearly had encircled the town by September 6. "We want it to be understood that we are Southern gentlemen, and not marauders," broadcast Col. Bradley T. Johnson, a native Marylander who formerly practiced law in Frederick. Gen. Lee astutely assigned Johnson as the Confederate officer in charge of the first columns that arrived at Frederick. Proudly leading the 1st Maryland C.S. Infantry into the city, upon his return home, Johnson assumed the duties of provost marshal.[287]

The Rebel colonel then issued a proclamation: "After 16 months of oppression . . . the victorious army of the South brings freedom to your doors. Its standard now waves from the Potomac to Mason and Dixon's line. The men of Maryland, who have been crushed under the heel of this terrible despotism, now have the opportunity of working out their own redemption."

Ensuring a long-time commitment, Johnson continued. "The government of the Confederate States is pledged . . . never to cease this war until Maryland has the opportunity to decide for herself her own fate, untrammeled and free from Federal bayonets."[288]

Local citizens were impressed with Johnson's passion, but even more by the respect shown to inhabitants by the Confederate army. "Everyone agrees in saying that the Rebel soldiers behaved remarkably well. When any one of them would meet a lady, she was saluted with a 'present arms,' or the cap was doffed with a 'good morning, madam.' At one place a Rebel brigade encamped between a peach orchard and a cornfield, and such was the rigid discipline enforced by their officers, that not a peach or a single ear of corn was taken." [289]

A Baltimore correspondent credited the army's commander. "Lee is thoroughly a gentleman in feeling, and has been considerate, as far as practicable, towards the property of others."[290]

Gen. Lee's army required food, supplies and clothing. "The army is not properly equipped for an invasion of an enemy's territory," he informed President Davis. "It lacks much of the material of war, is feeble in transportation, the animals much reduced, and the men are poorly provided with clothes, and in thousands of instances are destitute of shoes."[291]

Lee hoped to remedy these problems in Maryland — and the general intended to pay for everything. "I shall endeavor to purchase horses, clothing, shoes, and medical stores for our present use," Lee informed President Davis. "I find there is plenty of provisions and forage in this country, and the community has received us with kindness. There may be some embarrassment in paying for necessaries for the army, as it is probable that many individuals will hesitate to receive Confederate currency."[292]

Lee understood his problem of economics. Despite his good intentions, what value would Confederate money have once the Rebels departed? What bank in Maryland would accept inflated paper dollars from the South?

Purchases by Confederate quartermasters and commissaries started briskly. "The 30 flour mills around Frederick have been [emptied] of several thousand barrels, and the farmers on the northern, eastern, and southern side, where the rebels were encamped, have been well relieved of their forage, grain and cattle." When payments in gold ceased, and the limited supply of U.S. greenbacks became exhausted, Union-supporting merchants and farmers recoiled, and even refused to accept Confederate bills — "shocking bad money."[293]

Those espousing secession, however, accepted the Rebel scrip in allegiance to their cause. Some even became wealthy (temporarily) selling their products to the Southerners. "One credulous tobacconist sold his whole stock for $30,000. He paid $10,000 for it. . . . But his fortune cannot be appreciated, as it is all in Confederate money." Merchants who sold caps, shoes, and clothing collected between $30,000-$40,000 in Confederate notes, "of which 10% is good, 40% indifferently bad, and 50% wholly worthless." Unionists predicted that the "credulous fools" would become "chop-fallen" when they tried to exchange their Rebel dollars once the United States reclaimed its soil.[294]

Many Confederate enthusiasts soon lost their enthusiasm for the Rebel presence about Frederick. "Their coming to Frederick has been a sad visitation to the middling classes, many of whom have lost everything in exchange for Rebel scrip, especially the storekeepers."[295]

Shoes were one commodity Lee's army desperately needed. Months of campaigning had ruined the Rebels' footgear; and through failures in the Confederate subsistence department, shoe manufacturing had broken down. Some estimated nearly 50 percent of Confederate soldiers marched and fought without shoes.

The principal supplier of shoes had become dead and wounded Union soldiers. "Every battle contributes to human comfort in this respect, but it is not every man who is fortunate enough to 'foot' himself upon the [battle]field," revealed a correspondent with the *Charleston Courier*. "It has become a trite remark among the troops, that 'all a Yankee is now worth is his shoes,' and it is said . . . that some of our regiments have become so expert in securing these coveted articles, that they can make a charge and strip every dead Yankee's feet they pass without coming to a halt."

The Charleston correspondent estimated "at least 40,000 pairs of shoes are required today to supply the wants of the army." [296] They weren't found in Frederick.

Absence of shoes was only one debilitation for the Confederate soldier. The destitution of the Rebels was obvious.

"The privates were shoeless, hatless, and largely out at the knees, elbows, and unmentionable parts of their systems," reported one witness. Another confirmed the Confederates had been "sorely in want of garments to cover their nakedness, as we observed pantaloons and under clothing made out of United States tents." [297]

Their physical appearance was shocking. "These lack and pallid individuals, with matted hair and twisted whiskers, look but little like men, much less have they the appearance of soldiers." They contrasted sharply with the well-uniformed Union soldiers. "They pretend to despise the United States Volunteers, because they affect cleanliness. Their argument is that no man can be a soldier and keep clean."

A Frederick correspondent for the *Baltimore American and Commercial Advertiser* filed a detailed account. "They have no uniforms, but are well armed and equipped, and have become so inured to hardships that they care but little for any of the comforts of civilization."

He then described the general appearance of the Confederate soldiers. "They were the roughest set of creatures I ever saw; their features, hair, and clothing matted with dirt and filth; and the scratching they kept up gave warrant of vermin in abundance. . . . Whenever a Unionist met a Secessionist on the street he would commence to scratch, which all understood."

The Baltimore reporter encountered six young men who had come to Frederick to join the Rebel army, "but after 'seeing and smelling it,'" had concluded to return home.

"What did they mean by smelling it? They meant exactly what they said. I have never seen a mass of such filthy strong-smelling men. Three of them in a room would make it unbearable, and when marching in column along the street the smell from them was most offensive."[298]

The condition of the Confederate soldier did not entice many Marylanders to join the Confederate army. This proved disappointing to Lee. "I do not anticipate any general rising of the people in our behalf," he informed President Davis from his headquarters near Frederick.[299]

It proved humiliating to Bradley Johnson — the native son — who had invited his fellow Marylanders to join him in his arrival proclamation. "You must do your part. We have the arms for you. I am authorized immediately to muster in companies and regiments." Calling forth the memories of the occupation and martial law imposed by the Lincoln government, Johnson appealed to defense of their liberties. *"Rise at once!* Remember the cells of Fort McHenry. Remember the dungeons of Fort Lafayette and Fort Warren; the insults to your wives and daughters; the arrests, the midnight searches of your houses. Remember these, your wrongs, and rise at once in arms and strike for liberty and right."

Curious men looked at enlisting with the Confederates, but they did not like what they saw. Even if spurred by Johnson's appeal, they were not attracted to his description of army life. "Let each man provide himself with a stout pair of shoes, a good blanket and a tin cup — Jackson's men have no baggage."[300]

Perhaps 500 Marylanders joined Lee's army during the four days it was posted at Frederick. When Lee invaded western Maryland, he encountered the most pro-Union portion of the state. "The disappointment of the Rebels over what they called the cowardly apathy of Maryland was outspoken and bitter," recalled a Union sympathizer. "Brad Johnson's 'rising proclamation' brings even a lugubrious smile to the face of a Secessionist. Poor Brad! Maryland wouldn't rise, and he went down."[301]

The twin facts that the Confederates had failed to attract new recruits and descriptions of the deplorable condition of the Confederate soldier became fodder for jokes in newspapers throughout the North. This led the editor of the *Philadelphia Inquirer* to issue a stern warning. "We do not exactly perceive the fun in such disparaging descriptions, nor do we appreciate the joke. . . . The practical question for us is simply this — If our foes, hatless, shoeless, ragged, famished and ill armed, have, with such success, defended the soil of their State, what should we — with our ample military appliances — be able to accomplish when our homes are, in turn, invaded?"

The editor expressed admiration for the Confederate soldier, and demanded an equal response from the Union army. "If these men endure such privation and still fight on and march on with such skillfulness of plan and boldness of execution, we may as well at once make up our minds that their 'extermination' is going to involve us in business more serious than that of a military picnic."[302]

THE THREAT OF CONFEDERATE victories on Northern soil remained a dangerous reality. All wondered where the big battle would occur — the contest that could determine the future of two countries.

Gen. Lee had made a decision. It would not be Washington.

"I had no intention of attacking [the enemy] in his fortifications, and am not prepared to invest them," Lee informed President Davis.[303] The Rebel commander desired Pennsylvania as his objective, but few knew this goal. Lincoln and his generals certainly didn't know the Confederate plans, and neither did the press or the public. Anxiety ruled in the North the second week of September.

Confederate enthusiasts publicly declared they could "swallow Washington at one mouthful." More temperate and practical Southern leaders understood the impracticality and improbability of capturing the U.S. capital. "The chief prize of the late victories is not the possession of Washington, but the opportunity for the commencement of an offensive campaign in the enemy's territory," argued the *Richmond Examiner*. "The capture of Washington would produce an immense sensation, but if unattended by an immediate advance into Pennsylvania, and a menace of the Northern capitals, it is impossible to say that the sensation would be altogether and necessarily to our advantage."

The newspaper completed its analysis: "Possession of Washington is only desirable as the open door to invasion. . . . We hope that this precious season will not be consumed in picking the lock or battering it down, while the wall is full of breaches through which we may pass as well."[304]

One of those potential breaches was Baltimore. Signs indicated prospects for a Confederate thrust toward Baltimore. Stonewall Jackson and his divisions — Lee's rapid deployment force — had positioned themselves east of Frederick, along the National Road leading to Baltimore. Southern commanders boldly announced their target was Baltimore. The Southern press rejoiced that the army was "now on a tour to the most important and inviting point between Baltimore and Washington." The men in the ranks cheerfully proclaimed "they would go to church next Sunday in Baltimore."[305]

Union sympathizers residing in Baltimore noticed something strange in their city during September's second week. "A great many families here have received large accessions to their numbers. Various ones who have been missing for a number of months past are home again, having been 'away on business.'"

The reuniting of families and an influx of visitors attracted attention. "Some of the old residents are quite excited about the increase of strange faces in their midst, and are not willing, judging from their sun-burns and dark complexions, to believe that they can *all* be [refugees] from the invaded portions of the State."

Suspicions were strong that Confederate scouts were prowling Baltimore's avenues. "Nearly all the prominent Rebels here have very full information of the enemy's movements from day to day. There are now, daily, walking the streets of this city, officers of the Rebel army in disguise."[306]

Baltimore was having a bad September. Due to the proximity of the Confederate army, all the barrooms were closed, "so that it was difficult to get anything by which to inflame the passions." Bulletin boards outside the newspaper offices, typically posted full of news, were devoid of information, and "the people became weary of waiting for that they knew they could not get." Even the oyster season was bad. The delicacies from the Chesapeake were "generally poor and unfit for use" due to the protracted drought of the summer which had prevented them "from fattening as rapidly as if the season had had more rain."[307]

As the Confederate army continued its nearby menacing, Baltimore Unionists determined to display their loyalty to the United States. National flags began flying everywhere. From houses to hotels, from offices to oyster saloons, from churches to street corners, Old Glory colored the city in red, white, and blue. "No Rebel rag is permitted to see the light," and "the nearer traitors come towards us, the stronger grows the Union sentiment." They remembered the last time Baltimore figured in the defense of the country. It was against the British, 48 years before — almost to the same September date — during the War of 1812. That defense produced the lyrics to *The Star Spangled Banner*; and once again, Baltimoreans prepared to protect the flag.[308]

The editor of the *Baltimore American and Commercial Advertiser* painted a stark picture of Baltimore's fate if battle erupted over the city. Assuming the Federals would refuse to surrender, he anticipated a Confederate attack. "Solid shot, shell and canister would soon be flying over our domiciles, and store-houses, and some of them struck and others fired by incendiary shells. Even some of our tall buildings might be shattered."

Assuming a Confederate investment, with eventual Rebel success, he predicted the retreating U.S. troops "would order the destruction of every foundry, machine shop and workshop — they would fire all the Government stores, and destroy the railroad depots and remove the cars and locomotives — in short, they would take care to leave nothing to fall into the hands of the enemy, in the way of food, clothing, munitions of war, public or private, that fire could consume." Meanwhile, he envisioned "'bombs bursting in air'" fired from the artillery of Fort McHenry and the gunboats in the harbor, "whilst the flames might be spreading from the burning storehouses in every direction."

He hoped the city would avoid disaster; for if the Confederates came to Baltimore, there was "no room for doubt that death and destruction would be showered upon our city."[309]

MYSTERY OVER GEN. LEE'S target intensified when he didn't move from Frederick for four days. What was he thinking? What was he waiting for?

Hopeful Northern newspapers began postulating that the Confederates intended no invasion, but merely a temporary "raid." "The general impression is that the invasion of Maryland is for food and other supplies, and not for a general raid into the State of Pennsylvania," theorized the press. The belief was that Lee intended to return to Virginia with bountiful provender and clothing and shoes, but at the same time lure the Union army out of its Washington defenses to a place of Lee's choosing.[310]

The theorists were wrong. Lee expected to spend weeks on Yankee soil — most of it in Pennsylvania.

But Lee faced an unexpected problem: Harpers Ferry.

Located 20 miles southwest of Frederick, Harpers Ferry concerned the Confederate commander. Nearly 14,000 U.S. soldiers garrisoned the mouth of the Shenandoah Valley — the umbilical cord between Lee's invasion force and his supply base in Virginia. Lee could not utilize this line of supply as long as the Federals remained at Harpers Ferry and nearby Martinsburg. Their presence presented serious threats to Lee's plans to carry the war into Pennsylvania.

Gen. Lee had expected the Yankees would withdraw from the Shenandoah Valley once he occupied Frederick. His Frederick position effectively isolated Harpers Ferry, cutting its garrison off from communication and support from either Washington or Baltimore. Common sense dictated to Lee that the Federals would abandon Harpers Ferry, thus opening his supply route by their departure. The general decided to exercise patience.

Lee waited. While he waited, he rested his army. He also purchased food and clothing and (some) shoes. During his wait, he issued his own proclamation to Marylanders: "The people of the South have long wished to aid you in throwing off this foreign yoke, to enable you again to enjoy the inalienable rights of freemen, and restore independence and sovereignty to your State."

Tuesday, September 9 arrived. Four days at Frederick, and still the Federals at Harpers Ferry and Martinsburg had not budged. Lee determined he would wait no longer. He devised a plan.

Since the Federals would not remove themselves, Lee would remove them.

He summoned Stonewall Jackson. He instructed Jackson to march his foot cavalry to Harpers Ferry. Jackson would receive support from three other divisions in the army. In sum, two-thirds

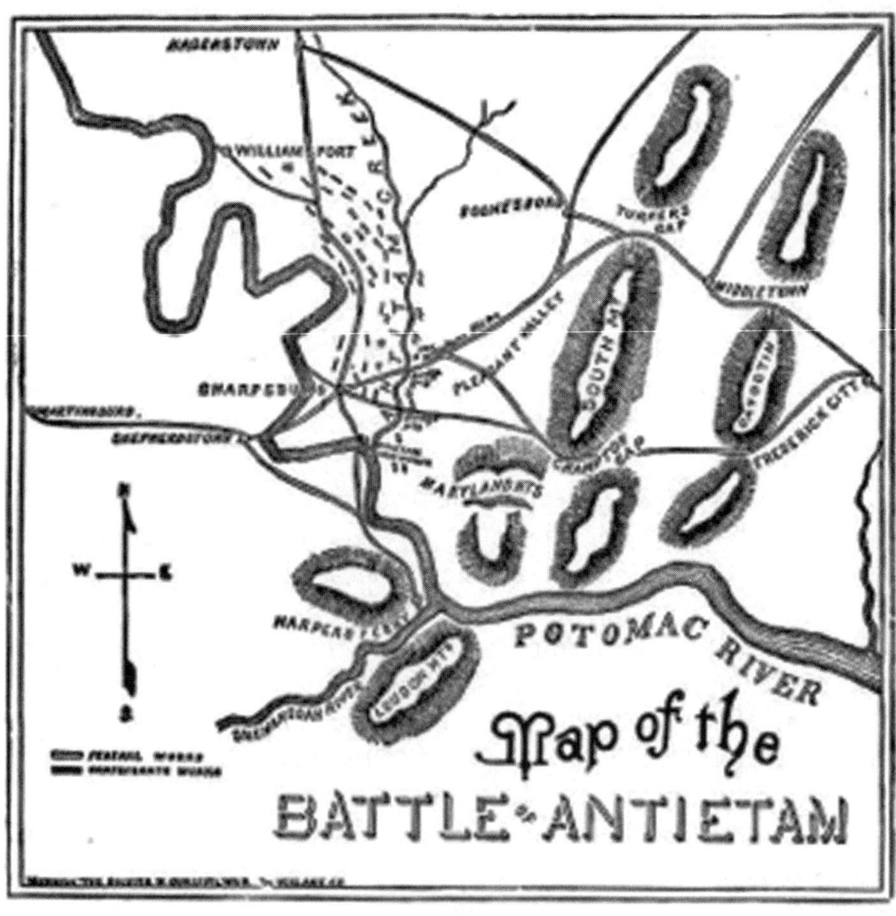

The theater of operations as General Lee moved west from Frederick. *(Frank Leslie's Illustrated Newspaper)*

of the Confederate army would descend upon Harpers Ferry. This small border town at the confluence of the Potomac and Shenandoah rivers would be the invasion's first target.

The plan called for the seizure of the three mountains surrounding Harpers Ferry. This would trap the doomed Federals in a natural hole where they would have the option of surrender, or destruction. Jackson would command the operation. Lee gave him three days to snap the trap upon the Ferry.

Gen. Lee was aware of Jackson's intimate familiarity with Harpers Ferry. He had assigned Jackson command of the post during the war's first week in 1861. No one was better qualified for this mission than Stonewall Jackson.

Once Jackson had eliminated the U.S. garrison, his expedition would reunite with Lee in Maryland. With the supply line thus secured in the Shenandoah Valley, the way was open to Pennsylvania. Lee gave little concern to any danger from Yankee reinforcements. Jackson would complete his assignment well before the Federals passed too far from their Washington defenses.

Lee labeled his instructions "Special Orders 191."[311]

Never could he have imagined how it would alter the course of American history.

CHAPTER 11

Quakers Quaking

Let every man arm himself and forget comfort, ease and cloth, in preparing for the worst.

—*Philadelphia Inquirer,* September 5, 1862

Hagerstown is six and one half miles from the Pennsylvania border.

On September 11, this small German farming community, in the heart of western Maryland, became a center of attention in the United States. Confederates! Robert E. Lee had arrived in Hagerstown. He found himself positioned at the county seat of Washington County. Ironically, Lee would launch his invasion — designed to secure Confederate independence — from the *first* county in the country named after the general who had attained American independence.

Lee's plans were working perfectly. Accompanied by his senior lieutenant, Maj. Gen. James Longstreet and his command, Lee was poised for his advance into Pennsylvania. Stonewall Jackson, meanwhile, had achieved his first mission 23 miles south of Lee — removing the Federals from their outpost at Martinsburg. Lee's supply route was now open, connecting the Confederate army with Winchester, Virginia, Lee's base of operations in the Shenandoah Valley.

Now Lee waited. Jackson was on his way to Harpers Ferry to remove the final hurdle to the invasion of Pennsylvania. Two out of every three soldiers in the Rebel army were with Jackson, and Lee needed his Confederates reunited before crossing the Mason-Dixon Line. Stonewall, Lee assumed, would be along shortly.

"Our advance pickets are at Middleburg, on the Pennsylvania line," Lee informed President Davis in a matter-of-fact report, disguising any excitement. "I await here the results of the movements upon Harper's Ferry."[312] Seldom had Lee felt so confident; no need for any worry.

Worry was the best weapon in the arsenal of Pennsylvania Gov. Andrew Curtin, according to the Pennsylvania press.

> We begin now to realize that our own valleys and riversides may be made the scene of the conflict; that instead of invaders, we are to become the invaded; that flame, and pillage, and slaughter, which have wasted distant regions, may ere long hold high carnival upon the peaceful fields and around the quiet homes of our own State; and we be called upon to stand in literal defense of our firesides, granaries and warehouses. This may be the final ordeal through which it may be ours to pass.[313]

No one could ignore the danger. No one could avoid the threat. The war was coming to Pennsylvania.

"Let every man be a Home Guard, in the use of individual and collective preparation to succor his country, in defending his home. An army of peaceful citizens, thus urged by patriotism and self-defense, and preparing to defend their wives and children, the altars of their God, and the ashes of their fathers, will be enduing with a power which will demand universal respect, awaken the fears of Traitors, and insure success."[314]

The editor of the *Philadelphia Inquirer*, aware that the "distant war" had become long and stale, witnessed the passions of Pennsylvanians erupt with the Confederates near their border. "This, after all, is perhaps just what was needed; that we required some imminent danger, some pressing necessity, to supply us with fresh motives and stimulate us with a new enthusiasm."

He predicted the approaching Rebels "shall join together the promptings of religion, the calls of patriotism, and the instinct of self-preservation, so that each man shall be all ablaze with the blended enthusiasm of hero, saint and martyr."[315]

The opportunity for martyrdom came on September 11, when Gov. Curtin issued General Orders No. 36: "Fifty thousand of the freemen of Pennsylvania are hereby called for immediate service to repel the now imminent danger from Invasion by the enemies of the country."[316]

"The Governor's Proclamation is the trumpet call at the moment of danger. . . . [Pennsylvania's] sons are now called upon to defend their State and their homes, and to maintain the strength and symmetry of the beautiful keystone in the arch of our Union."[317]

Every post office (2,300) in the state received the governor's militia call out, and most of the daily newspapers published it as quickly as they could run their presses. The response was rapid.

In Philadelphia, Pennsylvania's largest city, the city's largest newspaper displayed these headlines: "To Arms! To Arms!"

"Men of Philadelphia, will you intercept the traitors in their march and drive them back across your border! There can be but one response. You will!"[318]

The bell at the Baldwin Locomotive Works clanged at 9 a.m., and the workers left their jobs and assembled into four military companies (about 100 men each). They proceeded to the mayor's office for instructions, many of them "carrying their dinner kettles with them, not knowing but they would be sent off immediately."

Employees of the stove and hollow-ware factories formed a full company, and the city fire companies mustered their firemen. Neighborhood civilians organized as well. One company from Tenth and South streets began to drill "in the saloon of the Odd Fellows' Hall there." Laborers at Whitney's car wheel factory left their machines and headed to the mayor's office. Owner James

Whitney vowed to go with the company as a private. "Every man who goes to defend the State from the establishment of Mr. Whitney will receive his pay while absent."[319]

Mechanics and laborers employed in the construction industry "laid aside their shovels, trowels, and jack planes and shouldered muskets and proceeded to the armories preparatory to going to Harrisburg." The workmen of the "celebrated piano manufactory" formed a company, shouting, "Give us arms, we are ready." At the Hope Hose House, the firemen mustered the "Athlete Guards."

The *Philadelphia Press* described the martial scene. "The streets yesterday were alive with soldiers — some with uniforms, some without, and some with portions of uniforms. Judging from the appearance of some of the squads, every available 'soger' coat, vest, trousers, must have been brought into requisition."

The paper concluded external appearances were immaterial. "It is not the handsome uniforms or the gaudy epaulets that make the true soldier. It is a firm and courageous heart, such as that possessed by our many civilian soldiers, who have left good and comfortable homes in response to the Governor's call — in many homes, active preparations were in progress to fit out fathers, husbands, and brothers, for their departure . . . to the field of active service."[320]

This outpouring of patriots evinced a positive reaction from the press. "We have every reason to be thankful for the threats of invasion which the Rebels have uttered, and for the Napoleonic ardor with which they are endeavoring to carry them out. It was the very thing needed. It is making a vast army of reserves, and it is the readiest possible way to seal the doom of the Rebellion."[321]

Independence Square in Philadelphia transformed into the country's largest outdoor recruiting station.

Christened "Camp Independence," the avenue through the Square was lined with 25 large Sibley tents that were "brilliantly illuminated with lanterns of various colors and devices, stretched from tent to tent and tree to tree. The spacious avenue on each side of which the tents were placed was densely thronged with ladies and gentlemen, promenading, examining the different tents, and listening to the music. Drums were beating up recruits in various parts of the ground, and the whole formed an ensemble the very opposite of the scenes usually produced by 'grim-visage war.'"[322]

At nearby Independence Hall, "rolls of honor" would be perpetually recorded listing the names of Pennsylvanians who enlisted in the state's regiments. "No other permanent record will be extant and its utility will be incalculable hereafter, to bereaved relatives and friends, in ascertaining the precise military status of the deceased and wounded, for the purpose of securing pensions."[323]

An odd irony occurred in Philadelphia in the midst of the war fervor. "Constitution Day" (September 17), an annual remembrance to honor the adoption of the U.S. Constitution in 1789, had to be postponed "in view of the present State emergency, and the absence of the men who have gone to defend the Commonwealth."[324]

In response to the threat of invasion, Philadelphia had "the appearance of a vast military encampment. The sound of the drum and fife is heard at any moment up to a late hour at night, and all are slowly realizing what the great stir and excitement, constantly taking place around them, indicates."[325]

This flood of exuberant recruits nearly ended with a literal flood. Heavy rains drenched Philadelphia throughout the night of September 11, and by next morning, the Cohocksink Creek had "burst its bonds" and deluged at least 1,000 houses. "While the city bells were calling the people to arms yesterday, an invader, against which no ordnance can prevail, was sweeping through two Wards of the city, carrying devastation in its train."

The torrent of water, as deep as four feet, "dashed with immense power against all obstacles, pouring into cellars like waterfalls, destroying frame tenements and undermining walls that we thought to be able to withstand all shocks." In some places, the water pooled to 18 feet deep. Damage in the 17th and 18th Wards was extensive.

"Stray animals floated through the streets on impromptu rafts; pedestrians were overtaken by the rush of waters, and either stood in speechless amazement, or selected the nearest accessible place of refuge. Families were imprisoned in the second stories of their dwellings. Steam fire-engines were at work during the entire afternoon clearing the cellars of water."

Three children died — all from the same family. Mary (age 7), Wilhelmina (age 10) and Frederica (age 12) were crushed instantly when their tenement at No. 1532 N. Sixth Street crumbled into ruins. The mother had left home just before the flood, gone to secure board for her children at a neighbor's. For a moment, Philadelphia paused and grieved.[326]

INSPIRED BY patriotic fever and a phobia of the Rebels, thousands turned out to defend Pennsylvania from Lee's invaders. Thousands more did not. Their absence in the ranks aroused indignation and charges of cowardice.

> If ever an opportunity was afforded you to prove your love of country, the present hour supplies it. . . . *The enemy is at your very door*, and yet many of you shrink from your duty. Your State is invaded by a foe to whom revenge is most sweet, and yet you stand idle spectators. . . . If you have health and strength, you *must* be with us, or be content to be branded as undeserving the respect of the meanest soldier in our ranks. There is no alternative. For God's sake, arouse from your lethargy before it is too late.[327]

The response to the governor's militia call was remarkable — almost miraculous. Over 200 companies (20,000 men) organized and offered their services within one day. Six thousand were arriving from Pittsburgh. Farmers flocked in from the rural areas. The Pennsylvania Railroad deposited thousands in Harrisburg, transporting all militia men free, either singly or in companies.[328] In one September week, an estimated 75,000 volunteers turned out to defend the Quaker State.

"These gallant volunteers of the Keystone State deserve all applause for the alacrity with which they have sprung to arms and the splendid patriotism they have shown," admired the *New York*

Times. "General Lee did not expect to have this vast additional army to contend with."[329]

The Pennsylvania governor had militiamen, but he did not have trained soldiers. How would they respond to Lee's veterans? How would they react in battle? The governor did not wish to depend exclusively upon his citizens to defend the Commonwealth. He wanted the help of the U.S. Army.

Gov. Curtin had been soliciting Federal support ever since the Confederates had reached Frederick. "What can be done for the protection of our border," he wired the Secretary of War Edwin M. Stanton on September 7. The response from Washington was vague and bureaucratic. "The attention of the military authorities is clearly directed to the movements of the enemy, and every effort will be made to overcome him."[330]

Dissatisfied, and desiring a firmer commitment, Curtin pleaded once more to Secretary Stanton. "Any number of regiments that can be spared from Washington or Baltimore could be advantageously employed."

Stanton snapped back. "We have no troops in Washington or Baltimore to send to Harrisburg." The Secretary maintained "the best defense of Harrisburg is to strengthen the force now marching against the enemy under General McClellan."[331] McClellan, at that moment, was just northwest of Washington, still about 30 miles distant from Lee, who was then at Frederick.

As word arrived in Harrisburg that the Confederates were marching toward Hagerstown, Curtin escalated the pressure on the Lincoln government to assist him in the defense of his state. "It is fair to presume their object is the capture of the capital of Pennsylvania. What can you do to aid with forces to meet this movement?"

The governor's office begged for help. "We are destitute of artillery to defend the passage of the Susquehanna. Can you order guns and ammunition tonight, from Pittsburgh and eastern points, to concentrate at Harrisburg immediately, using special trains on the railroads? Please answer."

This time General in Chief Henry W. Halleck returned the message with an emphatic *no*. "If there should be any real necessity to send guns and ammunition from Pittsburgh, it will be ordered."[332]

Washington did not dismiss Harrisburg as a legitimate Rebel target. Lincoln and his military authorities understood the psychological boost the capture of the capital of Pennsylvania would yield for the Rebels. They also were concerned about the network of railroads that passed through Harrisburg. They knew the Confederates could disrupt a nerve center of Northern transportation and commerce. They also were aware that every day Lee stayed in Pennsylvania — a state governed by a Republican — he vacuumed votes away from the Republican Party in the forthcoming elections.

The Washington strategy, however, adopted *concentration of its forces* as the best antidote against Lee. It depended upon McClellan's army — a force of mobility — as the best hope to stop or even destroy the Confederate invaders.

Gen. Halleck, the chief deviser of this strategy, explained his methods to Gov. Curtin. "It is not deemed advisable to assemble troops at so many different points. For the present we want all

Pennsylvania militiamen rush into Harrisburg to defend the state against Confederate invasion. (*Harper's Weekly*)

troops here [with McClellan]. We can protect Harrisburg better from this vicinity [Washington] than to weaken our force by [sending] them there."[333]

Unconvinced, Curtin tried once again. "The Cumberland Valley is entirely undefended, and we are entirely without force here."

Halleck again refused to hedge his strategy. He reinforced his thinking. "The best way to defend Pennsylvania now is to concentrate our forces on the enemy, and not to scatter them in weak parties at several points."[334]

When the Confederates arrived in Hagerstown — making it obvious that Pennsylvania was their invasion target — an exasperated Curtin carried his plea for U.S. troops to President Lincoln. "The whole of the Rebel army has been moved from Frederick, and their destination is Harrisburg or Philadelphia. . . . Send here not less than 80,000 disciplined forces."

The President replied promptly. "Please consider we have not to exceed 80,000 disciplined troops . . . this side of the mountains." He then adhered to Halleck's strategy of concentration. "Start half of [the troops] to Harrisburg and the enemy will turn upon and beat the remaining half, and then reach Harrisburg before the part going there, and beat it, too. The best possible security for Pennsylvania is putting the strongest force possible into the enemy's rear."

Curtin finally relented. "Your message received. Reasons for not sending force entirely satisfactory."[335]

Lincoln did agree, however, to mollify Gov. Curtin (somewhat) by acquiescing to his request for an experienced combat general from Pennsylvania to lead the burgeoning, but undisciplined, Quaker State militia. The U.S. dispatched Brig. Gen. John Reynolds, a native of Lancaster and commander of the Pennsylvania Reserves division in the Army of the Potomac, to Harrisburg on September 11.

This outraged Gen. McClellan. He considered Reynolds one of his best division commanders, and indispensable. It also brought an outburst of disgust from Reynolds' boss, Maj. Gen. Joseph Hooker.

"A scared Governor ought not to be permitted to destroy the usefulness of an entire division of the army, on the eve of important operations." Hooker was convinced the Lincoln government had overreacted. "It is satisfactory to my mind that the Rebels have no more intention of going to Harrisburg then they have of going to heaven." Hooker lost his bid for Reynolds, however. "It is only in the United States that atrocities like this are entertained."[336]

When Reynolds arrived at the Pennsylvania capital, he deemed the situation dire. "I am fully impressed that the intention has been for some time entertained by [the enemy] to invade this section of the State." He then asked if his own troops he left behind in McClellan's army could be sent to join him. "I think if the [Pennsylvania] Reserve Corps could be spared from the army in front of Washington and dispatched here, it would be of great assistance in forming and organizing the new troops assembling at this point." Reynolds then responded to his own appeal. "I have no hope that this request will meet with the favor from the commanding general."[337]

President Lincoln also assented to Gov. Curtin's request that the Pennsylvania militia be federalized. "It is my anxious desire to afford, as far as possible, the means and power of the Federal Government to protect the State of Pennsylvania from invasion by the Rebel forces. . . . I sanction the [militia] call that you have made, and will receive them into the service and pay of the United States to the extent they can be armed, equipped, and usefully employed."[338]

GOV. CURTIN ALREADY was usefully deploying his militia by sending them toward the Pennsylvania-Maryland border.

The precarious position of Franklin County, just north of Hagerstown, especially troubled him. Chambersburg, the county seat, stood directly in the path of the invaders. It appeared destined to be the first major Northern town that would fall into the clasp of the Confederates.

Chambersburg also was an important rail junction, connecting Harrisburg with Hagerstown. If the Confederates captured Chambersburg, it would eliminate opportunities for rapid transport of troops south toward the border. Hours of movement via locomotives could change into days of marching, opening more time for Confederate mischief in southern Pennsylvania.

"We are indeed in the midst of a frightful panic," Chambersburg resident Benjamin Schneck informed his sister. "More than half our people have left and are leaving. Just think, I left for the Far West a week or 10 days ago — got to Cincinnati in a similar confusion — and . . . I heard of the contemplated (or rather, expected) march of the Rebels from Hagerstown to Chambersburg."

Schneck assessed the situation, and he sensed the desperation. "Should they come, we must just submit — we are defenseless."[339]

Hagerstown "refugees" were the first to alarm the citizens of Chambersburg. Hundreds of pro-Union people fled north as the Confederates approached, escaping via the Cumberland Valley Railroad or roads heading across the Mason-Dixon Line. The Hagerstown Bank, the Hagerstown Savings Bank, and the Washington County Bank removed their species, knowing the Rebels were in short supply of gold and U.S. dollars. This inspired the Bank of Chambersburg to follow suit, sending its holdings to Harrisburg. The Cumberland Valley Railroad removed its locomotives and cars from the Hagerstown line, considering it unsafe to continue its operation.[340]

"Any number of rumors became rife of the advance of the Rebel army upon our State border. Each additional report brought confirmation of the former ones, until our community was considerably excited and alarmed at the prospect of having the Rebel hordes in our midst."

Businesses shut down. Martial law was declared. Large bodies of armed men began pouring in from north, east, and west, in response to the governor's call for troops. Joining the cause were the editor and employees of the *Valley Spirit*, a weekly newspaper published in Chambersburg.

"We perhaps owe an apology for not issuing a paper," explained the editor. "We issued no paper because we couldn't. Stonewall Jackson was threatening to invade our State and capture and perhaps sack our town. Martial law was declared and every able-bodied man and boy was required to shoulder the musket, and assist in repelling the invader from our homes and altars."

The editor justified his excuse for shutting down the press. "We succumbed to the necessities of the case, closed the office, postponed all business till a more convenient season, and all hands about the establishment, from Editors down to devil, shouldered their guns (ours was a shot-gun). . . . This is our apology. We feel sure our readers will excuse us."[341]

People of southern Pennsylvania were concerned for their property and their livelihoods. Rumors circulated that the Rebels intended "to make Pennsylvania howl," and that Chambersburg was "to be the recipient of their first favors." Everywhere in the town, "faces were anxious, and the streets grew alive with groups discussing the probabilities of Rebel conduct."

"The fact of their having behaved civilly in Maryland proved nothing. It was a slave State and was considered as their own soul. The question was what would they do in the country of avowed enemies?"

"Nearly everyone has passed a sleepless night, and those who did not chiefly slept in their clothing, ready at a moment's notice to rise." A letter writer to the *Philadelphia Press* expressed that Chambersburg "saw its darkest hour" since its perilous existence as a frontier town during the French and Indian War.

The correspondent detected one calming influence, however. "It is odd that far less anxiety was exhibited by women than by men. They sat tranquilly on their door-steps, and only the elder ones appeared desirous and leaving. The young ones had heard that Southerners were gentlemanly, and often good-looking. Female curiosity was excited, and anticipated no harm. The girls, therefore, were as lively as at a strawberry festival, and trotted about with supreme indifference."[342]

One group that felt extreme anxiety was the 126th Pennsylvania Infantry. Many of the regiment's men hailed from Chambersburg and Franklin County, and they had enlisted less than a month before to fight the Confederates *in Virginia*. Lee's invaders now threatened their own homes, but they were still within the Washington defenses, nearly 100 miles distant.

"We are all anxious to be with you, in this hour of trial; and on our native hills, defending our homes against a foreign foe. . . . But it is otherwise ordered, and you and your neighbors must, in a great measure, rely upon yourselves. You have all we can give — our hopes and our prayers. Let every man do his duty, and then, whatever be the result, you will at least have no cause to reproach yourselves."

Where, exactly, was the U.S. Army as the Confederates prepared to cross the Pennsylvania border?

Much of George McClellan's Army of the Potomac was still near the Potomac. On the day Lee landed in Hagerstown, McClellan was still two days from Frederick. The Rebels had a significant head start, and McClellan attempted to assuage the fears of Gov. Curtin.

"Call out the militia, especially mounted men, and do everything in your power to impede the enemy by the action of light troops," McClellan advised the governor. "Attack them in flank, destroying their trains and any property which must inevitably come into their possession."

McClellan attempted to assure the governor that it was not too late. He and his army were coming.

"You may be sure that I will follow them as closely as I can, and fight them whenever I can find them. It is as much my interest as yours to preserve the soil of Pennsylvania from invasion, or, failing in that, to destroy any army that may have the temerity to attempt it." [343]

Gen. McClellan soon would be presented his best opportunity.

CHAPTER 12

Fortune Found

I think Lee has made a gross mistake. . . I have all of the plans of the Rebels, and will catch them in their own trap.

—Gen. George B. McClellan, September 13, 1862

George McClellan received an unexpected favor from Robert E. Lee.

The Confederate commander had abandoned Frederick, without a fight.

Lee's Fredericktown halt had McClellan and the Lincoln government theorizing for a week over Rebel intentions. "They are in a position to take . . . three or four roads, to Chambersburg, to Hagerstown, to Gettysburg, to Baltimore, or to re-cross the Potomac," explained the bewildered U.S. department commander stationed at Baltimore. "Where the Rebel army is going is more than I can conjecture."[344]

Gen. Lee's elongated stay at Frederick convinced some that he was trying to lure McClellan out of the Washington fortifications; then choose a fight along the north-south line of the Monocacy River. Intelligence coming to Gov. Curtin in Harrisburg seemed to confirm this notion. He informed Gen. McClellan, "From all we can learn, the enemy has selected his ground and massed his force near Frederick, to give you battle, the result of which will probably decide the future of our country."

"Everything that we can learn induces me to believe that the information you have received is substantially correct," McClellan responded.[345] On the same day both men were predicting the determinant battle at Frederick, Lee's army was departing. The military intelligence was wrong.

Even as Lee moved to Hagerstown, just over six miles from the Pennsylvania border, uncertainty plagued Washington. General in Chief Halleck was convinced that any Confederate move north was a ruse to weaken Washington's defenses and make the capital vulnerable. He shared his theory with Gen. McClellan. "It may be the enemy's object to draw off the mass of our forces and then attempt to attack from the Virginia side of the Potomac. Think of this."[346]

The Union high command had received troubling reports about Virginia. Tens of thousands of additional Confederates, according to intelligence sources, were on their way to join Lee. These extra Rebels were concentrating in northern Virginia and the Shenandoah Valley, and were en route, but had not yet crossed the Potomac. This presented concerns, not only for the safety of the capital, but to the possible weakness of the Union army, which could be overpowered by superior Confederate numbers.[347]

"I am by no means satisfied yet that the enemy has crossed the river in any large force," McClellan wrote to Halleck on September 8. "Our information is still entirely too indefinite to justify definite action. . . . The time occupied in ascertaining their position, strength, and intentions will enable me to place the army in fair condition."[348]

Lack of good intelligence or conflicting intelligence frustrated Navy Secretary Gideon Welles. "The War Department is bewildered, knows but little, does nothing, proposes nothing."[349]

Despite uncertainties about Lee's intentions, Gen. McClellan understood his assignments. His first two goals were the protection of Washington and Baltimore. Both of these depended upon success with his third assignment: rebuilding and reorganizing two shattered armies.

The summer battles around Richmond and during the Manassas campaign had taken heavy tolls on McClellan's Army of the Potomac and John Pope's Army of Virginia. The 29,000 U.S. casualties included dozens of officers killed and wounded, including generals. Unit strengths in many cases had been reduced by 70 percent, a result of battle losses and depletion through diseases. Regiments that commenced the war with 1,000 men now were reduced to an average of 350. Resting, refitting, and reorganizing were McClellan's tasks, but the Confederate invasion permitted little time for accomplishment.

The brigade of Samuel Crawford demonstrated McClellan's problem. Crawford's four regiments totaled 659 soldiers (the average brigade strength was 1,400). Three of the regiments had no field or staff officers, and were commanded by captains; corporals were in charge of companies (usually the captain's job).

"No time or opportunity has been allowed, from the necessities of the service, either to rest the men or to reorganize the companies and regiments," Crawford complained on September 9. "Every day adds to the report of the medical officers of these regiments, and they unanimously show that it is owing to the [campaigning], the great exposure they have suffered, the deprivation of proper food, and the want of absolute rest. . . . Depression of spirit adds greatly to the induction of camp diseases."

Every movement of the brigade presented a problem. "There are many men belonging to the command who cannot, from absolute want of muscular tone, follow in its marches. Men never known to fall behind, upon previous marches, do so now."[350]

Condition meant nothing to the Northern press. The Confederate invasion demanded an immediate response. "There is one thing the nation will insist upon, and that is: Action! Action! Action!"

Baltimore's *American and Commercial Advertiser* reserved no patience. "Instead of returning to the shelter of the fortifications to 'refatten our jaded horses, and respoke our tottering wagons' — to subside into chronic inaction, in other words, let a week's rest at furthest see the great army again seeking the foe — let [there be] blows."

The editor continued his diatribe against inaction. "Commended to idleness for even a few weeks now, who does not feel, with horror creeping over him, that the old bulletins concerning [excuses] will be repeated."

Only one solution to the Rebel invasion existed. "Force everything that is available into the field; every man, every gun, sword, revolver, and pound of powder, and *end the war*. We can do it, and do it soon. The nation is smarting under its needless reverses; it is worn out with delays. We have gone along leisurely. . . . We may talk of patriotism, of devotion, of singleness of purpose, but the Rebels themselves shame us."[351]

A POSTURE OF DEFENSE *was* an action for George McClellan. Defending Washington and Baltimore was his first charge from the Lincoln government. For the capital, McClellan quickly readied his veteran soldiers behind Washington's fortifications. But Baltimore presented a problem. No fortifications ringed the Chesapeake city. Only an army operating in the field could secure Baltimore.

McClellan contrived a three-wing strategy to defend against the Confederate menace in Maryland. His left wing would hug the Potomac, securing river crossings and ensuring no surprise Rebel approach from imagined enemy forces still in Virginia. The center wing would defend all roads leading from Frederick toward Washington. The right wing would start north to protect Baltimore. Each wing would be connected, with an ability to support one another. The Army of the Potomac would depart Washington's defenses and form a shield in the field — a shield that would deflect any strike by Lee.

McClellan reasoned Baltimore, and especially its railroads, most vulnerable. During the war's first month in 1861, Rebel sympathizers in Maryland had attempted to cut off troop transports to Washington by destroying vital railroad bridges. Even the Baltimore newspapers sensed that Lee intended "to make a dash on the railroads between here and Washington, at one or two points that might be damaged quickly." The press announced, much to the army's discomfort, that "sufficient protection is not afforded the large stone structure over the Patapsco [River], used by the Washington Railway Company. At such a period as this, too much importance cannot be attached to such matters."[352]

Maintaining the railroad artery from Baltimore into Washington was critical. As the president of the Baltimore & Ohio Railroad informed the secretary of war, his line could convey 28,000 men in one convoy, along with 50-60 pieces of artillery. He could repeat the operation every 18-24 hours.[353] McClellan knew he must launch toward Baltimore — and quickly.

Believing a confrontation likely in his advance toward Baltimore, McClellan chose the most experienced general in Washington (other than himself) to command his right wing: Maj. Gen. Ambrose Burnside. President Lincoln had such confidence in Burnside that he twice offered him command of the Army of the Potomac. But Burnside had refused, deferring to George McClellan.

Burnside and McClellan had been best friends since West Point, and Burnside had worked for McClellan in the railroad industry in the years prior to the war. Burnside had completed a complicated amphibious mission along the North Carolina coast, heralded by the press as one of the great Union exploits of the war (there hadn't been many thus far). With the Confederate invasion, Burnside was called to Washington, where McClellan promptly placed his most senior commander in charge of his most uncertain assignment — protecting Baltimore and its railroads.

Burnside began marching nearly 24,000 men from Washington on September 8, but not toward Baltimore. Instead he veered northwest, establishing his headquarters at Brookeville, some 20 miles from the capital the next day. From there, Burnside's tentacles stretched north toward the National Road, the main pike connecting Frederick and Baltimore. These maneuvers placed Burnside in position to block any Confederate raids toward Baltimore. In addition, they exposed Lee's southern flank to assault if he advanced toward Baltimore.

"I THINK THAT WE ARE NOW IN POSITION to prevent any attack in force on Baltimore," triumphed McClellan in a message to his superior, General in Chief Halleck. "They shall not take Baltimore without defeating this army."[354]

Jubilation turned to consternation late on September 9. McClellan received word from his cavalry chief that Stonewall Jackson and Jeb Stuart had located their headquarters well east of Frederick. "This indicates that the enemy intends moving on Baltimore." McClellan responded, sending definitive orders to Burnside. "Should the enemy make any demonstration toward Baltimore, let his column get well in motion, and then attack him vigorously on the flank."[355] Attack!

For a man with a reputation of overbearing caution and hesitance, this was an extraordinary order by McClellan. More remarkable was his trust in Burnside, in essence giving him independent command of an offensive operation without McClellan present. Perhaps most astonishing, McClellan was willing to initiate battle without his forces consolidated. Most of his army was not with Burnside.

Baltimore was just too important. McClellan had to act *now*. He trusted Burnside not to be rash, but prudent, discovering a weakness in Lee's flank, and striking there. That would slow, if not stop, the Confederate thrust toward Baltimore. McClellan would support Burnside from other positions along his line, if he could.

"How does it look now?" President Lincoln wired McClellan on the morning of the September 10.

"The information subsequently obtained from General Burnside's scouts, that the mass of the enemy was still at Frederick, induced me to suspend the movement of the right wing," responded McClellan.

Baltimore turned out to be a false alarm. The location of the Confederate generals' positions east of Frederick was correct, but the assumption proved incorrect. Not all was lost, however. Burnside's reconnaissance force seized the National Road and a north-south hill at Ridgeville. This not only ensured Baltimore's protection, but it offered McClellan an excellent defensive position, should Lee decide to attack him from Frederick.[356]

Unbeknownst to McClellan, Lee was headed the opposite direction. On the same day Burnside deployed at Ridgeville, the

Confederates began executing Special Orders 191, marching west toward Harpers Ferry and northwest to Hagerstown. There would be no fight near Frederick.

UNAWARE OF THE CONFEDERATE abandonment of Frederick, at this point, McClellan was pleased. Washington was safe; Baltimore secure. The principal move by the Union army had been Burnside's wing, reaching Ridgeville and marching about 30 miles in two days. The other two wings had progressed less rapidly, by intention. Anchored on the Potomac and spanning into central Maryland, their mission was defensive: protect Washington. With both cities now safeguarded, McClellan could focus his army toward the enemy at Frederick. But his posture remained defensive, clutching the approaches to Washington and Baltimore.

Most of the army had not marched great distances, but it had moved in sizzling heat under a sun that "scorched to withering — almost to burning," on roads piled in three inches of dust, rising "to fill the air almost to suffocation." Soldiers in the newest regiments, who had been in the army for less than a month, suffered the greatest, loaded by paraphernalia long ago discarded by veterans. The new recruits "were nearly all laden with knapsack, blanket, coat, etc., and the result was that very many of them became exhausted before reaching their destination. An old soldier knows better than to load himself down in warm weather and heavy or dusty walking."[357]

These laden soldiers attracted the attention of the Russian ambassador to the United States, who watched endless columns of the army marching out of northwest Washington. Minister Edouard de Stoeckl said that "we had the finest army in the world, but that no soldier could do his duty who carried so much luggage on his person. Twice as much, he said, as a Russian soldier was allowed to carry, and far more awkwardly and inconveniently placed than his load."[358]

A soldier in the 126th Pennsylvania (one of the new regiments) described his first Sunday in September, recalling his brigade march from the forts near Alexandria to the northwest side of Washington. "The hour of departure was six o'clock a.m. On we marched, knapsacks slung, and our spirits of the most joyous character. But as we advanced, the sun became more oppressive, the dust more blinding, our loads heavier, and strength and hilarity soon gave way to exhaustion and feebleness." The writer recalled some of his fellow soldiers "nearly lost their lives from sun-stroke," and that upon arrival at their destination, the brigade was "scarcely two-thirds full, the balance straggling at a slow pace back." He concluded, "That march will not soon be effaced from memory, and will be put down by every soldier who performed it as one of the heaviest and severest tasks of his life."[359]

The march from Washington to Rockville, constituting McClellan's center wing, was particularly memorable. "Officers and soldiers attest that the march to Rockville was the severest they have experienced — nothing they experienced on the Peninsula [Richmond Campaign] was so trying to them." Exhausted, men collapsed in the evening; but about 10 p.m., they suddenly were reinvigorated when Gen. McClellan rode into camp.

"Instantly the fact was known through the army, as if by telegraph, each man communicating it, joyfully and enthusiastically, to the one next him; and, as if by a new creation, the worn and wearied immediately became imbued with new spirit; music pealed forth its welcome, and loud huzzas made the air, and groves and woods resounded with the soldier's greeting." [360]

The next day, Rockville, the seat of Montgomery County, was blanketed with dust caused by the combination of drought and a moving army. "It seems as if Providence intended to punish the vicinity of this dusty village for some of the sins of the country, by withholding from it bountiful showers, and giving them a drouth."

The village looked like "Herculaneum dug from the ashes of Mount Vesuvius, as if it might have been excavated from some uncommon land slide. There was dust on the trees, dust on the houses, dust in the atmosphere, dust in the water you drank, and dust on all you eat, that made your teeth grit till it chilled you to the heart. It might have been called the village of dust."[361]

Despite the fact that "trees and cornstalks looked red" due to the powdered clay dust, and that "all the pumps on the road were nearly pumped dry," some comfort came to the soldiers as local farmers crowded along the roads, "with all sorts of venders of eatables and drinkables, from solace beer to apple tarts and watermelons." Peaches could be purchased at a good price — ten for five cents."[362]

The extreme weather that second week of September proved too much for debilitated U.S. soldiers. Hundreds dropped from their ranks. Straggling became so epidemic that it forced Gen. McClellan to issue a specific order to correct the evil.

"The mischievous practice of straggling, it is observed, is again instituted in this army, and this, in many cases, without the least apparent concern on the part of commanding officers or either the higher or lower grade. Straggling is habitually associated with cowardice, marauding, and theft. The straggler must now be taught that he leaves the ranks without authority and skulks at the severest risk, even that of death."[363]

Marauding and theft had become a problem — and an embarrassment — for McClellan's army. The Confederates had passed through much of the same region and had not stolen a chicken or burned a fence rail. The U.S. Army arrived, and Maryland citizens were subjected "to the pillage and plunder of our soldiers."

"Many of these characters ruthlessly invade the precincts of the kitchen and dining-room, and driving the family away from the table where the accustomed meal is spread, and proceed in the coolest manner to partake of the meal themselves."

One notorious example included 15-20 stragglers from the 82nd New York Infantry, who drove a farmer's hogs out of his yard, shot one of them, quartered it up, and then "impudently accosted the owner of the swine, and demanded a kettle in which to cook the meat." Other similar depravities occurred, not because soldiers were hungry, but "simply to appease a rascally desire to rob and plunder."[364]

The editor of the *Baltimore American and Commercial Advertiser* expressed disgust. "At this critical time, when the loyalty of Maryland hangs, as I believe, upon a very slender thread, this thieving is to me a cause of the most serious apprehension."

The writer could not explain the callous indifference of the Union army in a Union state. "We who profess to be [Maryland's] friends are destroying private property, touching the purse of every citizen in the vicinity of our army by allowing a shameful and unnecessary plundering of private property of every description. The other armies whom we claim are our enemies, most rigidly abstain from even the slightest infringement. . . . What is to be the effect of these wanton depredations upon this very doubtful state of sentiment in Maryland?"

The observer marveled at the good behavior and discipline of the Rebels and the misbehavior and ill-discipline of the Federals. "It is humiliating to record the superior sagacity and discrimination with which the Rebels have managed the sentiment of the people wherever they have been."

Finally, the editor blamed the generals. "Our Generals are responsible for it. Upon them must come the blame. It has now been quite long enough a stench in the nostrils of every right-minded soldier or citizen." He concluded, "Their present course is equivalent to winning victories for the Rebels."[365]

Gen. McClellan recognized the indiscretions of his army, and he also acknowledged his public relations problem. He ordered his officers to post guards on the flanks and the rear of each division. He placed armed men at all road junctions with the authority to shoot stragglers. He instructed provost marshals to send cavalry into the country, scouring every habitation and corner for stragglers. For any marauder caught trespassing, he instructed an immediate trial, and a possible sentence of public death before the army.

"The safety of the country depends upon what this army shall now achieve; it cannot be successful if its soldiers are one-half skulking to the rear, while the brunt of battle is borne by the other half, and its officers inattentive to observe and correct the grossest evils which are daily occurring under their eyes."[366]

ON SEPTEMBER 11, George McClellan proclaimed some good news: no more Confederates were expected from Virginia. "This uncertainty, in my judgment, exists no longer," he explained to General in Chief Halleck.

Then McClellan shared the bad news. "All the evidence that has been accumulated from various sources since we left Washington goes to prove most conclusively that almost the entire Rebel army in Virginia, amounting to not less than 120,000 men, is in the vicinity of Frederick City."

How many Confederates? 120,000?[367]

This presented a problem. As McClellan approached Frederick, he was outnumbered. "They are probably aware that their forces are numerically superior to ours by at least 25%. . . . The momentous consequences involved in the struggle of the next few days impels me, at the risk of being considered slow and overcautious, to most earnestly recommend that every available man be at once added to this army." [368]

Gen. Halleck, McClellan's superior, appeared to confirm McClellan's estimate. "What force, in your opinion, has the enemy?" inquired Treasury Secretary Salmon Chase during a discussion with Halleck on September 11.

"From the best evidence I have — not satisfactory, but the best — I reckon the whole number in Maryland and the vicinity of Washington at 150,000."

Chase asked for clarification. "How many in Maryland? . . . Two thirds probably, or 100,000." [369] McClellan, concerned about his perceived deficiency, requested that his army be bolstered by 48,600 veterans from three corps still behind the defenses of Washington. Lincoln expressed concern this would "sweep everything" from the Virginia defenses of the capital, but he promised some support. "I am for sending you all that can be spared." One corps, but no more, was dispatched from Washington.[370]

Meanwhile, at 8 p.m. on September 11, McClellan received news concerning Frederick from Gov. Curtin in Pennsylvania. "We have advices that the enemy broke up whole encampment at Frederick yesterday morning, 3 o'clock, and marched in direction of Hagerstown. . . . Men all believed they were going to Pennsylvania. We shall need a large portion of your column in [the Cumberland Valley] to save us from utter destruction."[371]

McClellan already suspected the Confederates' departure. His signal observatory atop Sugar Loaf Mountain, established earlier that day, could detect no large encampments or enemy movements about Frederick. He informed Halleck, "I have ordered [Burnside] to advance tomorrow, if possible, to Frederick and occupy it. . . . I shall follow up the Rebels as rapidly as possible."[372]

Burnside moved west toward Frederick along the National Road on Friday, September 12, appointed by McClellan to capture the city. Five days ago, he was departing Washington. Now he was leading the U.S. Army into the territory seized by Lee.

Burnside approached cautiously, encountering Confederate rear-guard resistance. When he arrived at the Monocacy River, resistance increased momentarily at the four-arch stone bridge carrying the National Road over the river. But the Rebels were too few, and the bridge fell quickly to the Yankees. At about 4 p.m., the U.S. advance entered the east end of town, and the Federals hoisted the Stars and Stripes once again over the city. The Associated Press reported: "Frederick is ours."[373]

At any early hour on Saturday morning, Burnside came into Frederick. He was heralded as a liberator, and welcomed by "the most enthusiastic demonstrations of the people."

Burnside had not received any similar civilian greeting since the war commenced. Understandable, considering he rode into North Carolina coastal towns as a conqueror. But here in Frederick, a nest in Union country, Burnside felt appreciated. In response to the cheers and the waving of flags and handkerchiefs, Burnside "rode through the streets with his hat off, giving and receiving orders as he moved along to the messengers who were constantly approaching him."

Burnside warmed up the crowds; but when Gen. McClellan entered town about 11 a.m. on Saturday the 13th, the people were "almost wild with joy." McClellan had been cheered by his troops, but the outpouring of affection in Frederick matched his favorite martial moments.

"Men, women and children thronged the streets, and to such an extent obstructed the way, that [McClellan] was compelled to rein up his horse to prevent doing any injury to them. They not only cheered, but fairly screamed with joy, and the waving of flags and handkerchiefs appeared almost universal."[374]

Gen. McClellan enters Frederick amidst wild celebration. (*Harper's Weekly*)

The Frederick women made McClellan's reception especially memorable. "They gave [him] such a welcome as ladies know how to give to a hero. They saluted him with kisses (figuratively I mean — but they would have been actual ones have the General come within reach); showered flowers upon him; waved their flags over his head, and cheered him with their good wishes."[375]

The ardor hardly cooled as tens of thousands of U.S. soldiers passed through the town. Even the writer for the *New York Herald*, who hailed from a city known for the fervor of its mass meetings, seemed impressed. "My pen fails when I would attempt to describe the glorious reception we met with from the citizens of Frederick. Our march through the streets was one grand ovation. Old men hobbled into the streets to call us deliverers. The richest and fairest of the beauties of the fair sex soiled their dainty feet with the mud of the street to wave myriads of Union emblems in our faces, while the young men and the children actually laughed until they cried for joy." [376]

Throughout the ranks, ladies and children crowded among the troops, serving them hot coffee and refreshments. Unlike when the Confederates occupied the town — when doors were locked and windows shuddered — everything was open, with flags flying from windows and hoisted from roof tops. "The effect of this reception on the troops was most inspiring and the whole city was vocal with cheering."[377]

The scene was the antithesis of the Rebels leaving town. In fact, among the last to depart was Confederate Brig. Gen. Howell Cobb, former speaker of the U.S. House of Representatives and former secretary of the treasury, who concluded his stay with a threatening speech in the square at Patrick Street. He proclaimed "he knew the name of every Union man in Frederick; that he would soon return; and that if they had turned over any of his friends to the fury of the Lincoln Government, he would revenge himself and his Government tenfold."[378]

ROBERT E. LEE had Pennsylvania in sight as he waited at Hagerstown on Saturday morning, September 13.

Artillery thundered from the distant mountains south of Hagerstown. Something was happening at Harpers Ferry. Lee expected the sound of cannon soon would herald reports of success from Stonewall. Jackson was about 24 miles distant, via the most direct route. A day's march for the celebrated "Foot Cavalry" would reunite Lee with most of his army. Then onward into the North.

All was now ready for the expedition across the Mason-Dixon Line. His supply line now was operational, thanks to Jackson chasing away the U.S. garrison at Martinsburg, clearing the supply route into the Shenandoah Valley. The Potomac River was so low that the ford at Williamsport presented an ideal crossing, and Lee expected wagon trains of provisions soon to be rumbling north to Hagerstown and beyond.

He needed their arrival. Lee had been disappointed in efforts to supply the army from western Maryland. "The army has been received in this region [Hagerstown] with sympathy and kindness," Lee informed President Davis. "We have found in this city about 1,500 barrels of flour, and I am led to hope that a supply can be gathered from the mills in the country, though I fear we shall have to haul from the Valley of Virginia."

Food remained a problem for the hungry Confederates. Livestock had been rustled north into Pennsylvania or into the mountains to the west by Unionists, and Lee's strict prohibitions against plundering made it difficult to obtain meat. "The supply of beef has been very small, and we have been able to procure no bacon."

Thousands of Confederates remained shoeless. Shoe manufacturing was not a big industry in western Maryland, and Lee now knew it. "A thousand pairs of shoes and some clothing were obtained in Fredericktown, 250 pairs in Williamsport, and about 400 pairs in this city. This will not be sufficient to cover the bare feet of the army."[379]

The discomfort of Confederate soldiers was mollified by their proximity to Pennsylvania, and for the moment, by a rousing reception in Hagerstown.

"Who can describe the wild delight manifested along the streets; the deafening shouts of the populace once more beyond the control of the despot? I'm sure our soldiers never felt happier since the war began — feeling that their presence had created so much joy."

The scribe for the *Savannah Republican* especially enjoyed the food. "Women fed the soldiers as they marched along, from baskets filled with provisions prepared for their advent; the little boys shouted hurrahs for Davis, and the men plainly told by their firm looks that their day had come and the Unionists had better stand clear. . . . The fact that our soldiers had soiled clothes, and many were barefooted, only served to strengthen the admiration of our Confederate friends for our army. They wore the aspect of toiling, enduring men, just such as they desired to see."[380]

Hagerstown offered the Georgian everything he had expected. Hagerstown was "the warmest Secession town we have entered in Maryland. Certainly two-thirds of the citizens are Southern, judging from the enthusiastic reception given us. Our cause is in great favor here, if we can satisfy the people that we will hold the country."[381]

Gen. Lee had no intention of long-term occupation, but his invasion faced bright prospects. He had, however, two worries.

"One great embarrassment is the reduction of our ranks by straggling," he notified President Davis from his Hagerstown headquarters. "Our ranks are very much diminished — I fear from a third to one-half of the original numbers." Lee knew the reasons. Forced marches. Hard duty. Little good food. Bare feet. Many just quit. Lee loved and admired his army. "The material of which it is composed is the best in the world," but some of the material had broken. "One of the greatest evils, from which many minor ones proceed, is the habit of straggling."[382]

Lee's other concern: the U.S. Army.

"The enemy have doubtless occupied Frederick since our troops have abandoned it, and are following our rear," Lee's military secretary informed Maj. Gen. Lafayette McLaws on September 13.

Lee had chosen McLaws to coordinate with Jackson in the investment of Harpers Ferry. Special Orders 191 charged McLaws with seizure of Maryland Heights, the highest mountain overlooking the Ferry. This was supposed to have been accomplished by now. In fact, Lee had expected Jackson's mission to Harpers Ferry to be concluded. Delay was not good.

If, indeed, the Federals had occupied Frederick, as Lee suspected, they were nearer McLaws (19 miles) than Jackson was to Lee (24 miles). Plus a good road from Frederick to Harpers Ferry led through the Potomac's river gaps, making McLaws vulnerable to attack. Lee did not expect such a Federal initiative; but if the Unionists learned that their Harpers Ferry garrison was endangered, they may stage a rescue attempt.

"The commanding general hopes that the enemy about Harpers Ferry will be speedily disposed of, and the various detachments returned to the main body of the army."[383]

Little did Lee know how much McClellan knew about his plan.

GEORGE MCCLELLAN was worried about Harpers Ferry. The telegraph had been cut. No word had come from that quarter. What was happening?

Even before arriving in Frederick, he had concerns about the situation of the U.S. garrison at the Ferry. He notified Gen. Halleck on the evening of September 12, "I this morning ordered cavalry to endeavor to open communication with Harper's Ferry, and in my orders of movement for tomorrow, have arranged so that I can go or send to [its] relief. . . . I think I cannot only relieve [Union commander Dixon Miles], but place the Rebels who attack him in great danger of being cut off."[384]

The next day, McClellan experienced his joyous reception in Frederick. Even more joy awaited him. At some point on September 13, he was delivered an order. But it wasn't to him; nor was it from him. It was Lee's Special Orders 191!

"I have all the plans of the Rebels, and will catch them in their own trap," a confident and exuberant McClellan informed President Lincoln.

"Will send you trophies."[385]

CHAPTER 13

Sabbath Surprise

A few days will decide all this; will tell, perhaps, the whole future story, not only for our own State, but even for the nation.

—*Baltimore American and Commercial Advertiser,* September 13, 1862

Time was not George McClellan's ally.

He had Lee's plans in his hands, but was it too late?

Cannon firing could be heard echoing off the mountains from the direction of Harpers Ferry, 20 miles west of Frederick, on September 13. That convinced McClellan that the Confederates were investing the post, just as prescribed in Lee's Lost Orders. The roar of cannon also encouraged McClellan that the Federals at the Ferry were still fighting. Could they hold on?

A 42-year veteran of the U.S. Army commanded the Harpers Ferry position. Col. Dixon Stansbury Miles had worn an army uniform seven years longer than McClellan's age. Now 59, Miles had graduated from West Point and distinguished himself in the Mexican War, rising from captain to brevet lieutenant colonel in the first four months of that war. Prior to the Civil War, Miles achieved the rank of full colonel of infantry — one of only 19 line

Harpers Ferry looking east through the Potomac River gap in the Blue Ridge. The armory ruins are in the foreground. Maryland Heights hovers over the town to the left. The Harpers Ferry operation delayed Lee's invasion plans. (*Harper's Weekly*)

colonels in a very small standing army. Miles, in fact, outranked Robert E. Lee in the United States Army.

McClellan had placed Miles in command at Harpers Ferry in March 1862. Due to its strategic location at the mouth of the Shenandoah Valley and the passage of the east-west Baltimore and Ohio Railroad, Miles maintained a U.S. presence in the Valley, and his jurisdiction spanned 380 miles of track. He christened his command the "Railroad Brigade."

Miles knew he was a potential Rebel target from the outset of Lee's invasion. His cavalry was the first to report Confederates crossing the Potomac; and shortly thereafter, Lee had juxtaposed himself between Washington and Harpers Ferry, placing Miles in complete isolation.

On the first day of the Southern invasion, Miles received these instructions from his commander in Baltimore: "Be energetic and active, and defend all places to the last extremity. There must be no abandoning of a post, and shoot the first man that thinks of it."

Later the same day, he received another frantic message. "Have your wits about you, and do all you can to annoy the Rebels should they advance on you. Activity, energy, and decision should be used. You will not abandon Harper's Ferry without defending it to the last extremity."

There was no equivocation in these orders. No room for discretion. Miles *must* hold his ground.

"I am ready for them," responded Miles.[386]

Then the Confederates sliced the telegraph wires, and Miles went silent.

The sudden isolation of Harpers Ferry concerned President Lincoln. He wired the department commander in Baltimore on September 7, "What about Harper's Ferry? Do you know anything about it?"[387] Lincoln knew some 14,000 U.S. soldiers now were separated from support and communication.

McClellan recognized Miles's possible predicament; but the Railroad Brigade was not assigned to his command, and while the Confederates remained at Frederick, Miles appeared unchallenged.

That changed when McClellan received definitive information on September 11 that the Rebels had abandoned Frederick and were moving west toward Harpers Ferry and northwest toward Hagerstown. "Miles can do nothing where he is, but could be of great service if ordered to join me," McClellan requested of General in Chief Halleck. Halleck refused. "There is no way for Colonel Miles to join you at present. His only chance is to defend his works until you can open communication with him."[388]

Halleck was not being intransigent, but practical. Where could Miles go? He already was surrounded at a distance. He couldn't move west. Jackson was in that direction after his seizure of Martinsburg. He couldn't go north. Lee would nab him at Hagerstown. He couldn't go east. Confederates held those routes, separating Miles from McClellan. The only path apparently open was from the south — the wrong direction for an attempted U.S. escape.

Perhaps the Confederates would ignore Miles. Not in Gen. Lee's book.

Lee needed every Yankee cleared from the Shenandoah Valley. This was essential to establishing the Rebel line of supply between his base in Virginia and the army, now in Maryland, and soon in Pennsylvania. The Harpers Ferry garrison menaced this arrangement. It potentially threatened the invasion. Lee informed Davis on September 12 that he had expected the enemy's forces to depart from the Valley. "In this I was disappointed." Lee then conceived Special Orders 191 to eradicate the Harpers Ferry problem.[389]

Unless help arrived, Miles and his garrison were in peril.

He, himself, knew it by Saturday afternoon, September 13. Confederates were everywhere in sight. The maneuvers prescribed by Lee in Special Orders 191 were in full affect. Loudoun Heights, overlooking the Shenandoah, was the first to fall (Miles didn't have enough troops to defend that position). Stonewall Jackson then seized School House Ridge, where he began menacing Miles's lines on Bolivar Heights, a higher ridge paralleling Jackson.[390]

Atop Maryland Heights — the tallest mountain hovering over the Ferry, and the key to the position — Miles fought his battle. His men *must hold Maryland Heights*. But after nine hours of defending the rugged mountain crest on the 13th, the worst occurred. The Bluecoats were abandoning the Heights. "God Almighty!" screamed the astonished colonel from his command post on Bolivar Heights, more than two miles from the Maryland Heights position. "What does that mean? They are coming down! Hell and damnation!"[391]

Miles was now surrounded, but not yet surrendered. The veteran colonel, in desperation, attempted to inform U.S. authorities of his predicament on the night of September 13. He instructed a Maryland cavalry officer who was familiar with the locale to pass through the enemy lines, and "try to reach somebody that had ever heard of the United States Army, or any general of the United States Army, or anybody that knew anything about the United States Army, and report the condition of Harpers Ferry." Miles told the messenger, assuming he would succeed in his mission to locate McClellan, to inform the general that "he could hold out for 48 hours."[392]

McClellan, meanwhile, was planning Miles's rescue. His nearest force was about 15 miles from Harpers Ferry. Through his fortunate possession of Special Orders 191, McClellan knew exactly that six of nine infantry divisions in Lee's army were at Harpers Ferry. Two of those divisions had been assigned the task of taking Maryland Heights. If McClellan could recapture Maryland Heights — or engage that force long enough to permit an opening for Miles's escape — he would spoil Lee's Harpers Ferry operation.

McClellan prepared specific instructions for Sixth Corps commander Maj. Gen. William B. Franklin. "I have now full information as to movements and intentions of the enemy. . . . The firing [at the Ferry] shows that Miles still holds out. . . . You will move at daybreak in the morning. . . I have reliable information that the [South Mountain] pass . . . is practicable for artillery and wagons. If this pass is not occupied by the enemy in force, seize it as soon as practicable . . . in order to cut off the retreat of or destroy [Confederate General] McLaws' command. . . . Having gained the pass, your duty will be first to cut off, destroy, or capture McLaws' command and relieve Colonel Miles."

McClellan dated the order at 6:20 p.m. It was almost dark, and the cannon booming in the distance at Harpers Ferry had ceased. If Miles could hold, the fate of Harpers Ferry depended upon Franklin. McClellan's final sentence expressed urgency: "I ask of you, at this important moment, all your intellect and the utmost activity that a general can exercise."[393]

ON A RIDGE west of Harpers Ferry, Stonewall Jackson was frustrated.

First, he was behind schedule. Special Orders 191 called for the investment to commence on September 12. It was now the 13th, and Jackson's Confederates were just arriving on the mountains surrounding the town. Other than being late, all was according to plan; though Jackson faced a communications problem. Three mountains and two rivers separated his command, with a Union garrison positioned in between. He attempted to remedy this problem through signal flags, but when that failed, he dispatched couriers in all directions of the compass. "Before the necessary orders were thus transmitted, the day [the 13th] was far advanced."

Jackson's greatest frustration was the uncooperative Federals. Miles had not yielded simply at Stonewall's presence. Even though Jackson had a noose around Miles, the Union commander was not ready to drop through the trap door.

Complicating matters, Jackson realized that his infantry weapons on the mountain tops were far too distant to cause any harm. Although the Confederates held superior elevations from Maryland and Loudoun Heights, bullets from their rifle-muskets could not reach the Yankees down below. In addition, Rebel infantry from these heights could not be employed, as the Potomac and Shenandoah Rivers flowed between Miles and the mountains, thus preventing Confederate infantry access to Miles on Bolivar Heights. Jackson realized this was becoming complicated.

Matters worsened late on the night of the 13th when a disturbing message was sent via courier to Gen. McLaws from Gen. Lee at Hagerstown. "From reports reaching him [Lee], he believes the enemy is moving toward Harper's Ferry to relieve the force they have there. You will see, therefore, the necessity of expediting your operations as much as possible."[394]

Jackson may not have received a copy of this urgent message, but he knew he had to force the issue. Stonewall reverted. He returned to his days as an artilleryman in the old U.S. Army, and he recalled his time as an instructor of artillery at the Virginia Military Institute. An artillery blast would force Miles to submit.

Sunday, September 14 arrived with the Confederates laboring feverishly to haul cannon up the rugged and precipitous slopes of Maryland and Loudoun Heights. Miles did not anticipate this; in fact, he considered the feat impossible. But Jackson excelled at turning impossible into possible; and by early afternoon on the 14th, long-range rifled cannon were in position.

"Should we have to attack, let the work be done thoroughly; fire on the houses where necessary. The citizens can keep out of harm's way from your artillery. Demolish the place if it is occupied by the enemy, and does not surrender."[395]

Confederate cannoneers began yanking their lanyards as 1 p.m. approached, and for the next five hours, iron shells hailed upon the hapless U.S. garrison trapped beneath the mountains.

"I saw two, three, four, half a dozen puffs of smoke burst out," recalled Capt. Edward Hastings Ripley of the 9th Vermont Infantry from his post on Bolivar Heights. Suddenly, in the very center of the Union lines, "there was a crash, then another and another, and columns of dirt and smoke leaped into the air, as though a dozen young volcanoes had burst forth."

"At first," recorded Lt. James H. Clark of the 115th New York Infantry, "their missiles of death fell far short of our camp; but each succeeding shell came nearer and nearer, until the earth was plowed up at our feet, and our tents torn to tatters."

Even Col. Miles's aide-de-camp, Lieutenant Henry Binney, was rattled by the intensity of the iron storm cascading from the mountaintops. "The cannonade is now terrific. The enemy's shell and shot fall in every direction; houses are demolished and detonation among the hills terrible."

Local resident Mary Clemmer Ames scampered to her Camp Hill cellar and entrenched herself in an empty piano box "to escape the earthquake from above." "The windows rattled; the house shook to its foundations," she wrote. "Heaven and earth seemed collapsing."[396]

Nightfall brought an end to the merciless pounding. Still, no white flags. The Yankees remained obstinate.

Worsening the situation for Jackson, he had received word that Gen. McLaws and his Maryland Heights position were in danger of approaching Federals. "General McLaws informs . . . that the enemy is in his rear, and that he can do but little more than he has done."[397] Jackson had to do something fast.

Thus far, Jackson had been reluctant to utilize his infantry. The only place he could advance his foot soldiers was across a low valley between School House Ridge and Miles's position atop Bolivar Heights. Miles held the height advantage, buffered by a near perpendicular slope elevating nearly 300 feet. The space across the valley was open pasture, making Jackson's men easy targets for Union gunners. A frontal assault may not work — may even prove fatal.

Jackson recalled from his days in command at Harpers Ferry 17 months earlier that a level plateau called the Chambers Farm, overlooking the rapids of the Shenandoah, constituted the extreme southern edge of Bolivar Heights. If he could move men and cannon to that location, he would be behind Miles and in rear of the U.S. line. Jackson summoned his most experienced division commander, Maj. Gen. A. P. Hill, and ordered him to skirt the Shenandoah in the darkness and to seize Miles's left flank.

In an amazing conquering of terrain — and unbeknownst to Miles — Hill moved 5,000 men and 20 cannon during the night of the 14th, quietly posting them behind the Union line. There he waited for the sun to rise.

Jackson was feeling confident. He believed the morrow would bring him victory.

Miles, meanwhile, knew the noose was tightening. He realized he was running short on time. He had heard nothing from his attempt to communicate with the Union army the previous day. Where was McClellan's army?[398]

GEORGE MCCLELLAN anticipated great success on the morrow, Sunday the 14th.

"An order from General R. E. Lee . . . which has accidentally come into my hands this evening — the authenticity of which is unquestionable — discloses some of the plans of the enemy, and shows most conclusively that the main Rebel army is now before us."

He continued his report to his superior, General in Chief Henry Halleck, an hour before midnight on the 13th. "This army marches forward early tomorrow morning, and will make forced marches, to endeavor to relieve Colonel Miles . . . I shall do everything in my power to save Miles if he still holds out."[399]

Halleck expressed no enthusiasm for McClellan's discovery. He remained concerned that the entire Rebel movement was a ruse to draw troops away from the protection of Washington. He especially was worried that McClellan — in his ardor to move upon Harpers Ferry — had pulled all Union troops away from guarding the Potomac. The river crossings were now vulnerable.

"Scouts report a large [Confederate] force still on Virginia side of the Potomac, near Leesburg. If so, I fear you are exposing your left flank, and that the enemy can cross in your rear."[400]

McClellan, now more than 50 miles from Washington, remained focused on the Rebels in his front rather than a supposed enemy in his rear. Shortly after his cavalry confirmed the Confederate positions outlined in Special Orders 191, he devised a two-pronged offensive. Franklin would move to relieve Harpers Ferry. At the same time, Gen. Ambrose Burnside would drive against the Rebels at Boonsboro, strike them, defeat them, and beat them to the Potomac, cutting off their avenue of escape.

Boonsboro, Maryland, was a small farming village of about 1,000 inhabitants astride the National Road, located beneath the western shadow of South Mountain. Lee had identified Boonsboro in Special Orders 191 as the original objective of Longstreet's command, as it was only 12 miles north of Harpers Ferry — a good rendezvous point for Jackson upon his conquering of the Ferry's garrison. Lee, however, had shifted Longstreet to Hagerstown on September 11, leaving only the rear guard of the army at Boonsboro.

McClellan grasped his unprecedented opportunity. If he could sweep away this rear guard with Burnside's thrust, and then rush to the Potomac at Williamsport, he could severe Lee's line of retreat and entrap Lee in Maryland. Even better were his numerical odds. McClellan usually believed the Confederates outnumbered him; but in this case — with Lee's army divided and scattered, and its wings separated by more than 20 miles — McClellan sensed a numbers advantage. Never had he felt so confident.

GEN. LEE WAS ANYTHING but confident.

Jackson was behind schedule. His army was scattered across all points of the compass. Reports arriving in Hagerstown from his cavalry scouts showed the uncharacteristically aggressive Federals moving west from Frederick toward South Mountain. Lee recognized his vulnerability. If the enemy crossed that mountain, his position in Hagerstown became untenable. Even worse, Gen. McLaws' command north of Harpers Ferry would become trapped.

What was happening?

Lee turned his attention away from Pennsylvania, at least for the moment. Late on the night of the 13th, he determined to remove Longstreet's command away from Hagerstown and reverse its tracks, marching it south toward Boonsboro and placing it in a position where it could support Maj. Gen. Daniel Harvey Hill's rear guard near South Mountain. The next morning (Sunday the 14th), Lee received more disconcerting news. The Federals were approaching South Mountain in mass numbers. He responded by moving Longstreet even closer to the range. It appeared the Yankees intended to flood over the mountain.[401]

South Mountain is a north-south ridge that starts at the Potomac River and runs the length of Maryland (37 miles) before crossing into Pennsylvania and continuing north to Carlisle. The Confederates were concerned with its five southern-most gaps, spread over 14 miles. If the U.S. penetrated any of them, or only one gap, it could bring disaster to Lee. None of them could be lost.[402]

Lee never anticipated this problem. The unexpected resistance Jackson met at Harpers Ferry had stalled the army. Now the invasion of Pennsylvania was deferred. Lee needed Harpers Ferry to collapse. If, indeed, the Federals were determined to advance against South Mountain, Lee must stop them. He had no other choice.

"THE MORNING CHURCH BELLS rang out clearly," observed a cheerful John M. Gould of the 10th Maine Infantry as his regiment marched through Frederick on Sunday, September 14. "It was the most pleasant sound I have heard for a long time. . . . After all, civilization is a fine thing."

He was impressed with his new impression of Frederick. "Last winter when I visited this place I thought it dirty and shabby; but this morning everyone was out dressed in the Sunday clothes. From the windows and roofs swing the American flag, and the women and children were waving handkerchiefs and giving water to our soldiers. Boston couldn't make a more lively exhibition or display more Union sentiment than did Frederick this morning."

Gould was marching near the rear of the army when his unit arrived at the top of Braddock Gap in the Catoctin Mountain. Before him was the panorama of the lovely Middletown Valley, bordered on its western edge by South Mountain. Gould could see powder smoke rising from the mountain. He heard the thumping discharges of artillery. Battle was underway.

For the first time since September 1, the Union army was engaged. For the first time on Maryland soil, battle now raged. Burnside's men clawed their way up South Mountain's eastern slopes, but the operation became difficult. Lee's Confederates refused to yield. For 12 hours at Fox's Gap — from 9 a.m. until almost three hours after dusk — Burnside's Ninth Corps men attempted to breech and hold the gap. They failed.

One mile north at Turner's Gap, Lee's soldiers made a resolute stand against a U.S. brigade. The Rebels held, maintaining control of the gap and the critical artery of the National Road. Success for the Yankees finally came one mile further north at Frosttown Gap, where Joseph Hooker's First Corps overwhelmed a greatly outnumbered Alabama brigade; but darkness stalled the momentum. When the firing finally ceased, men from opposing sides were so near they could speak to each other without raising their voices.[403]

Lee still held the crest of South Mountain.

Further south at Crampton's Gap, Gen. Franklin's rescue mission to Harpers Ferry was underway. McLaws was focused upon Harpers Ferry. He had not prepared, and his rear guard was dangerously outmanned and outgunned. But Franklin didn't know McLaws' disposition, and he approached Crampton's Gap with deliberation and caution.

Three hours passed as he employed his civil engineer's mind to calculate advantages and disadvantages of striking the gap. Once he moved, it ended quickly. There were too many Yankees for the Confederates to withstand. They fled up the mountain's east slope, with the Federals in rapid pursuit. McLaws and Jeb Stuart arrived to mend the hole, but they were too late. Franklin owned the gap, along with 400 POWs from 17 different Rebel units.[404] The late hour prevented further Confederate catastrophe. Darkness settled over Pleasant Valley. Indications were it would be unpleasant there the next morning.

ROBERT E. LEE'S first retreat as commander of the Army of Northern Virginia occurred when he abandoned Fox's and Turner's Gaps at South Mountain late on the evening of September 14.

Lee's men had fought well, and fought desperately. He had achieved one goal: the enemy did not break through his mountain fortress. But that was not on Lee's accomplishment list. A defensive battle at South Mountain never was part of Lee's invasion strategy. He never expected a fight there. It was forced upon him.

Lee saw his invasion crumbling. Thirty-six hours earlier, at 10 a.m. on the 13th, he was poised to cross the Pennsylvania border. At 10 p.m. on the 14th, he was heading back to Virginia.

"The day has gone against us," explained Lee's adjutant general. *The day has gone against us*.

Never before had the Confederate commander been compelled to this admission. The sentence had double connotation. Not only was Lee withdrawing his army from a battlefield, but the entire invasion had turned negative for the Confederates. The most important matter now was not Pennsylvania, but preservation of the army.

"This army will go by Sharpsburg and cross the river."

Sharpsburg was Lee's quickest route of escape. Two good roads led from the Boonsboro area to the western Maryland village straddling the Antietam Creek. A night retreat would protect the army from Union detection and harassment. The march to the Potomac would be about 10 miles, not overly taxing, but difficult in the darkness. Lee knew his men were fatigued. Some had been awake for 24 hours with little or no food. If he could return the army to Virginia, he presumed it would be safe. Surely McClellan would not follow him into the Confederacy.

Retreat also had advantage in reuniting the army. Lee would cancel the Harpers Ferry investment, and bring two-thirds of his prodigal soldiers back into his comforting hands. Momentum would be lost, but the army would be saved. Plenty of fight and enthusiasm remained for a future renewal of an invasion.

Return to the offensive could, potentially, happen quickly. Once reunited in Virginia, Lee could race his Rebels to Williamsport and launch into Maryland once more. This option assumed McClellan had not seized the Williamsport crossing first. Or, Lee could simply terminate the campaign, rest and reorganize his army, and consider another venture into Yankee country at a more opportune time.

But this *was* the opportune moment. The previous week, the Confederacy was charged with confidence. Bold proclamations to end the war were issued. The Confederate Congress and the Rebel press demanded invasion. Southern peace terms were presented publicly. What would retreat mean for the rising surf of the South?

If Lee ended the campaign, how would it affect the upcoming Northern political campaigns? Surely Lincoln and the Republicans would trumpet Lee's withdraw, claiming it as proof that competent Republicans are managing the war and should be returned to office. And what of the diplomatic front? Europe had been impressed with the recent flurry of Confederate triumphs. Would a retreat perhaps defeat recognition of Southern independence, especially after the bravado of invasion had stirred editors of British and French newspapers?

During the somber and sullen night march to Sharpsburg, Gen. Lee changed his mind. Not for the purposes pondered above, but for a practical reason. He needed to ensure a path of escape for Lafayette McLaws and his 8,000 Confederates, now trapped in Pleasant Valley. "It is necessary for you to abandon your position tonight [Sunday the 14th]," Lee ordered McLaws. "Your troops you must have well in hand to unite with this command." McLaws' only route to safety was due west, via mountain roads that led to Sharpsburg. Lee altered his original retreat plan, but just a bit. The army would stop near Sharpsburg, but only momentarily. Lee would halt, await McLaws, and then return to Virginia.[405]

Lee did not know it, but he was cancelling the Harpers Ferry operation at the same time Jackson felt confident of victory. "Through God's blessing, the advance, which commenced this evening, has been successful thus far, and I look to Him for complete success tomorrow."[406]

God had not, however, shown blessing to the Confederates on this Sunday.

CHAPTER 14

Mars's Moment

All gloomy forebodings and anxious solicitude gave place to joyous feelings and bright anticipations.

—*Philadelphia Inquirer,* September 16, 1862

Something was missing from South Mountain at sunrise on September 15.

Confederates. They were all gone — except for the Rebel dead.

"I have seen a thousand and one sights this morning. Only one is worth mentioning. It was the battlefield."

John Mead Gould had been in the U.S. Army since the first week of the Civil War. He had never witnessed anything like what he saw at South Mountain.

"The Rebels were sheltered but little by [stonewalls], and being laid down [while firing], were all without exception shot in the head and the blood of course covered their faces and necks. It was the same in every instance and I must have seen more than a hundred for they literally lined the road on both sides of both walls in both the roads."

The stunned soldier from Maine continued his tour of the Maryland battlefield. "They were laying there, a mass of grey flesh, loose dust, blood, blankets, grey cloth rags, guns and equipment. Vast quantities of biscuit and other rations were loose too. The waste of property was not unlike that seen after a fire, but the waste of life, human beings, was so new, so awful, so revolting that I lost all heart for rejoicing and all hate for my foes."

Gould could not cease his study. "They look very unlike our dead who have swollen a trifle and appear very hale and hearty. Theirs are mere skeletons and have an ashy hue against which the dust that here is ash colored hardly shows. I saw a little fellow scarcely 14 years old. . . . He had died upon his back with his hands folded on his breast. Someone had turned him over and he was on his side now, nestled with the other corpses, his stiffened arm and hand lay over another man and but for the blood you would have thought him in sound and peaceful sleep."

Gould's curiosity carried him to a section of the stone wall, where he pushed back some bushes that revealed a Confederate corpse. The sight was shocking.

> His eyes were wide open and staring. His head was covered with blood, so was the greater part of his body. The bushes had caught him as he was falling backward and he was nearly in a standing attitude. There he was, with his hands thrown to the front, apparently shrinking from something he feared, and with his staring eyes and bloody face, made the most horrible and frightful sight I ever witnessed. . . . I had seen enough now and came off as quick as my legs could carry me.[407]

Word of the Battle of South Mountain rapidly reached the Northern press. Headlines soared with excitement:

> *Prospects Brightening*
> *Retreat of the Rebels*
> *A Glorious Victory for the Union*
> *Lee Acknowledges Himself Badly Whipped*
> *General McClellan in Hot Pursuit*[408]

The headlines screamed, but a relieved North cheered even louder.

"*There is now no fear of an invasion of Pennsylvania,*" proclaimed the *Philadelphia Inquirer*, adding emphasis to its type. "The cheerful news transmitted to us over the telegraphic wires . . . thrilled the heart of every patriotic citizen of Philadelphia." The city celebrated, in part, by serenading the mother of George McClellan (at her residence in the western part of town), with rousing patriotic tunes from members of the Corn Exchange Association, accompanied by a local patriotic band.[409]

Baltimore also rejoiced. "We hope every Union man will take occasion today to hang out the Stars and Stripes which have been so gloriously honored in the late successes of the National troops. Let the city put on its gala appearance in honor of the great 'deliverance' — so different from that invoked for us by the traitors of Richmond. The most memorable victory during the war, let us begin that commemoration of it today which will be a memory with our children to the end of time."[410]

They celebrated in New York. "The city today is wild with joy over the glorious news from Maryland. The brilliant victory achieved by McClellan has summarily brushed away the gloom and despondency which pervaded the public mind all last week. . . . Wall Street is radiant with smiles. There is scarcely a stock on the list that has not experienced an improvement. The bears were nowhere for the moment."[411]

Washington's joy was interrupted by a momentary panic when the chief executive had a close call. As Abraham Lincoln was riding into the city from his retreat at the "Soldier's Home," the president had a narrow escape. "His steed, a spirited and powerful beast, ran off with him, and came very near throwing him in the [canal] race, in which Mr. Lincoln lost his hat but succeeded in checking the animal's career at the cost of a sprained wrist in so doing."[412]

Marylanders, espousing pro-Northern proclivities, particularly were relieved by the proclaimed U.S. victory at South Mountain. "The sympathizers with Secesh, who have been jubilant of late, and some of whom have uttered threats of what they intended to do with Union neighbors, are today rather downcast. One can walk . . . without hearing anyone whistle *Maryland, My Maryland*, and the ladies who have sported red, white, and blue rosettes in their [Southern] bonnets have taken them out or they remain at home."[413]

Much was made in the Northern press of the cold reception of western Marylanders to the Confederates' invasion. "Their march through Maryland was attended with no manifestations of welcome or gratification on the part of the citizens. In lieu of a great uprising of the people, but few were found sufficiently ignorant or traitorous to forsake their comfortable homes and unite their fortunes with those of an army of half clothed, half famished marauders."[414]

The Yankee press attempted to embarrass the South's expectations in Maryland. "When the Rebel armies crossed into the State they expected . . . at least 50,000 new recruits [to] aid them in transferring the battleground of the war to the loyal States. In this they have been most grievously disappointed." Gen. Lee and Jefferson Davis must be "pretty well convinced by this time that 'Maryland, My Maryland' is *our* Maryland."[415]

Pennsylvanians paraded in Harrisburg and sighed relief on their southern border. Forty-eight hours earlier, Lee was positioning on the Mason-Dixon Line. Now he was rearing toward the Potomac. "Everybody's face looked bright at the new aspect of affairs. . . . The news of our successes was eagerly read. The effect upon the people was to re-inspirit and reassure them."

More than 50,000 Pennsylvania militiamen who had rushed to defend the Quaker State, but had been denied the opportunity for a fight, pledged, "If the Government will guarantee to put [the] Rebellion down in six months, we will guarantee our services. . . . We want to see the Rebellion crushed, but we don't want to see *playing*. We can crush insurrection in six months *if the Government tries!*"[416]

The Confederate *invasion* — the pervasive and fearful term employed during the first two weeks of September in both the Northern and Southern press — abruptly changed in nomenclature immediately following South Mountain. It was downgraded to a *raid*. "The raid, for such it can only be called, cannot fail to have convinced the most treasonable skeptic of the integrity and loyalty of our sister State [Maryland], and forever set at rest all apprehensions of a repetition of an attempt to 'liberate' it from fancied oppression and persecution."[417]

One editor summarized the Federal success succinctly: "The Rebel army has, after a brief raid across the Potomac . . . sought the most accessible avenues of escape . . . and commenced an inglorious retreat."[418]

Newspapers acclaimed South Mountain as redemption of the U.S. Army. "The Union army is again triumphant. Weeks of disaster but increased the determination of our brave soldiers to crush the hopes of the traitors. Their sufferings . . . have inured them to hardships, and accustomed them to actual warfare of the most sanguinary character. From these struggles they came forth new men."

The results of the battle, from the Northern perspective, were incomparable. "The fruits of Sunday's fight are incalculable, not only for future benefit but as tending to shorten the duration of the Rebellion. Routed and demoralized, even [Rebel] devotion for their commanders will fail to inspire the fleeing vandals."[419]

The Union exuberance exploded across the North. But it was premature. Unbeknownst to the jubilant Yankees, Lee had halted his retreat, and Stonewall Jackson had executed a brilliant maneuver.

A DENSE FOG blanketed the Harpers Ferry water gap on Monday morning, September 15. Nobody, regardless of U.S. or Confederate uniforms, could see the enemy through the gray drapery. The mountains were invisible. Strings of wispy steam rose from the two rivers. It was quiet, too quiet. Following the deafening roar of more than 100 cannon the previous day, the natural seemed unnatural.

Dawn brought light, but no visibility. About 6:30 a.m., the gray vapor brightened, but still no distance perception. Two hours after sunrise, the sun remained invisible. Then just before 8 a.m., the fog lifted like a curtain on a stage, exposing thousands of U.S. soldiers.

Fire! echoed from Confederate battery commanders. In seconds, Stonewall Jackson's cannoneers opened a ferocious bombardment. The Rebel cannon blasted the helpless Federal garrison from five directions, pummeling them from three ridge crests and two plateaus, including from point-blank range on the Chambers Farm in the rear of the Union bastion on Bolivar Heights. The Federals had no place to hide. No place to run. No place to escape the merciless missiles.

"The infernal screech owls came hissing and singing, then bursting, plowing great holes in the earth, filling our eyes with dust, and tearing many giant trees to atoms."

James H. Clark of the 115th New York did not stand alone in his misery and fright. "We are surrounded by [the] enemy's batteries," recalled Lieutenant Henry Binney, the aide-de-camp to commander Dixon Miles. "Nothing could stand before such a raking cannonade. . . . Every inch of ground was being torn up by the enemy's fire."

"We are as hapless as rats in a cage," wrote 9th Vermont Captain Edward Ripley. The 32nd Ohio's Charles E. Smith shared Ripley's despondency: "The Rebels were all around us and our refuge was the open canopy of heaven."[420]

During eleven hours of darkness the previous night, Jackson had duped Col. Miles, deploying 5,000 infantrymen and 20 cannon on his left flank at close range, and positioning artillery at point-blank range to fire into the previously secure Bolivar Heights ravines. Jackson had outgeneraled his opponent.

The Federals attempted a response, but Miles's battery commanders reported their long-range ammunition exhausted. Without artillery to support his inexperienced infantry (most of his men were new recruits, in the army for only three weeks), Miles believed further resistance useless. Following a council of war, Miles and his commanders unanimously agreed to surrender.

Miles immediately began spreading the word. Traveling along the crest of Bolivar Heights with white handkerchiefs waving in the air, Miles exhorted his men to raise the white flag.

"Boys, we've got no country now," cried Eugene McGrath of the 5th New York Heavy Artillery. Louis Hull of the 60th Ohio reflected similar anguish: "15th Monday a rather dark page in the history of us."[421]

As white flags began bobbing along the crest of Bolivar Heights, the hopeful Confederates ceased firing — but only momentarily. Apparently uncertain of the Federal intentions or unaware of the displayed white flags, a Southern battery near the base of Loudoun Heights launched its shells once again toward the Union left.

"The rebels have opened on us again," Miles declared. "What do they mean?"

Immediately after this query, a shell whizzed past Miles and his aide, Lt. Binney, and exploded directly behind the two officers. A large piece of iron ripped the flesh entirely from Col. Miles's left calf. Miles fell mortally wounded. The man responsible for the surrender of Harpers Ferry would die the next day.

"Well, Mr. Binney, we have done our duty," Miles gasped after his wounding, "but where can McClellan be?"[422]

Actually, McClellan's rescue mission was six miles away, approaching from the north, but Miles had no idea of its proximity. Gen. William Franklin's Sixth Corps had seized Crampton's Gap in South Mountain on the 14th and deployed in Pleasant Valley early the next morning. But Franklin was too late, and he suspected it when the cannon booming silenced from the direction of the Ferry.

"If Harper's Ferry has fallen — and the cessation of firing makes me fear that it has — it is my opinion that I should be strongly reinforced." Franklin, much like other Union generals, suffered from the paranoia of Confederate troop strengths. Even after the U.S. surrender, Lafayette McLaws and his 7,000 effective Confederates still faced a serious hazard, as they remained bottled up in Pleasant Valley with his opponent immediately before him.

Yet, Franklin hesitated. Instead of assaulting McLaws, he sent an assessment to McClellan, then seven miles distant. "They outnumber me two to one. It will, of course, not answer to pursue the enemy under these circumstances. . . . I shall wait here until I learn what is the prospect of reinforcement."[423]

Back at Harpers Ferry, Jackson's victory was dramatic. He seized 73 cannon, 200 wagons, 1,200 army mules, about 13,000 small arms, and more than 12,700 Union prisoners — the largest surrender of United States troops during the Civil War.[424] No Confederate general ever matched these results in one battle.

As Gen. Jackson trotted toward Harpers Ferry to examine the fruits of his victory, the dreaded Stonewall became the featured attraction for thousands of Federals.

"Boys, he's not much for looks," shouted one Northerner, "but if we'd had him we wouldn't have been caught in this trap." The drab appearance of Jackson disappointed many within the Union ranks. "Old Stonewall dressed in the coarsest of homespun, and dirty at that," witnessed *New York Times* correspondent David Judd. In appearance, the reporter continued, Jackson could not be distinguished from "the mongrel, barefoot crew who follow his fortunes. I had heard much of the decayed appearance of the Rebel soldiers; but such a looking crowd! Ireland, in her worst straits, could present no parallel."[425]

Before surveying his success, Jackson scribbled a message to Gen. Lee: "Through God's blessing, Harper's Ferry and its garrison are to be surrendered. . . . To what point shall [we] move?"[426]

ROBERT E. LEE finally had something to cheer. "The victory of the indomitable Jackson and his troops give us renewed occasion for gratitude to Almighty God for His guidance and protection."[427] No doubt Gen. Lee would have preferred less stress from the Creator's plan.

The past 24 hours had been fraught with danger. The army was divided and scattered. McClellan had advanced aggressively. Battle raged unexpectedly at South Mountain. The mountain gaps could not be defended, but temporarily. McLaws had become entrapped in Pleasant Valley. Jackson uncharacteristically was late. Harpers Ferry had not fallen. Lee had ordered a retreat to Virginia. Invasion had turned from hopeful to hopeless.

Now Lee had new life. Despite the diversion at South Mountain and delay at Harpers Ferry, little was lost, other than momentum. Lee could continue forward. From a ridge overlooking the

Antietam Creek, the Rebel commander could see the mountains ranging north into Pennsylvania. Only 12 miles separated him from his previous location at Hagerstown, and then just another six miles into Pennsylvania. Pennsylvania still beckoned — and it was within reach.

A good road ran directly north. If Lee could reunite his army in Maryland, he could race up the Sharpsburg-Hagerstown Turnpike, and once again have Pennsylvania within his grasp. It could be risky, as McClellan may drive to the Potomac and attempt to cut off the Confederate line of supply and avenue of escape. But if McClellan chose, instead, to chase the Confederate army, Lee could lead him into Pennsylvania or match him in the vicinity of Hagerstown. Regardless, Lee would have battle on Northern soil, and the outcome could determine the future of his country.

Lee's first priority, however, was reuniting the army. Once he learned of Jackson's success at Harpers Ferry, about noon on Monday the 15th, Lee determined to wait at Sharpsburg until Jackson and two-thirds of the Army of Northern Virginia rejoined its commander. Via the Virginia approach, Jackson's columns needed to march about 17 miles to meet Lee at Sharpsburg. But that could be accomplished in a day, even though it included a crossing of the Potomac at Boteler's Ford near Shepherdstown. It was settled. Lee would wait.

Linger necessitated risk. What if McClellan attacked? With Lee without the majority of his army, the numerical odds against him were severe. Could he withstand a blow from McClellan with only three of his nine infantry divisions present at Sharpsburg?

Lee recognized the odds. He understood his risk. But Lee had nature as his ally.

The Antietam Creek meandered north-south from southern Pennsylvania into the Potomac. Lee had located himself on the western side of the creek, effectively establishing a moat between himself and McClellan. The creek was not deep, but the valley it carved was narrow and steep. Vertical bluffs paralleled the Antietam's banks, making access across it difficult. Three stone bridges spanned the stream along with several fords; but if Lee could temporarily hold these approaches it could deliver the time he required for the Harpers Ferry expedition to rejoin him.

Lee made his decision. About noon on Monday the 15th, he determined his destiny. He would wait.

GEORGE MCCLELLAN WAS BAFFLED. What was Lee doing?

Lee's halt at Sharpsburg seemed unreasonable. He was within two miles of returning home. His country was in sight. The Potomac could be crossed. Why had he halted? Lee's stubborn hold on the western slopes of the Antietam disappointed McClellan. Earlier in the morning, he had informed his superior in Washington, "The enemy is making for Shepherdstown in a perfect panic; and General Lee last night stated publicly that he must admit they had been shockingly whipped."[428] Why would a panicked man stop running? Especially so close to the safety of his home?

Even President Lincoln expressed optimism. "I now consider it safe to say that General McClellan has gained a great victory over the great Rebel army in Maryland. . . . He is now pursuing the flying foe."[429]

McClellan's infantry began arriving on the eastern slopes of the Antietam Creek in the early afternoon of the 15th. His army was confident. "The men are in fine spirits and are anxious to be led forward to rid [Maryland] . . . of all invaders." Northern newspapers demanded action. "Not until the Potomac is re-crossed, its waters, in the passage, reddened with [Rebel] blood," would satisfaction prevail.[430]

The Irish Brigade led the Union pursuit, approaching the Middle Bridge over the Antietam, where Lee promptly greeted it with long-range artillery fire. The first Union corps commander on the scene was Maj. Gen. Joseph Hooker. Hooker witnessed the Confederates on the opposite side of the Antietam, "ostentatiously deployed in two lines," supported by artillery batteries. Lee's position paralleled the creek (but beyond it about one mile), stretching along a gradual ridgeline. Viewing the Antietam terrain, Hooker dismissed any immediate assault. "I did not feel strong enough to attack him in front."[431]

McClellan arrived by 3 p.m. and commenced his own examination of the situation. He had never seen the spot before, and the region's maps were imprecise concerning roads, fords, and topography. He knew where he was, but knew nothing about his location. That afternoon, McClellan's topographic engineers gathered intelligence, detailing ground elevations, creek crossings, enemy positions, and vulnerabilities — his own and Gen. Lee's.

McClellan was aware Harpers Ferry had surrendered. He surmised Lee would reunite his army. He expected Lee to return to Virginia, behind the safety of the Potomac. But what if the Confederates coalesced? McClellan had estimated Lee's army comprised 120,000 men. Joined together once again, would Lee attack him?

Monday the 15th disappeared into darkness, and Tuesday the 16th opened with thick fog. McClellan could see nothing. Was Lee still there? Or had he retired across the Potomac?

Unknown and unseen by McClellan due to the fog, Stonewall Jackson was crossing the Potomac, en route from Harpers Ferry to Sharpsburg. His famous "Stonewall Division" led the advance, leaving the Ferry at 1 a.m. on September 16. Jackson's men had little time to celebrate their victory as they marched in the predawn darkness. They pushed northward, and less than 12 hours later, Jackson's advance columns had united with Lee at Sharpsburg.

Lee's gamble was working. The fog helped disguise his gathering army's operations. McClellan had not crossed the Antietam. Lee possessed the Hagerstown-Sharpsburg Turnpike. The road to Pennsylvania remained open.

Gen. McClellan did not like what he saw by late morning when the sun finally burned off the cumbersome fog. The Confederates were still there. Lee had not budged.

McClellan sensed time was against him. Every hour that passed meant more Rebels arriving from Harpers Ferry. If he moved against Lee before the Confederates were at full strength, perhaps he had a chance.

But McClellan didn't necessarily have to engage Lee. What if he could maneuver him out of Maryland?

McClellan certainly was aware of the Hagerstown-Sharpsburg Turnpike. The major thoroughfare appeared on local maps and was heavily traveled by the area's populace. If McClellan could swing a portion of his army north of Lee (the Confederate left), he could seize the turnpike and eliminate Lee's most direct route north. By capturing that road, McClellan could force Lee to abandon the Pennsylvania objective, or at least compel Lee to return to Virginia to seek an alternative route north. By removing a strategic option, perhaps McClellan could induce Lee back across the Potomac.

This plan became more enticing when McClellan learned that the Rebels were not guarding the Antietam crossings to the north. This solved the problem of conquering the creek without facing opposition.

McClellan settled on his strategy. He would advance a portion of his army north, parallel to Lee, but out of his sight. A good country road crossed the Antietam at the Upper Bridge and headed north, then abruptly turned west toward the Turnpike, intersecting with it about two miles north of Lee's position. The march would be short and safe. And it had the potential to save Pennsylvania.

It also had the potential to turn Lee's left flank. If the Rebel leader insisted on remaining ensconced along the Antietam, McClellan's maneuver would go around him, making Lee's position untenable. The movement presented excellent possibilities.

McClellan chose Joseph Hooker and the veterans of his First Corps to accomplish the maneuver. Hooker moved out with about 9,000 men at 4 p.m. on the 16th, and McClellan soon joined in the march. Hooker expressed his desire for more soldiers, and McClellan accented. Soon, nearly one-third of the Federal army that had reached the Antietam vicinity was moving toward Lee's left. Two hours later, and just before dusk, the Federals had seized the turnpike. Lee's route north was sealed.

Hooker then turned south, almost as if to dare Lee to remain. He boldly announced his presence with a reconnaissance-in-force. Lee now knew the Federals were upon his left, and he turned to confront them. Darkness ceased the heavy skirmish. A light drizzle commenced. Pickets fired at noises and shadows throughout the tense night.

The next morning could determine the destinies of two nations.

CHAPTER 15

Sunrise Slaughter

The rebellion has at last gathered up all its resources and energies for a death struggle; it is determined to make one final effort to do all the damage it can before it finally succumbs to the mighty Union columns mustering for its overthrow.

—*Baltimore American and Commercial Advertiser,*
September 4, 1862

A dim light washed over South Mountain at 5:43 a.m. on Wednesday, September 17. After a tireless night, dawn had arrived.

Hooker scanned southward. Lee was *still* there. McClellan had severed his route north. Portions of his army had not yet arrived from Harpers Ferry. He was outnumbered.

Despite all of this, Lee was still at Sharpsburg.

Gen. Lee determined to stand. He would fight McClellan in Maryland along the Antietam Creek. He could not leave Northern territory without bringing to the enemy a decisive blow. He could not retreat twice in three days. He could not abandon the invasion — and its hopes engendered in Southern hearts and homes — on the day preceding Confederate Thanksgiving Day.[432]

Joe Hooker wasted no time. Before 6 a.m. he launched his first attack, smashing into Stonewall Jackson's men, who had arrived from Harpers Ferry the previous day. Waves of Union blue pushed forward. Waves of Rebel gray counterpunched. For nearly three hours, both sides bent, but neither opponent buckled. Ferocious fighting changed military dictionaries forever, adding to the lexicon of American history, "The Cornfield," "The East Woods," "The North Woods," and "The Sharpsburg Pike."

A correspondent from the *Philadelphia Inquirer* vividly reported from the scene:

> Front and flank, with musketry and artillery, are the death shots received thick and fast. The air is rendered thick and opaque with the fumes of saltpetre, the ground is shaken by the tremendous recoil of the guns; bullets are whizzing in every direction; and when, for a moment, the [deadly missiles] ceased their work of destruction, the ear is saluted with the groans of the dying strewn around in every direction; some begging "only for a drop of water," while others piteously importune you to kill them, that they may be put out of their misery.[433]

Gen. Hooker described the carnage in The Cornfield. "In the time I am writing every stalk of corn . . . was cut as closely as could have been done with a knife and the slain lay in rows precisely as they had stood in their ranks a few moments before." The veteran combat general was appalled. "It was never my fortune to witness a more bloody, dismal battlefield."[434]

Gen. Lee's morning had started with a draw in and around The Cornfield and East Woods. But his situation deteriorated. By 9 a.m., most of his original position had crumbled. Even worse, his left center had collapsed near a white-washed, single-room brick building called the Dunker Church. McClellan was driving Lee's Rebels. He called for reinforcements.

The Union Second Corps, McClellan's largest, comprised of nearly 17,000 men, snapped to attention. It needed to maintain McClellan's momentum, but it faced the difficult challenge of crossing the Antietam and its deep valley. It was taking too long. Maj. Gen. Edwin Sumner couldn't wait until everyone had crossed. The Rebels were on the run, and Sumner intended to keep them running.

With only one-third of his manpower in place, Sumner pushed forward, driving west across the Sharpsburg Pike, past the Dunker Church, and into the West Woods. He met little resistance. Where had the Confederates gone?

Gens. Lee and Jackson urgently had gathered their remnants from the early morning madness and redeployed upon Hauser's Ridge, about one-half mile in front of Sumner. But Lee was not convinced this new line could stop the Federal onslaught. He called upon Gens. Lafayette McLaws and John Walker, late of Harpers Ferry fame, to turn the Yankee tide. Lee posted them at the right place, just at the right time, and for the first time, the Federals went reeling backwards, racing out of the West Woods in a rout. Lee's left stabilized, but now he faced trouble elsewhere.

In the Sunken Road, one-half mile south of the Dunker Church and West Woods, Lee maintained a forward position along his right center. Here soldiers from Alabama and North Carolina knelt behind the cover of a deep and circuitous road cut. It offered a good defensive position, where earthen banks could stop bullets before they pierced human flesh. By late morning, more of Sumner's Federals, now finally across the Antietam, anxiously approached. When they came within 70 yards they were greeted with a hailstorm of Rebel lead. The firing at point-blank range sliced down the Union lines as if carved in half with a sickle.

"It is a murderous fire, that of the [Confederate] enemy; their shots are just high enough for the vital parts, and many patriot falls dead beneath their fire. Yet over the prostrate forms of their comrades our soldiers press on."[435]

Lee's Confederates fought desperately, holding the "Bloody Lane" for nearly four hours. But they could not maintain it as too many Federals kept advancing. By 2 p.m., McClellan's warriors had seized original Confederate positions on the northern portion of the field. From Lee's center to Lee's left, equal to nearly one and one-half miles, the battlefield belonged to George McClellan. His U.S. troops held it all.

Lee withdrew and regrouped, continuing his defense of Hauser's Ridge — a good defensive position anchored on the left by the Potomac. McClellan had pushed Lee backwards, but nowhere had he broken through. Lee, instead, attempted to break McClellan, staging his only offensive of the day near the Dunker Church. Lee's bold and most desperate attempt failed, however, with the timely arrival of William Franklin's Sixth Corps from Pleasant Valley (its morning position near Harpers Ferry).[436]

Meanwhile, Lee became concerned for his right. This was his strongest position. It included an elongated ridge running south from Sharpsburg, excellent for artillery and infantry. To approach this section of line, the enemy had to first cross the Antietam at the Lower Bridge, located in a narrow canyon of the creek. The Confederates established a forward detachment to guard the bridge and nearby fords, and for the first four hours of the battle, it was quiet in this sector.

That changed suddenly at 10 a.m. Maj. Gen. Ambrose Burnside received orders from McClellan to attack the bridge. As Burnside kept the Rebels defending the bridge busy in their front, he sent his primary attack column around the stronghold, flanking the Southerners out of their natural bastion. By 1 p.m., Burnside's men had seized the bridgehead, but his Ninth Corps had much hard work ahead.

Burnside then moved 10,000 men across the bridge and into a line of attack that spanned one mile. It was the largest coordinated U.S. attack of the day, and Gen. Lee knew he could not stop it. He tried to slow it, concentrating 40 cannon against Burnside's onslaught. But the wave of blue kept coming, like a tsunami, toward Lee's extreme right.[437]

Now Lee faced serious problems. He had no reserves. He could not shift troops from another location to bolster his weakly defended right. He understood that if his line ruptured here, his line of retreat to the Potomac was endangered. If he lost this position, his Army of Northern Virginia could become entrapped in Maryland. Never before had Lee faced such a desperate moment.

Almost miraculously came the arrival of A. P. Hill. Gen. Hill's division was the last of Jackson's force to depart Harpers Ferry. In response to an urgent plea from Lee, they had left the Ferry early that morning, Hill hustling his men northward, knowing battle was underway along the Antietam. They could hear the cannon thundering in the distance. Hill's men raced 17 miles in seven hours (including a Potomac River crossing), measuring the best of Jackson's "Foot Cavalry."

The fiery general, decked in his bright red fireman's shirt, rode ahead to inform Gen. Lee that his men were en route. Lee, relieved, calmly informed Hill to post his men upon Burnside's only vulnerability.

Though Burnside's attack line was one mile across, the southern end of his line constituted the extreme Union left. Nothing was out there to protect Burnside's left flank. And that was precisely where A. P. Hill struck. Hill smashed into Burnside's exposed left at about 4 p.m., striking with such ferocity that it broke Burnside's momentum, and eventually stalled his entire assault. Unable to sustain his attack, Burnside withdrew back toward the creek, with Hill holding the high ground on Lee's right. A. P. Hill's men had saved Lee from certain disaster.[438]

THE BATTLE ENDED AT DUSK. Americans had never witnessed such human carnage: *more than 23,000 casualties in only 12 hours.* Antietam had engraved itself as the bloodiest single day battle in American history.

Nightfall brought an end to the bullets and the shelling, but not the yelling for help. Thousands of Union and Confederate wounded, trapped between enemy lines, cried for water and medical aid. Any assistance was dangerous. The lines were close. Any movement could bring upon firing. The suffering persisted for all but the more than 4,000 dead.

The next day the two armies nervously eyed each other. Lee continued his hold upon an elevated ridge that ran north, east, and south of Sharpsburg. Paralleling him for three miles was McClellan, who also postured on defense. Exhausted, neither side renewed the attack.

September 18 arrived — and passed. Both sides stared down the other; both in a posture of defense; both daring the other to assault their positions. Trapped between the combatants were more than 18,000 wounded — 18 times the size of their host town Sharpsburg. No formal truce occurred, making it hazardous to lend any aid to the ailing soldiers from both sides.

"Sharpshooters were stationed on the outposts, and when parties from either side came too near the outer line in search of killed or wounded, the sharpshooters would crack away at them. It was dangerous business to engage in gathering in the killed and wounded. I saw several poor fellows just beyond the positions of the pickets lying wounded, on the field and piteously pleading for assistance, which it was dangerous to render."[439]

THE WOUNDED REMAINED MORIBUND, piled and scattered across acres of ground — most of it owned by members of a German religious sect known as Dunkers. The Dunkers practiced pacifism.

Under the cover of darkness, and without molestation from McClellan, Lee withdrew his army from the Antietam Battlefield during the night of September 18. Gen. Lee and his army were home — back in Virginia earlier than expected, and bloodied by the venture — but home once again.

Meanwhile on the battlefield, with the Confederates now gone, Union burial parties worked feverishly to bury the thousands of dead from both sides. John Mead Gould of Maine surveyed the ghastly landscape. "All wounded had been taken off, nearly all of our dead had been removed to heaps near the fences and all that remained were the Rebel dead. To the left of this cornfield where a pasture was and behind many projecting rocks they lay thick as grasshoppers."

Then Gould became a momentary philosopher. "After I had been about two hours among the corpses all sense of honor was lost. You look at them as so much trophy, so much evidence of the days' work, and of the uselessness of secession. It seemed as if human life was worth nothing and a man's soul a myth.

"The deviltry of one day is too tremendous to calculate."[440]

Confederate dead at Antietam. More than 23,000 casualties occurred in 12 hours in America's bloodiest single day battle. Here, Alexander Gardner photographs the dead of a Confederate battery near the Dunker Church. Antietam represented the first time in American history a large collection of photographs was taken of battlefield dead. *(Library of Congress)*

CHAPTER 16

Suspense Sustained

Someday a poet will arise who can do justice to such a scene and such events. We have to deal now with the meaning of the bloody business there transacted.

—*Philadelphia Inquirer*, September 24, 1862

No one in the Southern army expected Confederate Thanksgiving to be the day that terminated the invasion of the North.

Even on the following day, September 19, Lee's invasion ambitions did not end with his retreat from Maryland. Despite the loss of more than one-quarter of his army at Antietam — and the fact that he barely escaped with any army — General Lee determined to continue the campaign. Too much was at stake to quit.

The Confederate commander continued to eye Pennsylvania. He adjusted his plan. He would return the army to Maryland, via a safe route on the Virginia side of the Potomac. If Lee could reach Williamsport, about 25 miles upstream from his withdrawal point at Boteler's Ford, he could secure the Williamsport crossing, move back into Maryland, and once again return to Hagerstown. From there Pennsylvania beckoned.

But Lee quickly was disappointed. McClellan foiled his scheme. Union cavalry and infantry promptly seized Williamsport after a momentary Confederate occupation; and the Federals conducted a temporary chase into Virginia at Boteler's Ford, threatening the Rebel rear. When Lee learned that the Yankees had dared cross into the Confederacy, he ordered Stonewall Jackson to swat them back. Jackson did so during a brief but bloody engagement near Shepherdstown on September 20.

Lee's invasion thus ended. "A week of intense anxiety and apprehension happily terminated," exulted the *Philadelphia Inquirer*. "It was one week ago that the traitor Congress, intoxicated by their recent successes, and in the vain delusion that the armies of the nation were paralyzed, instructed their generals 'to advance their standards' into Pennsylvania. It was but a week that vain glorious [Rebels] proclaimed that in two days [they] would be in Harrisburg."[441]

The *Baltimore American and Commercial Advertiser* shared in the jubilation. "The invasion of Maryland and Pennsylvania is at an end. The full blown hopes that the disloyal here entertained that Washington was to be captured, Baltimore occupied, and the Rebel army furnished with winter quarters at Philadelphia, have been most ruthlessly crushed."[442]

New York cheered the conclusion of the invasion. "The news, the great news, from the Union Army in Maryland is on every tongue. But for the depressing thought about the lists of killed and wounded to come, I verily believe we should have a general illumination in the city in order to give the full measure of expression of the public exultation."

Perhaps the best barometer of the public pulse was the Stock Market. "As soon as the news reached Wall Street the excitement among the 'operators' there was intense. Prices went up rapidly, and there was a general scramble to buy. Uncle Sam's credit for the moment never stood stronger. . . . The oldest dealer on the corner said the excitement on all hands was without a parallel."[443]

General Lee expressed no celebration, but disillusion to President Davis. Though acknowledging the army had performed hard work, conducted long and laborious marches, and encountered large numbers of the enemy, Lee blamed much of his lost momentum on lost men. "A great many men belonging to the army never entered Maryland at all; many returned after getting there, while others who crossed the [Potomac] kept aloof. . . . This is a woeful condition of affairs, and I'm pained to state it."[444]

The great expectation in Maryland — and for an extended excursion in Northern territory — had ended badly for the Confederates. "I am frank to say I was in favor of the movement into Maryland. I am equally ready to admit that, under the circumstances, I now think it was a mistake."

The correspondent for the *Savannah Republican* detailed the reasoning behind his reversal. "This conviction gradually forced itself upon my mind after I came up with the army and saw the miserable condition in which it was. A fifth of the troops are barefooted; half of them are in rags; and the whole of them insufficiently supplied with food. Men in this condition cannot be relied on to the same extent as when they are properly clothed and subsisted." The Georgian concluded with a compliment and a complaint. "The best soldiers, under such circumstances, will straggle both on the march and in battle."[445]

Back in Sharpsburg, Maryland, victorious U.S. soldiers and curious civilians began surveying the battlefield. "The fence posts and panels and the trees of the woods were shivered and scattered around in every direction, covering the dead and the wounded that lay piled up and scattered over miles of country."

The observer noticed *Americans* on Antietam's acres. "Here lay a Wisconsin man with his hand and leg shot away with a round shot; here lay two Mississippi brothers, one with his head propped against a tree mortally wounded, and the other by his side locked in the embrace of death. I saw a Massachusetts man propping the head of a wounded South Carolinian, and filling his canteen with water by draining his own."[446]

Joining the soldiers scouring the battlefield was a "small army of curiosity seekers," coming daily, and from all sections of the North. Conveyances from nearby towns arrived loaded down, bringing "throngs of visitors" to the battlefield. "The owners of horse flesh in these towns are reaping a harvest. A seat in any sort of a vehicle has not only to be paid for, but sought and begged for."

Once upon the battlefield, "the curious crowd has an inexhaustible industry in searching for relics. They scour every thicket, gully and woods, and carry off with triumph broken and bent muskets, bayonets, ramrods, etc. The search is not without danger, as numerous unexploded shells lie about the field, and some of these adventurous sightseers may have a practical experience of one of the horrors of a battlefield."[447]

The spectators certainly witnessed horrors — especially yet-to-be buried Confederate dead who had been exposed for three to four days after the battle. "Some of them lay with their faces to the ground, whither they had turned in the agony of death, and in which position they had died; others were heaped in piles of three and four together, with their arms interlocked, and their faces turned upwards toward the sky. Scores of them were laid out in rows as though the death shot had penetrated their breasts as they were advancing to attack us."[448]

A Baltimore correspondent etched a vivid description into the minds of his readers. "There they lay in all conceivable positions and in all stages of revolting decomposition, a sight to appall the most courageous and to fill the memory of the most thoughtless beholder with impressions that must haunt the imagination many a day."[449]

Not all the dead were Confederates. One battlefield visitor discovered a fallen U.S. soldier, not yet laid in his grave. Upon the breast of the deceased was "a well worn Testament and a letter. I thought it no desecration to look for a moment at the document. It was from a fond father to his son, with words of affection — 'We hope and pray you may be permitted by a kind Providence, after the war is over, to return.' So has prayed many a father, many a mother."[450]

Though most of the wounded had been removed from the field prior to the arrival of visitors, no one could escape the horror and struggle of the injured survivors. In nearby Boonsboro, "the whole place [was] occupied with wounded soldiers. Every church and school house, and nearly every private dwelling, a hospital! What a sight — every degree of suffering that the human form can endure!" But the onlooker sensed humanity amidst the inhumane.

"This sad accumulation of woe was illumined with the bright beams of active heaven-born charity. The whole population, with but very few exceptions, seemed to be enlisted in the good work of ministering to the sufferers."[451]

Most of the wounded who could withstand the hard jostling of an ambulance wagon were removed from Sharpsburg within days, transported to more permanent hospitals in Frederick, Harrisburg, Baltimore, and Philadelphia. Some ended up in Washington, hospitalized in the U.S. Capitol or within the halls of the Department of Interior building. Three weeks previous the hospital at the Capitol held wounded from a defeated U.S. Army. This time the wounded were with the victors.[452]

NO ONE KNEW on September 17, 1862, that it would become the bloodiest day in America's bloodiest war. But many began to understand that the failed Confederate invasion had changed the course of the Civil War.

"The effect hereabouts of this series of national victories, culminating in the ignominious flight of the enemy . . . is very marked and easily interpreted," editorialized the *Baltimore American and Commercial Advertiser*. "Maryland is 'delivered.' The phrase has a mighty meaning. Maryland has been tried, tested — terribly tested. She has come out of the refining pot fine gold. The storm has swept her and leaves her steadfast beyond all our expectations."[453] Maryland, however, had been a disaster for the Confederates.

The Southern press did not acknowledge battlefield defeats or the failure of the invasion. "The operations of our armies during the past few months have been one unbroken series of splendid triumphs," proclaimed the *Charleston Mercury*. "Everywhere we have been gathering the fruits of that activity and energy of movement which the example of the invincible Jackson seems to have infused amongst our military leaders, and fortune seems still to smile and beckon onward our victorious columns to new and richer fields."

From the Confederate capital, the *Richmond Dispatch* quoted Alexander R. Boteler, a former U.S. congressman and resident of the Shenandoah Valley, reporting direct from Lee's army. "He represents the engagement [Sharpsburg] as resulting decidedly in our favor, and the victory obtained by our forces, if not complete, at least great and satisfactory. . . . He speaks in the most hopeful and cheering manner of the operations of our forces in Maryland and the Lower [Shenandoah] Valley, and entertains the belief that the enemy will not attempt an invasion for some time to come."[454]

The *Petersburg Express* reported the fight at Sharpsburg as "the most bloody and desperately contested engagement of the war," and summarized the battle with favor. "The Confederate army, though opposed by largely superior numbers, again illustrated their valor and invincibility by successfully repelling the repeated onsets of the enemy."[455]

The Confederate newspapers did extol the victories of Harpers Ferry and Shepherdstown while minimizing the retreats from South Mountain and Sharpsburg. They defined South Mountain as McClellan attacking "with his whole enormous force" the Confederate "rear guard." The action was described as "long, furious, and bloody"; and although "attacked by vastly superior forces, [we] stood our ground without yielding an inch." Reports heralded the arrival of Gen. Longstreet, who then drove the enemy. "But for the intervention of night, it is said that the rout would have been complete."[456]

Harpers Ferry received the greatest fanfare from the Rebel reporters. "These operations shed an almost unparalleled luster on the Confederate arms," declared the *Richmond Dispatch*. The *Charleston Mercury* claimed Jackson's victory "the most complete and valuable, and, at the same time, the least costly success that we have gained, thus far, during the war." The *Mercury* editor predicted great results. "In the sight of Europe, the fall of Harper's Ferry, following so closely upon our late successes, will be regarded as more than an offset to [our] disasters of Roanoke Island and Fort Donelson."[457]

The abandonment of Maryland and the return to Virginia was prudent, according to the *Petersburg Express*. "General Lee has very wisely withdrawn his army from Maryland, the cooperation of whose people in his plans and purposes was indispensable for success. They have failed to respond to his noble appeal in the desired way, and the victories of Boonsboro and Sharpsburg, purchased with torrents of blood, have been rendered unprofitable."

The *Express* best summarized the Southern perspective on the conclusion of Lee's invasion: "The re-crossing of the Potomac by our forces does not at all disturb us. Under the circumstances, it was a most judicious movement, and in no manner or degree prejudicial to our interests."[458]

These bold pronouncements in the Confederate press captured the attention of the Northern newspapers. "All the Rebel papers claim victories in all of the recent battles, and call upon the people of the Confederate States not to believe one word contained in the Northern papers of Federal successes. They say that Gen. McClellan's accounts of these battles fully equal Pope's dispatches in their misrepresentation of facts," opined the *Philadelphia Inquirer*.[459]

The *Inquirer* tossed some sarcasm toward the South. "It is rather amusing to see the facility with which the Rebels can put things so as to suit their own fancy. . . . A few more such 'glorious victories' for them and their ruin will be complete and final."[460]

ABRAHAM LINCOLN had his own plan to finish off the Southern rebellion.

Five days following the Battle of Antietam — bolstered by military victories and the termination of the Confederate invasion — the president issued his *Preliminary Emancipation Proclamation*. "There has been no more important and far-reaching document ever issued since the foundation of this Government than the proclamation of President Lincoln concerning slavery and slaves," proclaimed the *New York Times*.

"The gravity of this proclamation will strike everyone," announced the *New York Herald*. "It has been forced upon the nation by the Abolitionists of the North and the Secessionists of the South. It inaugurates an overwhelming revolution in the system of labor in a vast and important agricultural section of the country."

Horace Greeley's *New York Tribune* praised the president. "It is the beginning of the end of the Rebellion; the beginning of the new life of the nation. God bless Abraham Lincoln!"[461]

Lincoln had warned the South this was coming. Sixty days previous to the proclamation's issuance, the president — in conformity with the Congress' Second Confiscation Act — had announced that anyone who remained in rebellion by the third week of September would have their property (including slaves) confiscated by the United States. Lincoln's *Preliminary Emancipation Proclamation* gave rebellious Confederates one final chance. If any Confederate state agreed to seat members in good faith in the United States Congress by January 1, 1863 — and thus cease its participation in the rebellion — the U.S. government would consider payment for slaves, rather than abolition without compensation.

If, however, after January 1, any Confederate state had not rejoined the Union, then "all persons held as slaves within any State, or designated part of a State, whose people shall then be in Rebellion against the United States, *shall be then, thenceforward and forever free*."[462]

Lincoln knew that slave freedom without compensation would economically destroy the South. Investment in slave property far exceeded any other investments in the South. And Confederate inflation had driven slave prices even higher. The week Lincoln issued his proclamation, an enslaved brick layer sold for $1,500 in Charleston; and seven slaves, ranging in age from six to 35, sold for a total of $7,325 — the highest price ever obtained in Charleston.[463]

Not everyone in the North extoled Lincoln's action. "This new proclamation really amounts to little," explained the *New York World*. "It is unbecoming the dignity of a great Government to make such menaces as to what it will hereafter do in territory of which a powerful armed foe disputed the jurisdiction."

The *New York Journal of Commerce* was sorry the president issued the proclamation. "We have only anticipations of evil from it, and we regard it, as will an immense majority of the people of the North, with profound regret." The paper came to a dubious conclusion. "The only result which an adherence to the principles of this proclamation can lead to is a continuation of the war, in a dark future, in which the end is beyond our vision."

The *Baltimore American and Commercial Advertiser*, typically a friend of the Lincoln administration, expected a dull reaction. "As to the effects of the Proclamation in the most disloyal States, they will amount to little or nothing so far as any hopes of bringing them to terms." The editor presented an interesting perspective. "Even slavery in the perilous predicament in which it is placed may comfort itself with the reflection that paper proclamations will not overcome its artillery and other means of making war."

The Baltimore paper understood a position Lincoln himself had taken — that without the force of arms, the proclamation is meaningless. Union victories at South Mountain and Antietam, along with the retreat of the invaders from Maryland, offered Lincoln the demonstration of force he desired. But the *American and Commercial Advertiser* was not convinced it was enough.

"The Proclamation is little to the purpose if the Government finds itself unable to give effect to its provisions; and so in the yet untouched strongholds of the institution it may bid — for a yet considerable period — utter defiance to its assailants. It is the practical that must decide its fate at last, since military necessity is apt to bear down all before it when men are foolish enough to invite revolution to their aid."

The Baltimore editor advanced an idea more powerful, in his judgment, than the proclamation. "We do not think anything whatever is to answer in putting down the rebellion except the uttermost vigor in our military and naval movements. An advance of 70 or 80 miles from Cumberland Gap upon the Salt Works near Abington, Virginia — the only place in the whole South that furnishes salt in any quantity — would do more than any paper manifesto in bringing them to terms." [464]

AS EVENTFUL SEPTEMBER ENDED, no month of the war had equaled its tempo and its temperament. No single day had brought more terror across a broad front of the Union than September 11. No single day had been bloodier than at Antietam on September 17. No single day had been more transformative than *Preliminary Emancipation Proclamation* day on September 22.

"Looking back . . . we may well congratulate ourselves upon the utter failure and defeat of the Rebel plan of a Northern aggressive war," reflected the editor of the *Philadelphia Inquirer*. "East and West, [it] had its political as well as its military significance, which — after such prompt repulse in the West, and terrible punishment in the East — will scarcely be counseled again."[465]

He was wrong.

September ended, but the suspense — and the war — continued.

APPENDIX 1

On September 11, 1862, the following appeared in the *Philadelphia Inquirer.* The article was copied from an editorial in the *Richmond Enquirer.*

The Terms of Peace

It seems that the recent victories of the Confederate army have aroused a feeling for peace which is beginning to find public expression in Northern cities. We are informed that a late copy of the *New York Times* has been received that says: "If the combined armies of McClellan, Burnside and Pope are defeated, then we, for one, are for settlement." We have not seen the paper, and do not know whether or not any qualifications were added. Those who informed us of the *Times* expression, added that the whole tone of the article was that of disappointment and sorrow. Whether or not that statement is correct, we have no doubt that thousands at the North, who heretofore silently submitted to the popular cry, will now speak out and demand peace, since all their armies have been defeated, and no force intervenes between our victorious army and the Northern cities.

General Lee understands the Northern character well enough to know that the surest guarantee of an early peace is to the vigorous prosecution of present successes. He has shown himself to be a General who properly estimates the value of quick and rapid movements; he is pressing forward towards the enemy's country, and nothing but a speedy offer of the most favorable terms of peace will prevent an early invasion of Northern territory, carrying to the enemy's home the same kind of warfare that has been practiced by them in the South. When the fact of invasion is forcibly presented to the Northern mind, our own terms of peace will be offered us.

The only terms which the Confederate States can accept will be the immediate recognition of the present Confederate States, and the permission of the other States to elect their own destiny, and to decide whether their future shall be with the Confederate States or with the United States. We are of the opinion that the principle of election should be applied not only to the border slave States, but to each and all of the remaining United States. Not that any of the Northern States are wanted in the Confederacy, but as an acknowledgement of the right of Secession, for which this war has been waged.

The peace which ends this war should acknowledge the ends for which it was fought, and apply its principles to each and all of the United States.

We do not see the necessity for any proclamation to the Northwestern States about the free navigation of the Mississippi River; that has already been sufficiently declared, and the Northwestern States have, not withstanding that offer, as vigorously sustained the war as any of the other Northern States. We are unwilling to mitigate the force and effect of our victories by extending favors or offers to any portion of our enemies. The ability to conquer a peace has been demonstrated; let us do nothing that will appear like an effort to purchase it.

The earnest desire of the people of the Confederate States for peace is known to the North. Whenever the United States are prepared to have peace, it can be obtained upon proper terms. In the meantime, our army will speedily approach the enemy's territory, and be prepared to aid all peaceably disposed persons and communities, by cooperating against the enemy's forces.[466]

Editorial Response in the *Philadelphia Inquirer*

Terms of Peace

The *Richmond Enquirer* is to the full as boastful and insolent as in days of yore, before Virginia played the shameful, sneaking game from which she has since suffered so justly and heavily. The same cool contempt for the "mud-sills" of the loyal States pervades its articles.

It has enunciated its terms of peace, those which are to be, in some future day, dictated to the twenty millions of loyal people in Independence Square. It tells us how only the war can end; the only conditions on which the Rebels will consent to lay down their arms.

First. The Confederate States must be recognized. We must confess to the fact that they have successfully resisted our power; five and a-half millions have proved too much for twenty-one millions. We must confess that all we have said and hoped has been proved delusive. In fact, that we have been shamefully whipped.

Second. We must concede to "the other States" the right to say whether they will stay with us or whether they will cast in their lot with the victorious Rebels. By the "other States," we suppose he means Maryland, Delaware, Kentucky and Missouri, unless he claims the two latter as already part of the Confederacy. This is not only the admission of a fact, but the concession of a right.

Third. Having gone thus far, it is but a step to demand that not only "the other States," but all the remaining States should have the same right to forsake, if they choose, the beaten, and go with the victorious party. That is, having once conceded to "the other States" the right of Secession, it should be acknowledged as a universal right pertaining to every separate State.

These are the terms of peace which the *Richmond Enquirer* proposes as the only terms which the Rebels can accept. Of course they are pledged to fight till they are secured. To put the whole into plain English, we must admit that we were the aggressors in the war; that the treason of DAVIS, and THOMPSON, and

COBB, and the thieving of FLOYD, and even the petty villainy of the WIGFALLS, and WISES, the RHETTS and the KEITTS, or the masterly duplicity of BRECKINRIDGE, was all right, and proper, and virtuous. *We must give up the right to be a Government, and consent to see our country drop apart piecemeal,* like the victim of a foul leprosy.

If we mistake not the signs of the times, the swarming thousands of loyal Pennsylvanians who are now on their way, or preparing in hot haste to go towards our Southern counties, have little relish for such a suicidal policy as this. The revelation of the fell purpose of the Rebels, which the *Enquirer* so foolishly makes at this particular time, will only tend to nerve the arms of the thousands of our brave men who have said, and who mean to fulfill it, that this Rebellion shall be crushed, and the Government saved for themselves and for their children.[467]

APPENDIX 2

General Lee's Proclamation to the People of Maryland

Headquarters Army of Northern Virginia,
Near Fredericktown, Md., September 8, 1862

To the people of Maryland:

It is right that you should know the purpose that brought the army under my command within the limits of your State, so far as that purpose concerns yourselves. The people of the Confederate States have long watched with the deepest sympathy the wrongs and outrages that have been inflicted upon the citizens of a commonwealth allied to the States of the South by the strongest social, political, and commercial ties. They have seen with profound indignation their sister State deprived of every right and reduced to the condition of a conquered province. Under the pretense of supporting the Constitution, but in violation of its most valuable provisions, your citizens have been arrested and imprisoned upon no charge and contrary to all forms of law. The faithful and manly protest against this outrage made by the venerable and illustrious Marylander, to whom in better days no citizen appealed for right in vain, was treated with scorn and contempt; the government of your chief city has been usurped by armed strangers; your legislature has been dissolved by the unlawful arrest of its members; freedom of the press and speech has been suppressed; words have been declared offenses by an arbitrary decree of the Federal Executive, and citizens ordered to be tried by a military commission for what they may dare to speak. Believing that the people of Maryland possessed a spirit too lofty to submit to such a government, the people of the South have long wished to aid you in throwing off this foreign yoke, to enable you again to enjoy the inalienable rights of freedom, and restore independence and sovereignty to your State. In obedience to this wish, our army has come among you, and is prepared to assist you with the power of its arms in regaining the rights of which you have been despoiled.

This, citizens of Maryland, is our mission, so far as you are concerned. No constraint upon your free will is intended; no intimidation will be allowed within the limits of this army, at least. Marylanders shall once more enjoy their ancient freedom of thought and speech. We know no enemies among you, and will protect all, of every opinion. It is for you to decide your destiny freely and without constraint. This army will respect your choice, whatever it may be; and while the Southern people will rejoice to welcome you to your natural position among them, they will only welcome you when you come of your own free will.

R. E. LEE,

General, Commanding.[468]

APPENDIX 3

Counting Confederates

Determining the number of soldiers in the Confederate armies remained a mysterious affair for the North during the war's first three years. Even today, historians engage in intense debate on the numbers in Robert E. Lee's Army of Northern Virginia during September 1862.

The *Washington Star* shared its methodology for computing Confederates just prior to Lee's invasion of the North.

The Rebel Army

From the South we have the following data in relation to the strength of the Confederate forces from the date of the Confederate retreat from Manassas [early 1862]. Our informant states that Gen. Johnston left Manassas with 40,000 effective men. Gen. Magruder had Yorktown with 7,500 effective men, when the Union army landed. The Confederates, acting under the advice of Gen. Lee, left Yorktown with 67,000 men. On June 1st, 85,000 rations were issued to the Confederate army before Richmond. Detailed reports, by regiments, brigades, and battalions, of all but seventeen captains, showed that 6,357 soldiers were placed *hors du combat* in the battle of Seven Pines. On June 21st, 128,000 rations were issued to the Rebel army before Richmond. By July 20th, 30,000 new troops had reached Richmond from the South, most of whom were new levies, and not regarded as thoroughly safe. On the 13th of August there were six regiments of infantry at Savannah, and a force of 34,000 near Charleston. Gen. Lee and staff left Richmond headquarters (Tabb's Farm, Nine Mile Road), for Gordonsville, after telegraphing to Gen. Mercer, at Savannah, for the infantry at that post, and to Gen. Pemberton for as many as could be spared from the defense of Charleston. Deduct from 128,000, on June 20th, 10,000 for double rations and followers, which would leave 115,000. Losses in battles of Richmond say 15,000. Number remaining 100,000; to which add new troops 30,000, and deduct there from 20,000 for defense of Richmond, would make the Confederate army of Virginia opposite our lines to number 110,000 effective men.[469]

Notes

CHAPTER 1

[1] Andrew Curtin to Abraham Lincoln, September 11, 1862, *The War of the Rebellion: A Compilation of the Official Records of the Union and Confederate Armies*, Series 1, Vol. 19, Pt. 2 (Washington, D.C.: Government Printing Office, 1887), 268. Hereafter cited as *O.R.*

[2] *Philadelphia Inquirer*, September 12, 1862, p. 2, c. 2.

[3] *Philadelphia Inquirer*, September 11, 1862, p. 1, c. 4.

[4] *Philadelphia Inquirer*, September 12, 1862, p. 4, c. 1.

[5] *Philadelphia Inquirer*, September 11, 1862, p. 1, c. 1. The order was issued on September 10.

[6] *Philadelphia Inquirer*, September 6, 1862, p. 4, c. 3.

[7] *Baltimore American and Commercial Advertiser*, September 13, 1862, p. 1, c.7. This Baltimore newspaper had several names since it began publication in 1802. During the Civil War it was printed as the *American and Commercial Advertiser*. It is commonly cited as its alternate title, *Baltimore American*.

[8] *Philadelphia Inquirer*, September 8, 1862, p. 8, c. 8.

[9] *Philadelphia Inquirer*, September 6, 1862, p. 4, c. 1.

[10] *Philadelphia Inquirer*, September 11, 1862, p. 4, c. 1.

[11] *Philadelphia Inquirer*, September 11, 1862, p. 4, c. 2.

[12] *Philadelphia Inquirer*, September 10, 1862, p. 4, c. 1.

[13] *Philadelphia Inquirer*, September 11, 1862, p. 4, c. 1.

[14] *Philadelphia Inquirer*, September 8, 1862, p. 8, c. 8.

[15] *O.R.*, Committee of Bankers to Lincoln, September 11, 1862. Vol. 19, Pt. 2, p. 250.

[16] *Philadelphia Inquirer*, September 5, 1862, p. 3, c. 1. Tod issued the proclamation on September 2.

[17] *Philadelphia Inquirer*, September 3, 1862, p. 1, c. 6.

[18] *Philadelphia Inquirer*, September 11, 1862, p. 8, c. 1.

[19] *Philadelphia Inquirer*, September 3, 1862, p. 1, c. 6.

[20] *Philadelphia Inquirer*, September 8, 1862, p. 5, c. 1.

[21] *Philadelphia Inquirer*, September 3, 1862, p. 1, c. 6.

[22] *Philadelphia Inquirer*, September 10, 1862, p. 1, c. 5.

[23] *Philadelphia Inquirer*, September 10, 1862, p. 1, c. 5.

[24] *Philadelphia Inquirer*, September 8, 1862, p. 5, c. 1.
[25] *Philadelphia Inquirer*, September 10, 1862, p. 1, c. 5.
[26] *Philadelphia Inquirer*, September 6, 1862, p. 4, c. 1-2.

CHAPTER 2

[27] *Baltimore Sun*, September 4, 1862, p. 4, c. 1.
[28] *Philadelphia Inquirer*, September 15, 1862, p. 4, c. 3.
[29] *Philadelphia Inquirer*, September 9, 1862, p. 3, c. 1.
[30] *Baltimore Sun*, September 6, 1862, p. 4, c. 1; *Baltimore American and Commercial Advertiser*, September 5, 1862, p. 1, c. 5.
[31] *Baltimore American and Commercial Advertiser*, September 5, 1862, p. 1, c. 5; *Baltimore Sun*, September 4, 1862, p. 4, c. 1.
[32] *Baltimore American and Commercial Advertiser*, September 10, 1862, p. 4, c. 2.
[33] *Philadelphia Inquirer*, September 6, 1862, p. 7, c. 1.
[34] *Baltimore American and Commercial Advertiser*, September 10, 1862, p. 4, c. 2.
[35] *Philadelphia Inquirer*, September 6, 1862, p. 7, c. 1.
[36] *Baltimore Sun*, September 2, 1862, p. 2, c. 2.; p. 2, c. 3; p. 1, c. 7.
[37] *Baltimore Sun*, September 2, 1862, p. 2, c. 2.
[38] *Baltimore American and Commercial Advertiser*, September 3, 1862, p. 4, c. 2.
[39] *Baltimore Sun*, September 2, 1862, p. 2, c. 2; *Baltimore Sun*, September 3, 1862, p. 2, c. 2.
[40] *Philadelphia Inquirer*, September 8, 1862, p. 3, c. 4; *Philadelphia Inquirer*, September 3, 1862, p. 5, c. 2.
[41] John Mead Gould, *The Civil War Journals of John Mead Gould, 1861-1866*, ed. William B. Jordan (Baltimore: Butternut and Blue, 1997), 185.
[42] *Baltimore American and Commercial Advertiser*, September 2, 1862, p. 2, c. 1. The editor entitled the piece "An Affecting Letter from a soldier to His Family."
[43] www.civilwarpoetry.org/union/songs/chair.html. H.S. Washburn wrote the poem, sung to the music of G. F. Root.
[44] *Philadelphia Inquirer*, September 2, 1862, p. 4, c. 6. Both Northern and Southern newspapers extracted from the British press. Since no transatlantic telegraph line yet existed, news traveled via steamship. Ten days often elapsed before news was exchanged between England and America, and another 10 days vica versa.
[45] *Philadelphia Inquirer*, September 9, 1862, p. 4, c. 3.
[46] *Philadelphia Inquirer*, September 30, 1862, p. 2, c. 6. The original article appeared in the *London Times* on September 17. Due to the transatlantic lag, the reverses referred to were the fighting at the end of August at Manassas, the subsequent threat to Washington, and the invasion of Kentucky and threat to Cincinnati.
[47] *Baltimore Sun*, September 10, 1862, p. 2, c. 3. The Republican vote from the previous election reduced by 10,000 fewer voters, but the Republicans maintained their majorities in both branches of the Maine legislature.
[48] *Baltimore American and Commercial Advertiser*, September 5, 1862, p. 1, c. 3.
[49] Gould, 187.

[50] *Baltimore American and Commercial Advertiser*, September 6, 1862, p. 1, c. 4.
[51] Gould, 184.
[52] *Baltimore American and Commercial Advertiser*, September 6, 1862, p. 1, c. 5.
[53] *Philadelphia Inquirer*, September 3, 1862, p. 8, c. 1.
[54] *Baltimore American and Commercial Advertiser*, September 12, 1862, p. 4, c. 3. The article was reprinted from the *New York Post*.
[55] *Baltimore American and Commercial Advertiser*, September 12, 1862, p. 4, c. 3.
[56] *Baltimore American and Commercial Advertiser*, September 5, 1862, p. 1, c. 3.
[57] *Baltimore American and Commercial Advertiser*, September 6, 1862, p. 1, c. 4.
[58] *Baltimore American and Commercial Advertiser*, September 6, 1862, p. 1, c. 4.
[59] *Baltimore American and Commercial Advertiser*, September 6, 1862, p. 1, c. 4.
[60] *Philadelphia Inquirer*, September 9, 1862, p. 4, c. 4.
[61] George B. McClellan, *The Civil War Papers of George B. McClellan*, ed. Stephen W. Sears (New York: Tichnor & Fields, 1989), 135, 348, 374, 361, 363, 359.
[62] Gideon Welles, *The Diary of Gideon Welles, Secretary of the Navy under Lincoln and Johnson* (New York: Houghton Mifflin Co., 1911), 102. The entry is for September 1.
[63] McClellan, 389.
[64] Welles, 107, 104.
[65] Salmon P. Chase, *Diary and Correspondence of Salmon P. Chase in the Annual Report of the American Historical Association*, Vol. 2, p. 50 (Washington: Government Printing Office, 1902).
[66] Welles, 105.
[67] Welles, 105.
[68] Welles. 105.
[69] McClellan, 428. He writes this to his wife on September 2.

CHAPTER 3

[70] *Philadelphia Inquirer*, September 29, 1862, p. 7, c. 1. The article appeared under the title "The President and the Chicago Delegation," and was published in newspapers throughout the North.
[71] *Philadelphia Inquirer,* September 29, 1862, p. 7, c. 1.
[72] *Philadelphia Inquirer*, September 29, 1862, p. 7, c. 2.
[73] *Philadelphia Inquirer*, September 29, 1862, p. 7, c. 1.
[74] *Philadelphia Inquirer*, September 29, 1862, p. 7, c. 2.
[75] Samuel P. Wheeler, *The Prayer of Twenty Millions*, http://www.lincolnstudies.com/archives/80.
[76] *Philadelphia Inquirer*, August 25, 1862, p. 3, c. 1.
[77] *Philadelphia Inquirer*, August 25, 1862, p. 1, c. 1. The *Inquirer* ran Lincoln's response and Greeley's original letter on the same date, but Lincoln's retort appeared on page one, under the title: "He curtly Rebukes his Correspondent." The *Inquirer* rejected most of Greeley's opinions as too radical, seldom quoting him, but often berating him as too divisive during a time when American politics needed unity.

[78] Colonization," Mr. Lincoln and Freedom, http:// www.mrlincolnandfreedom.org/inside.asp?ID=34&subjectID=3
[79] *Harper's Weekly*, June 28, 1862, p. 402, c. 3.
[80] *Baltimore Sun*, September 3, 1862, p. 4, c. 1; *Philadelphia Inquirer*, September 4, 1862, p. 8, c. 5; *Philadelphia Inquirer*, September 15, 1862, p. 8, c. 4; *Philadelphia Inquirer*, September 15, 1862, p. 8, c. 6; *Baltimore Sun*, September 9, 1862, p. 4, c. 1.
[81] *Chambersburg Valley Spirit*, April 30, 1862, p. 5, c. 5. *Valley Spirit* was a weekly newspaper in Chambersburg, Franklin County, Pennsylvania. This article was a reprint of one that appeared in the *Harrisburg Patriot and Union*,http://valley.lib.virginia.edu/news/vs1862/pa.fr.vs.1862.04.30.xml.
[82] *Harper's Weekly*, June 28, 1862, p. 402, c. 2-3.
[83] *Chambersburg Valley Spirit*, April 30, 1862, p. 5, c. 4.
[84] *Chambersburg Valley Spirit*, April 30, 1862, p. 5, c. 4.
[85] "Colonization," *Mr. Lincoln and Freedom*, http: www.mrlincolnandfreedom.org/inside.asp?ID=34&subjectID=3
[86] *Philadelphia Inquirer*, August 15, 1862, p. 1, c. 4-5. The article appeared the day following the meeting under the title: "The Scheme of Colonization: Interview Between the President and a Committee of Colored Men — Remarks of the President."
[87] *Baltimore American and Commercial Advertiser*, September 15, 1862, p. 2, c.3. The article states "about four thousand of the more desirable of colored persons have already informed Senator Pomeroy of their desire to avail themselves of the President's Colonization Scheme."
[88] *Harper's Weekly*, June 28, 1862, p. 402, c. 1.
[89] Abraham Lincoln, "Appeal to Border State Representatives in Favor of Compensated Emancipation," *The Writings of Abraham Lincoln, 1862-1863,* Vol. 6, ed. Arthur B. Langley (New York: The Lamb Publishing Co., 1906), 87. Hereafter cited as Writings of Abraham Lincoln.
[90] Abraham Lincoln, "Letter to James A. McDougall," March 14, 1862, *The Collected Works of Abraham Lincoln,* Vol. 5, ed. Roy P. Basler (New Brunswick, NJ: Rutgers University Press, 1955), 160-161.
[91] Lincoln, *Writings of Abraham Lincoln*, 87.
[92] "Message from Border State Congressmen to Abraham Lincoln," July 15, 1862. Abraham Lincoln Papers at the Library of Congress. Transcribed and annotated by the Lincoln Studies Center, Knox College, Galesburg, IL. http://www.mrlincolnandfreedom.org/inside.asp?ID=35&subjectID=3
[93] *Philadelphia Inquirer*, July 31, 1862, p. 3, c. 3.
[94] "The Second Confiscation Act," July 17, 1862. Freedmen & Southern Society Project, http://www.history.umd.edu/Freedmen/contact2.htm.
[95] *Harper's Weekly*, September 6, 1862, p. 562, c. 1.
[96] George W. Wingate, *History of the 22nd Regiment of the National Guard of the State of New York* (New York: Edwin W. Dayton, 1896), 84-86.
[97] Chase *Diary*, August 26, 1862, 255.
[98] Chase *Diary*, September 9, 1862, 256.
[99] *Harper's Weekly*, July 19, 1862, p. 451, c. 1.

[100] *Baltimore Sun*, September 9, 1862, p. 4, c. 1.
[101] *Harper's Weekly*, August 9, 1862, p. 498, c. 2.
[102] *Harper's Weekly*, July 19, 1862, p. 451, c. 2.
[103] *Philadelphia Inquirer*, August 25, 1862, p. 1, c. 1.

CHAPTER 4

[104] *Baltimore Sun*, September 1, 1862, p. 3, c. 2.
[105] *Baltimore Sun*, September 3, 1862, p. 1, c. 5. The paper reprinted the article from the *Boston Post* on its front page under the headline: "Relief for Wounded Soldiers."
[106] *Baltimore Sun*, September 9, 1862, p. 2, c. 3.
[107] *Baltimore Sun*, September 9, 1862, p. 2, c. 3.
[108] *Philadelphia Inquirer*, September 18, 1862, p. 8, c. 6.
[109] *Philadelphia Inquirer*, September 24, 1862, p. 2, c. 6. The *Inquirer* copied the article from the *Boston Post*. The original communication from an army surgeon appeared widely in newspapers on September 22. The surgeon, who had practiced for more than a third of a century, claimed that lint was unnecessary to dress gunshot wounds, and that worn-out flannel, towels, sheets, or tablecloths sufficed as bandages, without the extra step of scraping lint. *Philadelphia Inquirer*, September 22, 1862, p. 8, c. 6.
[110] *Philadelphia Inquirer*, September 24, 1862, p. 2, c. 6.
[111] *Philadelphia Inquirer*, September 4, 1862, p. 8, c. 3.
[112] *Philadelphia Inquirer*, September 5, 1862, p. 4, c. 2.
[113] *Philadelphia Inquirer*, September 9, 1862, p. 3. c. 2.; *Philadelphia Inquirer*, September 26, 1862, p. 8, c. 4.
[114] *Philadelphia Inquirer,* September 22, 1862, p. 4, c. 5.
[115] *Philadelphia Inquirer*, September 17, 1862, p. 8, c. 6; *Philadelphia Inquirer,* September 16, 1862, p. 8, c. 3.
[116] *Philadelphia Inquirer*, September 9, 1862, p. 3, c. 1.
[117] The loyal state governors submitted their request for 300,000 new volunteers to President Lincoln on June 28, 1862. The president issued the call on July 1. Each state was given its own quota by the federal government. These troops were volunteering for a three year enlistment. Just over two weeks later, the Congress on July 16 authorized the president to raise an additional 300,000 men, via compulsory drafting, if necessary, if a state failed to meet its quota.
[118] *Philadelphia Inquirer,* July 16, 1862, p. 4, c. 5. The correspondent wrote for the *Inquirer* and was reporting on the mass meeting in New York on the previous day.
[119] *Philadelphia Inquirer*, July 16, 1862, p. 4, c. 3.
[120] *Harpers Weekly*, August 23, 1862, p. 539, c. 4.
[121] *Philadelphia Inquirer*, July 26, 1862, p. 2, c. 3-4. The *Inquirer* reprinted an article that appeared in the *Petersburg Express* on July 22.
[122] *Baltimore American and Commercial Advertiser*, September 9, 1862, p. 2, c. 2. Article reprinted from the *New York World.*

[123] *Philadelphia Inquirer*, September 9, 1862, p. 2, c. 5. The article was entitled: "The Loyalty of Washington County"; *Chambersburg Valley Spirit*, August 13, 1862, p. 1, c. 1.

CHAPTER 5

[124] *Philadelphia Inquirer*, September 3, 1862, p. 4, c. 1.

[125] *O.R.*, Vol. 51, Pt.2, 765-766.

[126] *Chambersburg Valley Spirit*, August 20, 1862, p. 1, c. 4; *Chambersburg Valley Spirit*, August 27, 1862, p. 1, c. 1.

[127] *Baltimore Sun*, September 9, 1862, p. 4, c. 1.

[128] *Philadelphia Inquirer*, September 9, 1862, p. 3, c. 1.

[129] *Philadelphia Inquirer*, September 8, 1862, p. 5, c. 1.

[130] *Philadelphia Inquirer*, September 9, 1862, p. 3, c. 1.

[131] *Philadelphia Inquirer*, September 8, 1862, p. 5, c. 1. This was the analysis of Parson Brownlow.

[132] *Chambersburg Valley Spirit*, September 3, 1862, p. 4, c. 1.

[133] *Philadelphia Inquirer*, September 2, 1862, p. 4, c. 1-2.

[134] *Philadelphia Inquirer*, September 2, 1862, p. 4, c. 2.

[135] *Chambersburg Valley Spirit*, September 3, 1862, p. 4, c. 1.

[136] *Baltimore American and Commercial Advertiser*, September 11, 1862, p. 2, c.2

[137] *Chambersburg Valley Spirit*, September 3, 1862, p. 4, c. 1.

[138] *Baltimore American and Commercial Advertiser*, September 5, 1862, p. 4, c. 2.

[139] *Philadelphia Inquirer*, September 9, 1862, p. 4, c. 1. The *Inquirer* particularly criticized the two largest New York newspapers for their political partisanship. Horace Greeley's *New York Tribune* served as the mouthpiece of the Republicans. *The New York Herald*, owned by James Gordon Bennett, Jr., trumpeted the Democrats' positions. The two Gotham papers were the largest circulating papers in the United States, and their opinion pages often were reprinted in newspapers throughout the country.

[140] *Baltimore American and Commercial Advertiser*, September 5, 1862, p. 4, c. 2. This served as an example of a moderate paper, as did the *Philadelphia Inquirer* and the *Baltimore Sun*.

[141] *Chambersburg Valley Spirit*, 3 September 1862, p.4, c.1.

[142] Charles Ingersoll, "An Undelivered Speech on Executive Arrests," 1862 (Philadelphia: privately published, 1862), 7-8, http://www.archive.org/details/undeliveredspeec00inge.

[143] *Philadelphia Inquirer*, August 23, 1862, p. 4, c. 1.

[144] *Philadelphia Inquirer*, 28 August 1862, p.8, c.3.

[145] *Chambersburg Valley Spirit*, August 20, 1862, p. 4, c. 2; *Philadelphia Inquirer*, August 22, 1862, p. 1, c. 3; *Philadelphia Inquirer*, September 4, 1862, p. 5, c. 2.

[146] *Philadelphia Inquirer*, August 28, 1862, p. 1, c. 2-3. The judge was the Hon. John J. Pearson.

[147] *Philadelphia Inquirer*, August 12, 1862, p. 2, c. 4. The *Chicago Times* article is reprinted from August 9.

[148] *Baltimore American and Commercial Advertiser*, September 11, 1862, p. 4, c.4.
[149] *Baltimore American and Commercial Advertiser*, September 11, 1862, p. 4, c.4.
[150] *Philadelphia Inquirer*, September 5, 1862, p. 8, c. 2. The Delaware Democrats delegates (150 strong) held their convention at Dover on September 4, where they nominated a candidate for governor and for their one member of Congress.
[151] *Philadelphia Inquirer*, August 25, 1862, p. 8, c. 1-2. Excerpts from a speech given by F.W. Hughes at the Democratic rally in Independence Square on August 25 — the same event that resulted in the arrest of Charles Ingersoll.
[152] *Baltimore Sun*, September 10, 1862, p. 4, c. 3. The article was copied from the *Gettysburg Compiler*, and satirically was titled: "Well Done."
[153] *Philadelphia Inquirer*, September 9, 1862, p. 4, c. 1.
[154] *Philadelphia Inquirer*, July 26, 1862, p. 2, c. 4. Reprinted from the July 22 *Petersburg Express*.
[155] *Philadelphia Inquirer*, September 4, 1862, p. 8, c. 2. Reprinted from August 24 *London Times*.

CHAPTER 6

[156] *Harper's Weekly*, August 30, 1862, p. 547, c. 4.
[157] Orville V. Burton and Patricia D. Bonnin, "The Confederacy," *A Macmillan Information Now Encyclopedia*. http:// www.civilwarhome.com/kingcotton.htm.
[158] James Henry Hammond, excerpts from speech delivered before the U.S. Senate on the Admission of Kansas as a State, Under the Lecompton Constitution, March 4, 1858. http://teachingamericanhistory.org/library/index.asp?documentprint=1722.
[159] *Philadelphia Inquirer*, September 9, 1862, p. 4, c. 4. The article was entitled: "Increasing Distress in the English Manufacturing Districts" and was reprinted from the *London Times*, dated August 26, 1862. For comparison between shillings and dollars, if paid in shillings, the average American worker would make 40 shillings in a work week (6 days), *Baltimore American and Commercial Advertiser*, September 9, 1862, p. 1, c. 6.
[160] *Philadelphia Inquirer*, July 31, 1862, p. 8, c. 1-3. The debate occurred in the House of Commons on July 18.
[161] *Philadelphia Inquirer*, August 20, 1862, p. 4, c. 4-5. The debate in the House of Lords occurred on August 4.
[162] *Philadelphia Inquirer*, July 31, 1862, p. 8, c. 3. Reprinted from the *London Times*, July 18, 1862.
[163] *Philadelphia Inquirer*, July 18, 1862, p. 4, c. 2.
[164] *Philadelphia Inquirer,* July 18, 1862, p. 4, c. 2.
[165] *Baltimore Sun*, September 12, 1862, p. 2, c. 1. Secretary Seward dated his letter of invitation August 3, but it did not appear in English papers until nearly two weeks later, due to slow transmission over the Atlantic via steamship.
[166] Welles, 74. The diary entry is for August 10, 1862.
[167] *Philadelphia Inquirer*, August 29, 1862, p. 4, c. 6.
[168] *Harper's Weekly*, August 16, 1862, p. 514, c. 2.

[169] *Philadelphia Inquirer,* August 30, 1862, p. 2, c. 5. Article of Bishop E. Purcell, of Ohio, encouraging Irish to enlist and not to resist the draft.
[170] *Philadelphia Inquirer*, August 29, 1862, p. 5, c. 1-2. These comments purportedly came from a letter drafted by the *London Times* correspondent in New York City, mistakenly dropped on a New York street. Whether real or contrived, the letter was printed in Northern newspapers to rile up Irish recruits. The *London Morning Herald* labeled Corcoran "an insignificant Irishmen," and commented on the Corcoran procession and spectacle in its September 5 edition: "We only wish to observe what a dearth of leading men, what a perfect famine of heroes must there be in New York, when 250,000 men can wave their hats and shout themselves hoarse all day, for what? For an individual of the name of Corcoran!" Printed in the *Philadelphia Inquirer*, September 19, 1862, p. 4, c. 4.
[171] *Philadelphia Inquirer*, September 29, 1862, p. 8, c. 2.
[172] *Philadelphia Inquirer*, October 3, 1862, p. 8, c. 1 (reprinted from the *London Times*, September 18, 1862); *Baltimore American and Commercial Advertiser*, September 10, 1862, p. 4 , c. 1 (printed in the *Times*, August 30, 1862).
[173] *Philadelphia Inquirer*, July 31, 1862, p. 8, c. 3. Cited from the *Times*, July 18, 1862.
[174] *Philadelphia Inquirer*, August 27, 1862, p. 4, c. 1.
[175] *Harper's Weekly*, July 12, 1862, p. 434, c. 2.
[176] *Philadelphia Inquirer*, September 25, 1862, p. 4, c. 3-4.
[177] *Philadelphia Inquirer*, September 17, 1862, p. 2, c. 5.
[178] *Harper's Weekly*, August 23, 1862, p. 530, c. 3.

CHAPTER 7

[179] *Philadelphia Inquirer*, July 19, 1862, p. 1, c. 1-4. General Orders # 7 was issued by Maj. Gen. John Pope on July 18.
[180] "Another Stringent Order by Gen. Pope – Secession Sympathizers to be Sent South," *Philadelphia Inquirer*, July 24, 1862, p. 1, c. 1. General Orders # 11 was issued by Pope on July 23.
[181] "The New War Policy," *Philadelphia Inquirer*, July 26, 1862, p. 1, c. 1. General Orders # 13 was issued by Pope on July 25.
[182] "We are at Last Beginning to Wage War," *Philadelphia Inquirer*, July 24, 1862, p. 4, c. 1-2.
[183] *Philadelphia Inquirer*, July 15, 1862, p. 1, c. 2. Pope addressed his soldiers on July 14.
[184] *Philadelphia Inquirer*, July 15, 1862, p. 4, c. 1.
[185] *Philadelphia Inquirer*, August 9, 1862, p. 4, c. 7. Reprinted from the *Richmond Dispatch*, August 9, 1862. The article includes General Orders No. 54, the South's response, issued on August 1 by Gen. Samuel Cooper, commander of the Confederate Adjutant and Inspector General's Office.
[186] *Philadelphia Inquirer*, August 25, 1862, p. 2, c. 3. Davis delivered the speech to the C. S. Senate on August 18.
[187] *Philadelphia Inquirer*, August 14, 1862, p. 4, c. 4-5. Lee wrote his letter on August 2.

[188] *Philadelphia Inquirer*, August 14, 1862, p. 4, c. 5. General in Chief Henry W. Halleck responded to Lee on August 9.
[189] "The Second Confiscation Act," approved July 17, 1862. Freedmen & Southern Society Project, http://www.history.umd.edu/Freedmen/contact2.htm.
[190] *Philadelphia Inquirer*, August 8, 1862, p. 2, c. 2-3. Reprinted from the *Richmond Examiner* (date not given).
[191] *Philadelphia Inquirer*, August 25, 1862. Excerpt from Davis speech to the C.S. Senate on August 18. The two U.S. generals remained unnamed by Davis, but he was referring to David Hunter along the South Carolina coast near Port Royal and Benjamin Butler in New Orleans.
[192] John Brown attacked the U.S. Armory and Arsenal at Harpers Ferry, Virginia, from October 16-18, 1859 to seize arms for the purpose of initiating a war against slavery. Brown failed in his attempt, but his subsequent trial and execution impassioned Southerners and Northerners alike.
[193] *Philadelphia Inquirer*, August 11, 1862, p. 2, c. 3. The article appeared in the *Richmond Enquirer* on August 5.
[194] *Chambersburg Valley Spirit*, July 30, 1862, p. 4, c. 1.
[195] "The Declaration of Causes of Seceding States," http://civilwar.org/education/history/primarysources//declarationofcauses.html.
[196] *Harper's Weekly*, August 30, 1862, p. 547, c. 1.
[197] *Philadelphia Inquirer*, July 30, 1862, p. 2, c. 1. Copied from an article entitled, "The Exchange of Prisoners," from the *Richmond Dispatch*, July 25, 1862.
[198] *Philadelphia Inquirer*, August 8, 1862, p. 2, c. 3. Reprinted from the *Richmond Examiner* (no date given).
[199] *Philadelphia Inquirer*, July 30, 1862, p. 2, c. 2. Reprinted from an editorial entitled, "A Military Despot," in the *Richmond Dispatch*, July 25, 1862.
[200] "Rebel Retaliation for Gen. Pope's Orders," *Philadelphia Inquirer*, August 9, 1862, p. 4, c. 7. The paper reprinted General Orders No. 54 (issued August 1) from the Confederate Adjutant and Inspector General's Office.
[201] *Philadelphia Inquirer*, July 31, 1862, p. 6, c., 1. Cited from the *Richmond Enquirer*, July 25, 1862.
[202] *Philadelphia Inquirer*, August 9, 1862, p. 4, c. 7.
[203] *Philadelphia Inquirer*, August 25, 1862, p. 2, c. 3. Davis speech to C. S. Senate, August 18, 1862.
[204] "Jefferson Davis on Retaliation," *Philadelphia Inquirer*, August 11, 1862, p. 4, c. 3.
[205] "Davis and his Lex Talionis," *Philadelphia Inquirer*, August 15, 1862, p. 4, c. 2-3.
[206] *Philadelphia Inquirer*, August 16, 1862, p. 3, c. 1; September 11, 1862, p. 1, c. 6.
[207] "Retaliation," *Harper's Weekly*, September 6, 1862, p. 563, c. 2. "General Pope's Captured Officers," *Philadelphia Inquirer*, August 16, 1862, p. 3, c. 1.
[208] *Philadelphia Inquirer*, July 30, 1862, p. 2, c. 2. Copied from the *Richmond Dispatch*, July 25, 1862.
[209] *Philadelphia Inquirer*, July 19, 1862, p. 1, c. 1-2. The Confederate government authorized guerrilla, or "partisan ranger" units on July 16, 1862, and

proclaimed them part of the Provisional Army of the Confederate States. Two days later, Pope issued his anti-guerrilla General Orders No. 7 on July 18.

210 "The Rebel Endorsement of Guerrillas," *Philadelphia Inquirer*, July 30, 1862, p. 4, c. 2.

211 *Philadelphia Inquirer*, September 1, 1862, p. 2, c. 1. Breckinridge was vice president under Lincoln's predecessor, President James Buchannan. Breckinridge attacked Baton Rouge on August 5, but was repulsed.

212 *Philadelphia Inquirer*, September 1, 1862, p. 2, c. 1-2. Paine's response ended the matter.

213 *Baltimore American and Commercial Advertiser*, September 8, 1862, p. 4, c. 1.

214 *Philadelphia Inquirer*, July 30, 1862, p. 2, c. 1. The article appeared in the *Richmond Examiner* on July 25.

215 *Harper's Weekly*, August 30, 1862, p. 546, c. 4.

216 *Philadelphia Inquirer*, August 28, 1862, p. 1, c. 5. Quoted from the *Richmond Whig*, August 23, 1862.

217 *Philadelphia Inquirer*, August 28, 1862, p. 1, c. 5.

CHAPTER 8

218 Thomas Jonathan Jackson graduated from West Point in 1846 and served with meritorious distinction in the Mexican War. When the Civil War erupted, he was teaching physics and artillery at the Virginia Military Institute. Lee chose Jackson to command Southern forces at Harpers Ferry during the war's first months, and here Jackson organized and drilled the 1st Virginia Brigade. These troops held the line on Henry Hill during the First Battle of Manassas on July 21, 1861, and here's where Jackson earned the nickname "Stonewall." Jackson defeated multiple Union armies in Virginia's Shenandoah Valley during the spring of 1862 before uniting with Lee to drive the Federals away from Richmond in the Seven Days Battles June 25-July 1. Jackson defeated another Union army at Slaughter Mountain (also known as Cedar Mountain) on August 9, and from there he circled behind Pope to destroy his supply base and trains on August 27. Jackson initiated the Battle of Second Manassas with Pope on August 28, and defended his position against repeated Union assaults on August 29. Lee then arrived, and with his reinforcements, he defeated Pope on August 30, forcing a Federal retreat to the defenses of Washington.

219 Jackson pursued, but the Union rear guard halted his advance in the Battle of Chantilly on September 1.

220 *Philadelphia Inquirer*, September 13, 1862, p. 2, c. 4. Copied from September 8 *Richmond Enquirer*. The panic in Washington was exaggerated.

221 *O.R.*, Vol. 19, Pt. 2, p. 590-591. Lee to Davis, September 3, 1862.

222 *O.R.*, Vol. 19, Pt. 2, p. 592. Lee to Davis, September 4, 1862.

223 *O.R.*, Vol. 19, Pt. 2, p. 591. Lee to Davis, September 3, 1862.

224 *O.R.*, Vol. 19, Pt. 2, p. 590. Lee to Davis, September 3, 1862.

225 *O.R.*, Vol. 19, Pt. 2, p. 590. Lee to Davis, September 3, 1862.

226 *Philadelphia Inquirer*, August 28, 1862, p. 1, c. 5. Copied from the *Richmond Whig* (no date given). The Confederate Congress adopted The Second

Conscription Act on September 27, expanding the draft age from 35 to age 45. The First Conscription Act passed six months earlier. For information on U.S. recruitment efforts, one paper Gen. Lee scanned was the *Baltimore Sun*. It reported on the front page of its September 6 edition that a "very heavy force of new levies have been arriving here [Washington] for three weeks past, by the thousands daily." *Baltimore Sun*, September 6, 1862, p. 1, c. 1.

[227] *Philadelphia Inquirer*, September 11, 1862, p. 2, c. 1-2. The article appeared in the *Richmond Examiner* on September 5.

[228] *O.R.*, Vol. 19, Pt. 2, p. 590. Lee to Davis, September 3, 1862.

[229] *Baltimore American and Commercial Advertiser*, September 16, 1862, p. 1, c 5. Reprinted from the September 13 *Richmond Whig*, entitled: "The Redemption of 'My Maryland.'"

[230] *O.R.*, Vol. 19, Pt. 2, p. 591. Lee to Davis, September 4, 1862.

[231] Samuel D. Buck, *With the Old Confeds: Actual Experiences of a Captain in the Line* (Baltimore: H.E. Hauck & Co., 1925), 59.

[232] The lyrics are sung to the song, *O Tannenbaum*, and were written by poet James Ryder Randall in 1861. The poem consists of nine stanzas. Stanzas 6 and 9 are presented here. http:www.msa.md.gov/msa/mdmanual/01glance/html/symbols/lyricsco.html.

[233] *Philadelphia Inquirer,* September 13, 1862, p. 2, c. 4. Article reprinted from the *Richmond Enquirer*, September 8, 1862.

[234] *Philadelphia Inquirer*, September 12, 1862, p. 3, c. 2. Article from the September 4 *Richmond Dispatch*.

[235] *Baltimore Sun*, September 16, 1862, p. 1, c. 4-5. Copied from the September 13 *Richmond Whig*.

[236] *Philadelphia Inquirer*, October 2, 1862, p. 2, c. 4.

[237] *Philadelphia Inquirer*, August 15, 1862, p. 3, c. 1. The article appeared in the *Richmond Examiner* on August 9.

[238] *O.R.*, Vol. 19, Pt. 2, p. 592. General Orders No. 102, issued September 4 from Leesburg, Virginia.

[239] *O.R.*, Vol. 19, Pt. 2, p. 593. Lee to Davis, September 5, 1862.

[240] *O.R.*, Vol. 19, Pt. 2, p. 598-599. Davis' proclamation was not prepared until September 7, three days after Lee had invaded Maryland. By the time it reached Confederate headquarters in Maryland on September 13, it was too late. Gen. Lee had issued his own explanatory proclamation on September 8. *O.R.*, Vol. 19, Pt. 2, p. 601-602, 605.

[241] *O.R.*, Vol. 19, Pt. 2, p. 600. Lee to Davis from his headquarters near Frederick, September 8, 1862.

CHAPTER 9

[242] Lincoln's quote is from http://www.quotesstar.com/quote/i/i-hope-to-have-god-3171.html.

[243] Kentucky was admitted into the Confederacy on December 10, 1861, at the request of the state's provisional government. The Confederate battle flag was a square St. Andrew's cross pattern, originally adopted only with 12 stars, and the center of the cross left void.

[244] "The Movement towards the Queen City," *Philadelphia Inquirer*, September 4, 1862, p. 4, c. 1.
[245] *Baltimore Sun*, September 3, 1862, p. 2, c. 1-2. *Baltimore Sun*, September 5, 1862, p. 1, c. 2.
[246] *Baltimore Sun*, September 5, 1862, p. 2, c. 2. Copied from the September 2 *Cincinnati Gazette*.
[247] *Baltimore Sun*, September 5, 1862, p. 2, c. 3. Copied from the September 2 *Cincinnati Commercial*.
[248] Richmond, Kentucky, is located about 25 miles south of Lexington. Kirby Smith's Army of Kentucky annihilated Maj. Gen. William "Bull" Nelson's force of 6,500 (mostly new recruits) on August 29-30. Nelson was wounded, and five out of six U.S. soldiers engaged were casualties, with nearly two-thirds captured or missing. Smith's army entered Lexington on September 2 and Frankfort on September 3.
[249] *Baltimore American and Commercial Advertiser*, September 6, 1862, p. 4. c. 2. Copied from the September 2 *Cincinnati Commercial* and September 2 *Cincinnati Gazette*.
[250] Smith's Army of Kentucky had strength of 11,000 men. U.S. estimates often doubled Confederate numbers.
[251] "The Great Tumult," *Baltimore American and Commercial Advertiser*, September 8, 1862, p. 4, c. 5. Copied from report submitted to the *New York World* on September 4.
[252] *Philadelphia Inquirer*, September 16, 1862, p. 2, c. 1. The correspondent wrote the article on September 10.
[253] *Philadelphia Inquirer*, September 12, 1862, p. 1, c. 2. The dispatch was written on September 11. The reinforcements were coming north from Nashville and commanded by Maj. Gen. Don Carlos Buell.
[254] *Philadelphia Inquirer*, September 17, 1862, p. 1, c. 4.
[255] *Baltimore American and Commercial Advertiser*, September 8, 1862, p. 1, c. 2.
[256] *Charleston Mercury*, August 26, 1862, p. 1, c. 3. *Newspaper Research, 1861-1865*. http://www2.uttyler.edu/vbetts/charleston_mercury.htm.
[257] *Southern Confederacy*, November 20, 1862, p. 1, c. 5-6. Reprinted from the November 15 *Richmond Enquirer*. The *Southern Confederacy* was published in Atlanta. *Newspaper Research, 1861-1865*. http://www2.uttyler.edu/vbetts/southern_confederacy.htm.
[258] *Savannah Republican*, March 22, 1862, p. 1, c. 3. *Newspaper Research*, 1861-1865. http://www2.uttyler.edu/vbetts/savannah_republican.htm.
[259] "The Perils of the Hour," *Baltimore American and Commercial Advertiser*, September 8, 1862, p. 1, c. 3.
[260] http://www.historynet.com/capital-defense-washington-dc-in-the-civil-war.htm.
[261] *Philadelphia Inquirer*, September 5, 1862, p. 1, c. 3. *Baltimore Sun*, September 5, 1862, p. 2., c. 2.
[262] *Philadelphia Inquirer*, September 8, 1862, p. 4, c. 4.
[263] *Philadelphia Inquirer*, September 8, 1862, p. 4, c. 7.
[264] *Philadelphia Inquirer*, September 6, 1862, p. 8, c. 1.
[265] *Philadelphia Inquirer*, September 8, 1862, p. 4, c. 4.

[266] *Baltimore American and Commercial Advertiser*, September 9, 1862, p. 1, c. 8. McClellan received orders on September 3 to "immediately commence, and proceed with all possible dispatch, to organize an army for active operations." *O.R.* 19, Pt. 2, p. 169.
[267] "Reception of General McClellan," *Baltimore American and Commercial Advertiser*, September 4, 1862, p. 1, c. 3.
[268] "The Crises at Hand," *Philadelphia Inquirer*, September 8, 1862, p. 4, c. 7.
[269] *O.R.*, Vol. 19, Pt. 1, p. 1069. Confederate Secretary of War George W. Randolph to Loring, August 29, 1862. *O.R.*, Vol. 19, Pt. 1, p. 1068, Loring to Randolph, September 1, 1862.
[270] *Baltimore Sun*, September 3, 1862, p. 1, c. 4. Copied from the September 1 *Wheeling Argus*.
[271] *O.R.*, Vol. 19, Pt. 2, p. 218. General in Chief Henry W. Halleck to J.A.J. Lightburn, September 8, 1862.
[272] *O.R.*, Vol. 19, Pt. 1, p. 1058. Lightburn to Halleck, September 19, 1862. Loring decided against an immediate pursuit. He had outdistanced his supply trains, and he was concerned a forward advance would expose his own rear to counter-marching Federals who could use numerous roads that led from the Ohio River to Charleston. *O.R.*, Vol. 19, Pt. 1, p. 1071.
[273] *O.R.*, Vol. 19, Pt. 1, p. 1070. Loring announced this achievement to Secretary of War Randolph on September 11, two days before seizing Charleston. The Confederate cavalry commander was Brig. Gen. Albert Gallatin Jenkins.
[274] *O.R.*, Vol. 19, Pt. 1, p. 1071. Loring's report to Secretary of War Randolph, September 14, 1862.
[275] *O.R.*, Vol. 19, Pt. 1, p. 1072.
[276] *Philadelphia Inquirer*, August 29, 1862, p. 4, c. 5.
[277] *Philadelphia Inquirer*, August 30, 1862, p. 2, c. 5. The *Inquirer* copied articles from the *St. Paul Pioneer and Democrat.*
[278] *Baltimore Sun*, September 19, 1862, p. 1, c. 4. Gov. Ramsey presented these details to a special session convened in St. Paul on September 9.

CHAPTER 10

[279] *Philadelphia Inquirer*, September 11, 1862, p. 2, c. 1. Copied from the September 6 *Richmond Enquirer*.
[280] *Savannah Republican*, September 20, 1862, p. 1, c. 3. The letter was written from near Frederick on September 7 by an author identified only by his initials, "V.A.S.R." *Newspaper Research, 1861-1865*. http://www2.uttyler.edu/vbetts/savannah_republican.htm.
[281] *Baltimore Sun*, September 9, 1862, p. 1, c. 4.
[282] *Baltimore American and Commercial Advertiser*, September 12, 1862, p. 1, c. 4.
[283] *Philadelphia Inquirer*, September 13, 1862, p. 4, c. 3.
[284] *Philadelphia Inquirer*, September 13, 1862, p. 4, c. 4.
[285] *Savannah Republican*, September 20, 1862, p. 1, c. 3. *Newspaper Research, 1861-1865*. http://www2.uttyler.edu/vbetts/savannah_republican.htm.
[286] *Philadelphia Inquirer*, September 13, 1862, p. 4, c. 3.

[287] *Baltimore American and Commercial Advertiser*, September 9, 1862, p. 1, c. 3.
[288] *Baltimore Sun*, September 13, 1862, p. 1, c. 2. Johnson issued his proclamation on September 8.
[289] *Philadelphia Inquirer*, September 15, 1862, p. 4, c. 3.
[290] *Baltimore Sun*, September 15, 1862, p. 1, c. 2.
[291] *O.R.*, Vol. 19, Pt. 2, p. 590. Lee to Davis, September 3, 1862.
[292] *O.R.*, Vol. 19, Pt. 2, p. 596. Lee to Davis, from his headquarters two miles from Frederick, September 7, 1862.
[293] *Baltimore Sun*, September 15, 1862, p. 1, c. 2. *Philadelphia Inquirer*, September 10, 1862, p. 3, c. 3.
[294] *Philadelphia Inquirer*, September 18, 1862, p. 1, c. 4. *Baltimore American and Commercial Advertiser*, September 16, 1862, p. 1, c. 3. *Baltimore Sun*, September 15, 1862, p. 1, c. 2-3.
[295] *Baltimore American and Commercial Advertiser*, September 12, 1862, p. 1, c.2.
[296] *Mobile Register and Advertiser*, September 8, 1862, p. 1, c. 3. *Newspaper Research, 1861-1865*. http://www2.uttyler.edu/vbetts/mobile_reg_and_adv_61-6.htm.
[297] *Philadelphia Inquirer*, September 10, 1862, p. 1, c. 4. *Philadelphia Inquirer*, September 13, 1862, p. 4, c. 3-4.
[298] *Baltimore American and Commercial Advertiser*, September 12, 1862, p. 1, c. 2.
[299] *O.R.*, Vol. 19, Pt. 2, p. 596.
[300] *Baltimore Sun*, September 13, 1862, p. 1, c. 2.
[301] *Baltimore American and Commercial Advertiser*, September 16, 1862, p. 1, c. 4.
[302] "A Warning Instead of a Joke," *Philadelphia Inquirer*, September 12, 1862, p. 4, c. 3.
[303] *O.R.*¸ Vol. 19, Pt. 2, p. 590. Lee to Davis, September 3, 1862. Lee had determined he would not assault Washington prior to invading Maryland. Few knew that, however.
[304] *Philadelphia Inquirer*, September 8, 1862, p. 2, c. 4; September 11, 1862, p. 2, c. 1. Copied from the September 5 *Richmond Examiner*.
[305] *Philadelphia Inquirer,* September 13, 1862, p. 2, c. 4. *Baltimore American and Commercial Advertiser*, September 12, 1862, p. 1, c. 4.
[306] *Philadelphia Inquirer*, September 12, 1862, p. 2, c. 4. These observations were made by the correspondent of the *Inquirer* posted in Baltimore.
[307] *Baltimore Sun*, September 9, 1862, p. 1, c. 6.
[308] *Philadelphia Inquirer*, September 10, 1862, p. 1, c. 3. *Baltimore Sun*, September 12, 1862, p. 1, c.7. September 13, 1862, p. 1, c. 7. The Battle of North Point occurred on September 14, 1814, and resulted in a British defeat.
[309] "A Few Words to the Rebel Sympathizers of Baltimore," *Baltimore American and Commercial Advertiser*, September 6, 1862, p. 2, c. 2.
[310] *Philadelphia Inquirer*, September 11, 1862, p. 4, c. 6. *Baltimore American and Commercial Advertiser*, September 9, 1862, p. 1, c. 3.
[311] *O.R.*, Vol. 19, Pt. 2, p. 601-602. Lee dated the orders on September 9. He instructed Jackson to commence his march the next day.

CHAPTER 11

[312] *O.R.*, Vol. 19, Pt. 2, p. 605. Lee to Davis from his headquarters in Hagerstown, September 12, 1862.

[313] "The Lesson of a Northern Invasion," *Philadelphia Inquirer*, September 8, 1862, p. 4, c. 1.

[314] "What the Men of Philadelphia Should do," *Philadelphia Inquirer*, September 5, 1862, p. 4, c. 1. The *Inquirer* at the outset of the Confederate invasion anticipated that Pennsylvania was Lee's target.

[315] "The Lesson of a Northern Invasion," *Philadelphia Inquirer*, September 8, 1862, p. 4, c. 1.

[316] "Threatened Invasion of the State," *Philadelphia Inquirer*, September 12, 1862, p. 4, c. 1. The order was issued from Harrisburg on September 11.

[317] "The Governor's Proclamation," *Philadelphia Inquirer*, September 11, 1862, p. 4, c. 1.

[318] "To Arms! To Arms!" *Philadelphia Inquirer*, September 12, 1862, p. 4, c. 1. This was the lead editorial.

[319] "The Call to Arms — Response of the Citizens," *Philadelphia Inquirer*, September 13, 1862, p. 8, c. 3.

[320] *Baltimore American and Commercial Advertiser*, September 16, 1862, p. 4, c.3. Copied from the *Philadelphia Press* (no date given).

[321] "Getting Ready for War," *Philadelphia Inquirer*, September 13, 1862, p. 4, c. 1.

[322] "Camp Independence," *Philadelphia Inquirer*, September 10, 1862, p. 8, c. 6. The Square opened initially to spur recruitment for old and new regiments serving in the U.S. Army. Recruitment increased upon the governor's proclamation calling out 50,000 militiamen on September 11.

[323] *Philadelphia Inquirer*, September 11, 1862, p. 8, c. 2. The roll of honor applied only to men who enlisted in old or new Pennsylvania regiments serving in the U.S. Army, and not the militia.

[324] "Celebration Postponed," *Philadelphia Inquirer*, September 15, 1862, p. 8, c. 6.

[325] *Baltimore Sun*, September 13, 1862, p. 4, c. 1.

[326] "Destructive Flood in Philadelphia," *Philadelphia Inquirer*, September 13, 1862, p. 8, c. 1.

[327] "Young Men of Philadelphia," *Philadelphia Inquirer*, September 11, 1862, p. 5, c. 1. The plea was made by Col. Charles H.T. Collis, commander of the 114th Pennsylvania Zouaves Infantry.

[328] *Philadelphia Inquirer*, September 13, 1862, p. 1, c. 6.

[329] "Honor to Pennsylvania," *Philadelphia Inquirer*, September 22, 1862, p. 2, c. 3-4. Copied from the September 20 *New York Times*.

[330] *O.R.*, Vol. 19, Pt. 2, p. 203. Curtin to Stanton and Gen. John Wool, commanding U.S. troops in the district including Pennsylvania, September 7 at 2:00 a.m.; Stanton to Curtin, September 7.

[331] *O.R.*, Vol. 19, Pt. 2, p. 217, Curtin to Stanton, September 8; *O.R.*, Vol. 19, Pt. 2, p. 217. Stanton to Curtin, September 8 at 4:30 p.m.

[332] *O.R.*, Vol. 19, Pt. 2, p. 249-250. Thomas A. Scott (aid to Gov. Curtin and president of the Pennsylvania Railroad Company) to Stanton, September 10; *O.R.*, Vol. 19, Pt. 2, p. 250. Halleck to Scott, September 10.

[333] *O.R.*, Vol. 19, Pt. 2, p. 229. Halleck to Curtin, September 9.
[334] *O.R.*, Vol. 19, Pt. 2, p. 247. Curtin to Halleck, September 10; *O.R.*, Vol. 19, Pt. 2, p. 247, Halleck to Curtin, September 10.
[335] *O.R.*, Vol. 19, Pt. 2, p. 268. Curtin to Lincoln, September 11 (received in Washington at 8:30 p.m.); *O.R.*, Vol. 19, Pt. 2, p. 276. Lincoln to Curtin, September 12 at 10:35 a.m.; *O.R.*, Vol. 19, Pt. 2, p. 277. Curtin to Lincoln, September 12.
[336] *O.R.*, Vol. 19, Pt. 2, p. 252. Halleck to McClellan, assigning Reynolds to Harrisburg, September 11 at 10:20 a.m.; *O.R.*, Vol. 19, Pt. 2, p. 273-274. Hooker to Seth Williams, McClellan's AAG, September 12.
[337] *O.R.*, Vol. 19, Pt. 2, p. 288. Reynolds to Halleck, September 13. Reynolds arrived at Harrisburg on the 13th. The Pennsylvania Reserves division was not detached from the Army of the Potomac.
[338] *O.R.*, Vol. 19, Pt. 2, p. 267-268. Lincoln to Curtin, September 11.
[339] Benjamin S. Schneck to Margaretta S. Keller, September 12, 1862. http://valley.lib.virginia.edu.papers/F6081.
[340] "From Southern Pennsylvania," *Baltimore Sun*, September 11, 1862, p. 1, c. 2.
[341] *Chambersburg Valley Spirit*, September 24, 1862, p. 1, c. 1; p. 4, c. 1. http://valley.lib.virginia.edu/news/vs1862/pa.fr.vs.1862.09.24.xml.
[342] *Baltimore American and Commercial Advertiser*, September 13, 1862, p. 1, c. 5. Copied from the September 12 *Philadelphia Press*.
[343] *Chambersburg Valley Spirit*, September 24, 1862, p. 1, c. 1. The letter was written from Fort Albany, Virginia, on September 12, and signed "Kennedy." *O.R.* , Vol. 19, Pt. 2, p. 248-249. McClellan to Curtin, September 10, 10:30 p.m.

CHAPTER 12

[344] *O.R.*, Vol. 19, Pt. 2, 231. Maj. Gen. John Wool to McClellan, September 9, 1862. Wool's military department included Maryland, southern and central Pennsylvania, and the Shenandoah Valley in Virginia.
[345] *O.R.*, Vol. 19, Pt. 2, 248. Curtin to McClellan, September 10, 1862 at 10 a.m.; p. 248. McClellan to Curtin, September 10, 1862 at 10:30 p.m.
[346] *O.R.*, Vol. 19, Pt. 2, 201. Halleck to McClellan, September 7, 1862.
[347] *O.R*, Vol. 19, Pt. 2, 201, 233, 207. McClellan's cavalry chief reported 50,000 Rebels south of the Potomac on September 7. Scouts informed Halleck on September 10 that 40,000 under Gustavus Smith (in command of Richmond's defenses) and Beverly Robertson were massing on the Virginia shore at Edward's Ferry near the mouth of the Monocacy. Department commander John Wool reported from Baltimore on September 7 that 40,000 men under Braxton Bragg were advancing in the Shenandoah Valley. Bragg actually was approaching Louisville, Kentucky. The Federals lost considerable time chasing such rumors, and it added considerable caution to their actions.
[348] *O.R.*, Vol. 19, Pt. 2, 211. McClellan to Halleck, September 8, 1862, 8 p.m.
[349] Welles, 111. Diary entry for September 6, 1862.
[350] *O.R.*, Vol. 19, Pt. 2, 223-224. Crawford to division commander Alpheus S. Williams, September 9, 1862. Williams forwarded the report to McClellan's headquarters on the same day.

351 "The New Crisis in the Nation's Affairs," *Baltimore American and Commercial Advertiser*, September 5, 1862, p. 2, c. 1.
352 *Philadelphia Inquirer*, September 9, 1862, p. 4, c. 6. Lee often surveyed Northern newspapers for intelligence about U.S. positions and intentions. Isaac Ridgeway Trimble, now a brigadier general in Lee's army, was a railroad civil engineer and superintendent during the antebellum period who led efforts to destroy bridges north of Baltimore during the war's first month.
353 *O.R.*, Vol. 19, Pt. 2, 208-209. B&O President John W. Garrett to Secretary of War Stanton, September 7, 1862.
354 *O.R.*, Vol. 19, Pt. 2, 211. McClellan to Halleck, September 8, 1862, 8 p.m.
355 *O.R.*, Vo. 19, Pt. 2, 222-223. R. B. Marcy (McClellan's Chief of Staff) to Burnside at Brookeville, September 9, 1862, 10 p.m.
356 *O.R.*, Vol. 19, Pt. 2, 232-233. Lincoln to McClellan, September 10, 1862, 10:15 a.m.; McClellan to Lincoln, September 10, 1862, noon.
357 *Baltimore American and Commercial Advertiser*, September 12, 1862, p. 1, c. 5-6. *Philadelphia Inquirer*, September 15, 1862, p. 4, c. 2. The *Inquirer* report was dated September 13.
358 "What the Russian Minister Thinks of Our Army," *Baltimore American and Commercial Advertiser*, September 12, 1862, p. 4, c. 2.
359 "From the 126th Pennsylvania," *Philadelphia Inquirer*, September 12, 1862, p. 2, c. 4. The letter was written on September 8.
360 *Baltimore Sun*, September 12, 1862, p. 1, c. 2. The march occurred on Sunday, September 7. The distance between Washington and Rockville is 23 miles.
361 "Advance of Our Army," *Philadelphia Inquirer*, September 16, 1862, p. 2, c.2. The correspondence is dated September 12.
362 *Philadelphia Inquirer*, September 9, 1862, p. 4, c. 6.
363 *O.R.*, Vol. 19, Pt. 2, 226-227. McClellan issues General Orders No. 155 about straggling from his headquarters near Rockville on September 9.
364 *Philadelphia Inquirer*, September 12, 1862, p. 2, c. 1.
365 *Baltimore American and Commercial Advertiser*, September 15, 1862, p. 1, c.6.
366 *O.R.*, Vol. 19. Pt. 2, 227. General Orders No. 155, September 9, 1862.
367 Calculation of Confederate numbers remained a mysterious business for the Federals throughout the first three years of the war. During the Confederate invasion of Maryland, McClellan had received estimates from various sources, from as low as 40,000 to as high as 250,000.

In *O.R.*, Vol. 19, Pt. 2, 277, is a message Gov. Curtin sent to President Lincoln at 10 p.m. on September 12. It states that he had received information from a "reliable gentleman" from Hanover, Pennsylvania, who had spent a day in the Rebel encampments. The spy reported, in part, as follows: "Their force in Maryland was about 190,000 men. That they have in Virginia about 250,000 men, all of whom are being concentrated to menace Washington and keep the Union armies employed there, while their forces in Maryland devastate and destroy Pennsylvania." When Secretary of Treasury Salmon Chase learned of this report, he scribbled in his diary, "This is a specimen of information collected and believed!" Found in Chase, 63.

Lee's actual numbers remain a spirited debate among 21st century Civil War historians. The figures range from as low as 32,000 to as many as 50,000. Lee himself could not give reliable numbers, as he, like McClellan, was suffering from a severe straggling problem.

368 *O.R.*, Vol. 19, Pt. 2, 254. McClellan to Halleck, September 11, 1862. Received in Washington at 6:00 p.m.

369 Chase, 58.

370 *O.R.*, Vol. 19, Pt. 2, 253. McClellan to Halleck, September 11, 1862, 3:45 p.m. "Please send forward all the troops you can spare from Washington, particularly Porter's, Heintzelman's, Sigel's, and all the other old troops." The number of 48,600 is found on p. 264 and is derived from returns posted on September 11. Specifically,

Fitz John Porter	=	21,000
Samuel Heintzelman	=	16,000
Franz Sigel	=	9,800

Lincoln's quote is found on p. 253-254.

371 *O.R.*, Vol. 19, Pt. 2, 269. Curtin to McClellan, September 11, 1862. Received at 8 p.m.

372 *O.R.*, Vol. 19, Pt. 2, 255. McClellan to Halleck, September 11, 1862. Sent 11:30 p.m.

373 *O.R.*, Vol. 19, Pt. 1, 416. *Philadelphia Inquirer*, September 15, 1862, p. 4, c. 5. The *Inquirer* did not publish on Sundays, hence the delay in reporting it in the paper. The A.P. article was dated September 13.

374 *Baltimore American and Commercial Advertiser*, September 15, 1862, p. 1, c. 4.

375 *Baltimore American and Commercial Advertiser*, September 16, 1862, p. 1, c. 4.

376 *Baltimore American and Commercial Advertiser*, September 16, 1862, p. 1, c. 4. Copied from the *New York Herald* (no date given).

377 *Baltimore American and Commercial Advertiser*, September 15, 1862, p. 1, c. 4.

378 *Baltimore American and Commercial Advertiser*, September 16, 1862, p. 1, c. 4.

379 *O.R.*, Vol. 19, Pt. 2, 604-605. Lee to Davis, September 12, 1862, from his headquarters at Hagerstown.

380 "From Our Army in Maryland," *Savannah Republican*, September 23, 1862, p. 2, c. 2. The letter is dated September 13 from Hagerstown. *Newspaper Research, 1861-1865*. http://www2.uttyler.edu/vbetts/savannah_republican_1862.htm.

381 *Savannah Republican*, September 25, 1862, p. 2, c. 2. Another letter dated September 13 from Hagerstown. *Newspaper Research, 1861-1865*. http://www2.uttyler.edu/vbetts/savannah_republican_1862.htm.

382 *O.R.*, Vol. 19, Pt. 2, 606, 597. Lee to Davis, September 13, 1862, from Hagerstown; Lee to Davis, September 7, 1862, from Frederick.

383 *O.R.*, Vol. 19, Pt. 1, 606. A. L. Long (Lee's Military Secretary) to McLaws, September 13, 1862, from Lee's headquarters at Hagerstown.

384 *O.R.*, Vol. 19, Pt. 2, 271-272. McClellan to Halleck, September 12, 1862, 6 p.m.

385 *O.R.*, Vol. 19, Pt. 2, 281. McClellan to Lincoln, September 13, 1862, "12 m." Historians do not agree on whether the "12 m." means midnight or meridian, another term for noon. The topic has been debated for generations. We do know the order was received in Washington at 2:35 a.m. on the 14th.

The debate is important. If, indeed, it is the meridian, it establishes that McClellan had possession of Special Orders 191 by noon on the 13th. The order was discovered by members of the 27th Indiana Infantry, in a field southeast of Frederick, lying on the ground, wrapped around three cigars. It remains a mystery who, in the Confederate army, was responsible for the "Lost Orders."

CHAPTER 13

386 *O.R.*, Vol. 19, Pt. 1, 790-791. John Wool to Miles, September 5, 1862; Wool to Miles, September 5, 1862; Miles to Wool, September 7, 1862, 2:30 a.m.

387 *O.R.*, Vol. 19, Pt. 2, 207. Lincoln to Wool, September 7, 1862.

388 *O.R.*, Vol. 19, Pt. 1, 43-44. McClellan to Halleck, September 11, 1862, 9:45 a.m.; Halleck to McClellan, September 11, 1862 (no time).

389 *O.R.*, Vol. 19, Pt. 2, 605. Lee to Davis, September 12, 1862, from headquarters in Hagerstown.

390 Special Orders 191 instructed Confederate Maj. Gen. John G. Walker to seize Loudoun Heights, which he accomplished by late morning September 13, facing no opposition. Jackson arrived at School House Ridge by 11 a.m. on the 13th, marching southeast from Martinsburg. The capture of Maryland Heights was assigned to Maj. Gen. Lafayette McLaws. McLaws had the shortest and most direct route to Harpers Ferry, marching from Frederick west to Middletown, then south to Burkittsville, and across South Mountain at Brownsville Pass. This brought him into Pleasant Valley, directly north of Harpers Ferry. To attain Maryland Heights, McLaws sent two brigades up Solomon's Gap to the top of the Elk Ridge. Maryland Heights constitutes the southern extremity of Elk Ridge.

391 *O.R.*¸ Vol. 19, Pt. 1, 537, 576. Miles had placed about one third of his troops on Maryland Heights, where they engaged forces commanded by Confederate Gen. Lafayette McLaws. McLaws assigned the South Carolina brigade of Joseph Kershaw and William Barksdale's brigade of Mississippians to seize Maryland Heights. Miles delegated the defense of Maryland Heights to Col. Thomas H. Ford, a former lieutenant governor of Ohio, who commanded one of Miles's most veteran regiments, the 32nd Ohio Infantry. Ford made the decision to withdraw, fearing his force was overwhelmed. He was not present on the crest, however, where the Federals were holding their position. Incredulous over Ford's withdrawal order, the Union defenders refused it and remained in their defensive posture. Ford remained insistent, and the Federals commenced the retreat about 3:30 p.m. on September 13. Ford later was cashiered from the army for his ineptitude at Maryland Heights.

McLaws understood the importance of his mission. "So long as Maryland Heights was occupied by the enemy, Harper's Ferry could never be occupied by us." *O.R.*, Vol. 19, Pt. 1, 852.

392 *O.R.*, Vol. 19, Pt. 1, 720-721. The Maryland officer was Capt. Charles H. Russell, 1st Maryland Cavalry. Russell's hazardous mission eluded Confederates on three occasions. First, when he breached the enemy position along the Potomac at School House Ridge. He then encountered Confederate pickets when he crossed the Potomac into Maryland at the mouth of the Antietam Creek.

He ran into more Confederates near Boonsboro on the western side of South Mountain. Astonishingly, Russell and his nine hand-picked men made it to McClellan, arriving at his headquarters near Frederick at 9:00 a.m. on the 14th. McClellan was pleased to learn Miles still remained combatant, and he then directed Russell to proceed to Gen. William Buel Franklin, who was leading the Sixth Corps to relieve Harpers Ferry.

[393] *O.R.*, Vol. 19, Pt. 2, 45-46. Franklin commanded about 12,000 men. Previous to this, his Sixth Corps had been hugging the Potomac, ensuring no more Confederate river crossings, and blocking the routes toward Washington that paralleled the river. Franklin finished first in his class at West Point — the same class in which Ulysses S. Grant finished 21st. At the outset of the war, Franklin was in Washington directing the construction of the new Capitol dome.

[394] *O.R.*, Vol. 19, Pt. 2, 607. T. M. R. Talcott (Lee's aide-de-camp) to McLaws, September 13, 1862, 10 p.m.

[395] *O.R.*, Vol. 19, Pt. 2, 607. Jackson to McLaws, September 14, 1862, 7:20 a.m.

[396] Dennis E. Frye, *Harpers Ferry Under Fire: A Border Town in the American Civil War* (Harpers Ferry Historical Association, 2012), 88-89.

[397] *O.R.*, Vol. 19, Pt. 1, 958. This message about McLaws' predicament was conveyed, via signal flag, from Walker on Loudoun Heights to Jackson on September 14 (no time given).

[398] Miles knew nothing of McClellan's whereabouts. He knew nothing about McClellan's discovery of Special Orders 191. He knew nothing about McClellan's relief expedition by Franklin's Sixth Corps. In a desperate attempt to learn some intelligence, Miles directed his entire cavalry force of 1,400 men to break out of Harpers Ferry, rendezvous with the Union army, and convey Miles's fraught situation at Harpers Ferry. The cavalry departed at 8 p.m. on the 14th, crossing a Potomac pontoon bridge, then turning left at the base of Maryland Heights and heading north toward Sharpsburg, Maryland.

Unbeknownst to Miles, the Confederates were not guarding the Harpers Ferry-Sharpsburg Road at this moment, and the cavalry escaped unmolested. It never reached McClellan, as it kept running into Rebels throughout the night of September 14-15. It eventually arrived near Williamsport, about 40 miles up the Potomac bank from Harpers Ferry, where it encountered and captured a Confederate reserve ammunition train. The cavalry escorted its captured prize north to Greencastle, Pennsylvania, where they arrived as heroes on September 15.

[399] *O.R.*, Vol. 19, Pt. 2, 281-282. McClellan to Halleck, September 13, 1862, 11 p.m.

[400] *O.R.*, Vol. 19, Pt. 2, 289. Halleck to McClellan, September 14, 1862, 1:20 p.m. Halleck was not aware at this time that McClellan was engaged in battle on South Mountain. It is not known when McClellan received Halleck's response that expressed concern that no troops were guarding the Potomac. Halleck remedied this himself, informing McClellan on the afternoon of the 14th, "Hearing that you had withdrawn all troop from the river below Conrad's Ferry, I directed General Banks to supply their place [from Washington]." The force McClellan drew away from the river was the division of Darius Couch. McClellan ordered him to join Franklin's Sixth Corps.

[401] *O.R.*, Vol. 19, Pt. 2, 607. 608. T. M. R. Talcott (Lee's aide-de-camp) to McLaws, September 13, 1862, 10 p.m.; Lee to McLaws, September 14, 1862 (no time). Lee initially intended to deploy Longstreet along Beaver Creek, a good north-south defensive position midway between Hagerstown and Boonsboro. When he determined Jackson had not yet succeeded with his Harpers Ferry mission, Lee moved Longstreet into the Boonsboro Valley to offer more protection for McLaws and to support D.H. Hill.

[402] Beginning at the Potomac, and then heading north, the gaps are: 1) Weverton Gap – through this ran the road connecting Harpers Ferry and Frederick. It endangered McLaws; 2) Crampton's Gap – six miles north, the road ran from Burkittsville into Pleasant Valley. It endangered McLaws' rear; 3) Fox's Gap – six miles north, through it passed a road running from Middletown to Sharpsburg. It endangered D. H. Hill's position at Boonsboro and offered the Federals access to the Potomac River; 4) Turner's Gap – one mile north, through it passed the National Road, right at the heart of D. H. Hill at Boonsboro and the direct route to Lee at Hagerstown; 5) Frosttown Gap – one mile north, through it passed another road toward Hagerstown, endangering the Confederate left at Boonsboro.

[403] For detailed reports on the actions at Fox's Gap, see Jacob Cox's Ninth Corps report in *O.R.*, Vol. 19, Pt. 1, 423-427. For descriptions of the actions at Turner's and Frosttown Gaps, see Joseph Hooker's First Corps report in *O.R.*, Vol. 19, Pt. 1, 213-216. For a Confederate account of the defense of these positions, see D. H. Hill's report in *O.R.*, Vol. 19, Pt. 1, 1019-1022.

[404] About 800 Confederates held the eastern base of Crampton's Gap when Franklin ordered the advance. Franklin had 12,000 men in his Sixth Corps.

For a Confederate summary of Crampton's Gap, see report of Col. Thomas T. Munford, the initial Confederate commander at that position, in *O.R.*, Vol. 19, Pt. 1, 826-827. For a detailed Federal report of the Crampton's Gap action, see Franklin's post-battle report in *O.R.*, Vol. 19, Pt. 1, 374-376. Total casualties from the fighting at the South Mountain gaps were U.S. = 2,325; C.S. = 2,685.

[405] *O.R.*, Vol. 51, Pt. 2, 618-619. R. H. Chilton (Lee's assistant adjutant general) to McLaws, September 14, 1862, 8 p.m. McLaws had two routes of escape. One was a difficult mountain road that crossed Elk Ridge at Solomon's Gap. A second was the Harpers Ferry Road that ran beneath the southern nose of Maryland Heights and then shifted north to Sharpsburg. McLaws did not abandon his position. Instead, he stretched two battle lines across half-mile-wide Pleasant Valley, and prepared to meet Franklin in battle on the morning of the 15th. His battle lines formed north of Solomon's Gap, allowing McLaws to maintain this escape hatch, if needed. See McLaws' report, *O.R.*, Vol. 19, Pt. 1, 855.

[406] *O.R.*, Vol. 19, Pt. 1, 951. Jackson to Col. R. H. Chilton (Lee's chief of staff), September 14, 1862, 8:15 p.m.

CHAPTER 14

[407] Gould, 192.

408 *Philadelphia Inquirer*, September 15, 1862, p. 1, c. 1; September 16, 1862, p. 1, c. 1.
409 *Philadelphia Inquirer*, September 15, 1862, p. 1, c. 1; September 16, 1862, p. 4, c. 1. "Serenade to Mrs. McClellan," *Philadelphia Inquirer*, September 16, 1862, p. 8, c. 5.
410 "The Stars and Stripes," *Baltimore American and Commercial Advertiser*, September 16, 1862, p. 2, c. 1.
411 "Our New York Letter," *Philadelphia Inquirer*, September 15, 1862, p. 1, c. 6.
412 "Almost a Serious Accident to the President," *Philadelphia Inquirer*, September 15, 1862, p. 4, c. 3.
413 "Rather Downcast," *Philadelphia Inquirer*, September 16, 1862, p. 8, c. 1.
414 "Cheering News from Our Army — The Rebels Retreating," *Philadelphia Inquirer*, September 15, 1862, p. 4, c. 1.
415 *Baltimore American and Commercial Advertiser*, September 16, 1862, p. 1, c. 6. Copied from the *New York Herald*.
416 "Our Harrisburg Letter," *Philadelphia Inquirer*, September 16, 1862, p. 4, c. 3. The letter is dated September 15.
417 "Loyal Maryland," *Philadelphia Inquirer*, September 17, 1862, p. 4, c. 2.
418 *Philadelphia Inquirer*, September 15, 1862, p. 4, c. 1.
419 *Philadelphia Inquirer*, September 16, 1862, p. 4, c. 1.
420 Frye, 94-95. *O.R.*, Vol. 19, Pt. 1, 539.
421 Frye, 94.
422 *O.R.*, Vol. 19, Pt. 1, 539. With the death of Miles, Lieutenant Binney filed an official report of the Confederate investment and U.S. surrender on September 18.
423 *O.R.*, Vol. 19, Pt. 1, 47. Franklin sent his first message to McClellan at 8:50 a.m., indicating his fear that the Ferry had surrendered. He informed McClellan at 11 a.m. that he was outnumbered. Franklin actually outnumbered the Confederates, 12,000 to 7,000. McLaws stared down Franklin all day on the 15th. "The enemy did not advance, nor did they offer any opposition to the troops taking position across the valley." McLaws remained in Pleasant Valley until the morning of the 16th, when his command marched south, crossing the Potomac over a pontoon bridge at Harpers Ferry, and reuniting with Confederates on the Virginia side of the river. Franklin did not pursue. *O.R.*, Vol. 19, Pt. 1, 855-857.
424 *O.R.*, Vol. 19, Pt. 1, 951. Jackson's official report of his siege and capture of Harpers Ferry appears in *O.R.*, Vol. 19, Pt. 1, 953-955. Jackson estimates only 11,000 prisoners, but U.S. tallies increase the number to 12,737 (see *O.R.*, Vol. 19, Pt. 1, 549).

The POWs did not go to a prison camp. They were paroled at Harpers Ferry, marched to Annapolis, Maryland, and then either sent home temporarily or to Camp Douglas in Chicago. All the Harpers Ferry POWs were exchanged for equal numbers of Confederate prisoners by January 1863, permitting them to return to active duty again in the U.S. Army.

A complete listing of the U.S. property and sustenance captured by Jackson can be found in *O.R.*, Vol. 19, Pt. 1, 960-961. It included 1,315 pounds of salt-pork; 1,545 pounds of salt-beef; 19,267 pounds of bacon; 4,930 pounds of coffee; and 155,954 pounds of hard bread.

During the end of September through the first week of November, the Lincoln government conducted an investigation of the defense and surrender of Harpers Ferry. The Harpers Ferry Military Commission interviewed 44 witnesses, ranging in rank from lieutenant to General in Chief Henry W. Halleck. The Commission asked nearly 1,800 questions during 15 days of testimony, and it admonished three scapegoats: 1) McClellan had moved too slowly to rescue the garrison; 2) Col. Thomas H. Ford had improperly defended Maryland Heights, resulting in his cashiering; and 3) Col. Dixon Miles, who was dead and unable to defend himself, had surrendered through incapacity, "amounting to almost imbecility." The full investigation is found in *O.R.*, Vol. 19, Pt. 1, 549-803.

[425] Frye, 98.

[426] *O.R.*, Vol. 19, Pt. 1, 951. September 15, 1862. Jackson to Lee, near 8 a.m.

[427] *O.R.*, Vol. 19, Pt. 1, 141. September 16, 1862. Lee to President Jefferson Davis (no time).

[428] *O.R.*, Vol. 19, Pt. 2, 295. September 15, 1862. McClellan to Halleck, 8 a.m.

[429] *O.R.*, Vol. 19, Pt. 2, 295. September 15, 1862. Lincoln to J. K. DuBois, Springfield, IL, 3 p.m.

[430] *Philadelphia Inquirer*, September 15, 1862, p. 1, c. 1; September 16, 1862, p. 4, c. 1.

[431] *O.R.*, Vol. 19, Pt. 1, 217. November 8, 1862. Hooker's official report.

CHAPTER 15

[432] President Jefferson Davis had proclaimed, on September 4, a day of thanksgiving in the Confederacy on September 18.

[433] *Philadelphia Inquirer*, September 22, 1862, p. 2, c. 1. The correspondent dated the report on September 17.

[434] *O.R.*¸ Vol. 19, Pt. 1, 218. For Hooker's complete official report, see 216-219. The Union attacks decimated Jackson's defenders. One out of every two Rebels in Richard Ewell's division (commanded by Alexander Lawton) became a casualty; and 11 of the 15 regimental commanders in Lawton's command were either killed or wounded. Casualties in Hooker's corps equaled about 2,600, or nearly one-third of those engaged. For the Confederate perspective, see Jackson's official report, *O.R.*, Vol. 19, Pt. 1, 955-957.

[435] *Philadelphia Inquirer*, September 22, 1862, p. 2, c. 1. For action reports of the U.S. assaults at Bloody Lane, see William H. French, *O.R.*, Vol. 19, Pt. 1, 323-324; and Winfield Scott Hancock, *O.R.*, Vol. 19, Pt. 1, 277-283. The Confederate defense is detailed in the report of D. H. Hill, *O.R.*, Vol. 19, Pt. 1, 1022-1026.

[436] *O.R.*, Vol. 19, Pt. 1, 376-378. Franklin's report summarizes his arrival and deployment on the ridge overlooking the Sharpsburg-Hagerstown Turnpike and in position near the Union right-center at Bloody Lane.

[437] *O.R.*, Vol. 19, Pt. 1, 419-420 contains Burnside's account of seizing the bridge. Jacob Cox, who held temporary command of the Ninth Corps, offers a

more detailed report in *O.R.*, Vol. 19, Pt. 1, 423-425. Robert Toombs provides the best official account of the Confederate defense of the bridge in *O.R.*, Vol. 19, Pt. 1, 888-891.
[438] *O.R.*, Vol. 19, Pt. 1, 981 gives Hill's description of his assault. Burnside describes this phase of the battle in *O.R.*, Vol. 19, Pt. 1, 420-421.
[439] *Baltimore American and Commercial Advertiser*, September 23, 1862, p. 4, c. 3. Extract from an eyewitness account by a correspondent for the newspaper.
[440] Gould, 198.

CHAPTER 16

[441] "Victory — The Happy Termination of an Eventful Week," *Philadelphia Inquirer*, September 20, 1862, p. 4, c. 1.
[442] *Baltimore American and Commercial Advertiser*, September 20, 1862, p. 1, c. 2.
[443] *Philadelphia Inquirer*, September 20, 1862, p. 4, c. 3.
[444] *O.R.*, Vol. 19, Pt. 1, 143. Lee to Davis, September 21, 1862.
[445] *Savannah Republican*, October 1, 1862, p. 1, c. 2. *Newspaper Research*. http://www2.uttyler.edu/vbetts/savannah_republican_1862.htm. Letter written from Smithfield, Jefferson County, Virginia, on September 19. This section of Virginia — including Harpers Ferry, Shepherdstown, Charles Town, and Martinsburg — became the State of West Virginia on June 20, 1863.
[446] *Baltimore American and Commercial Advertiser*, September 23, 1862, p. 1, c. 5.
[447] *Baltimore American and Commercial Advertiser*, September 24, 1862, p. 1, c. 4.
[448] *Philadelphia Inquirer*, September 24, 1862, p. 1, c. 6.
[449] *Baltimore American and Commercial Advertiser*, September 23, 1862, p. 1, c. 4. Whoever held the field at the end of the battle was responsible for the burial of the dead from both sides. The victor buried their own men first; thus, at Antietam, most U.S. dead had been buried by September 19-20. The spectators witnessed mostly Confederate dead who were buried soon thereafter in mass trench graves. Nearly all of the Union dead were buried in graves "marked with boards, or stakes, and the spots selected are generally pretty, beside a clump of young trees and surrounded with railing, log-cabin fashion, and covered over with boards or rails. . . . Others are buried just under a ledge of rocks; other graves are under stately trees, whilst others are in rows along fences or in fence corners." *Philadelphia Inquirer*, September 30, 1862, p. 1, c. 6.
[450] *Baltimore American and Commercial Advertiser*, September 25, 1862, p. 1, c. 7.
[451] *Baltimore American and Commercial Advertiser*, September 23, 1862, p. 1, c. 4.
[452] *Baltimore American and Commercial Advertiser*, September 22, 1862, p. 1, c. 8.
[453] *Baltimore American and Commercial Advertiser*, September 24, 1862, p. 1, c. 8.
[454] *Philadelphia Inquirer*, September 29, 1862, p. 8, c. 1. Copied from the *Charleston Mercury* (no date given). The *Richmond Dispatch* article is dated September 24.
[455] *Philadelphia Inquirer*, September 27, 1862, p. 2, c. 5. The *Petersburg Express* account is dated September 23.
[456] *Philadelphia Inquirer*, September 24, 1862, p. 8, c. 1. Quoted from the *Richmond Dispatch*, September 20, 1862.

[457] *Philadelphia Inquirer*, September 24, 1862, p. 8, c. 1. Copied from the September 20 *Richmond Dispatch*. No date provided for the *Mercury* article.
[458] *Philadelphia Inquirer*, September 27, 1862, p. 2, c. 5. Copied from the September 23, 1862 *Petersburg Express*.
[459] *Philadelphia Inquirer*, September 27, 1862, p. 4, c. 1.
[460] "Ruined by Victories," *Philadelphia Inquirer*, October 2, 1862, p. 4, c. 2-3.
[461] "Comments of the Press Upon the President's Proclamation," *Philadelphia Inquirer*, September 24, 1862, p. 2, c. 1-2.
[462] *Philadelphia Inquirer*, September 24, 1862, p. 2, c. 1.
[463] *Philadelphia Inquirer*, September 24, 1862, p. 8, c. 2.
[464] *Baltimore American and Commercial Advertiser*, September 24, 1862, p. 4, c.1-2.
[465] "Failure of the Rebel Aggressive War, West as well as East — Its Political Significance," *Philadelphia Inquirer*, October 2, 1862, p. 4, c. 1.

APPENDICES

[466] *Philadelphia Inquirer*, September 11, 1862, p. 2, c. 5-6. The date of the *Richmond Enquirer* editorial is September 5, 1862.
[467] *Philadelphia Inquirer*, September 12, 1862, p. 4, c. 3.
[468] *O.R.*, Vol. 19, Pt. 2, 601-602.
[469] *Philadelphia Inquirer*, August 29, 1862, p. 4, c. 6. Copied from the *Washington Star.*

Bibliography

Civil War Newspaper Sources

Author's Note: I intentionally utilized Civil War newspapers as the primary sources for this book. Approximately 90 percent of the quoted sources are from newspapers dating from July through October, 1862. My goal was to present the history as it was happening, free from the prejudice of post examination and the lapsed memory of time. The newspapers draw you into their action and share with you their immediate reactions, bringing you closest to their initial impressions.

Baltimore American & Commercial Advertiser
Baltimore Sun
Boston Post
Chambersburg Valley Spirit
Charleston Courier
Charleston Mercury
Chicago Times
Cincinnati Commercial
Cincinnati Gazette
Dublin Evening Mail
Frank Leslie's Illustrated Newspaper
Gettysburg Compiler
Harrisburg Patriot and Union
Harper's Weekly
Liverpool Post

London Morning Herald
London Star
London Times
Mobile Register and Advertiser
New York Herald
New York Journal of Commerce
New York Post
New York Times
New York Tribune
New York World
Petersburg Express
Philadelphia Inquirer
Philadelphia Press
Richmond Dispatch
Richmond Enquirer
Richmond Examiner
Richmond Whig
Savannah Republican
Southern Confederacy
St. Paul Pioneer and Democrat
Wheeling Argus

Additional Sources

Basler, Roy P, ed. *The Collected Works of Abraham Lincoln*. Vol. 5. New Brunswick, NJ: Rutgers University Press, 1955.

Buck, Samuel D. *With the Old Confeds: Actual Experiences of a Captain in the Line*. Baltimore: H.E. Hauck & Co., 1925.

"Charleston Mercury, 1860-1862." *The University of Texas at Tyler/ UT Tyler/News, Events, Admissions, Academics*. 18 Nov. 2010. <http://www2.uttyler.edu/vbetts/charleston_mercury_pt1.htm>

Chase, Salmon P. "Diary and Correspondence of Salmon P. Chase." *Annual Report of the American Historical Association*. Vol. 2. Washington, D.C.: Government Printing Office, 1902.

"Colonization - Abraham Lincoln." Abraham Lincoln's Emancipation Proclamation & 13th Amendment. 14 Jan. 2012. <http://www.mrlincolnandfreedom.org/inside.asp?ID=34&subjectID=3>

"Compensated Emancipation." *Abraham Lincoln's Emancipation Proclamation & 13th Amendment*. 12 Jan. 2012. <http://www.mrlincolnandfreedom.org/content_inside.asp?ID=35&subjectID=3>

"Correspondence." *The War of the Rebellion: A Compilation of the Official Records of the Union and Confederate Armies.* Series 1, Vol. 19, Pt. 2. Washington, D.C.: Government Printing Office, 1887.

"Correspondence." *The War of the Rebellion: A Compilation of the Official Records of the Union and Confederate Armies.* Series 1, Vol. 51, Pt. 2. Washington, D.C.: Government Printing Office, 1887.

"Cotton is King by Sen. James Henry Hammond (D-SC)." *TeachingAmericanHistory.org -- Free Seminars and Summer Institutes for Social Studies Teachers*. 27 Nov. 2011. <http://teachingamericanhistory.org/library/index.asp?documentprint=1722>

"The Declaration of Causes of Seceding States." *Civil War Trust: Saving America's Civil War Battlefields*. 9 Feb. 2011. <http://civilwar.org/education/history/primarysources//declarationofcauses.html>

Frye, Dennis E. *Harpers Ferry Under Fire: A Border Town during the American Civil War.* Harpers Ferry Historical Association, 2012.

Gould, John Mead. *The Civil War Journals of John Mead Gould, 1861-1866.* Ed. William B. Jordan. Baltimore: Butternut and Blue, 1997.

"I hope to have God on my side, but I . . ." *Star Quotes*. 7 Jan. 2012. <http://www.quotesstar.com/quotes/i/i-hope-to-have-god-3171.html>

"King Cotton In The Civil War." *The American Civil War Home Page*. 27 Nov. 2011. <http://www.civilwarhome.com/kingcotton.htm>

Langley, Arthur B, ed. *The Writings of Abraham Lincoln, 1862-1863*. Vol. 6. New York: The Lamb Publishing Co., 1906.

Leepson, Marc. "Capital Defense — Washington, D.C., in the Civil War." *History Net: Where History Comes Alive - World & US History Online*. 2 Feb. 2012.<http://www.historynet.com/capital-defense-washington-dc-in-the-civil-war.htm>

"Mobile Register and Advertiser, 1861-1863." *The University of Texas at Tyler/UT Tyler/News, Events, Admissions, Academics*. 25 Nov. 2010. <http://www2.uttyler.edu/vbetts/mobile_reg_and_adv_61-63.htm>

McClellan, George B. *The Civil War Papers of George B. McClellan.* Ed. Stephen W. Sears. New York: Tichnor & Fields, 1989.

Randall, James Ryder. "Maryland, My Maryland - State Song lyrics." *Maryland State Archives*. 7 Jan. 2012. <http://www.msa.md.gov/msa/mdmanual/01glance/html/symbols/lyricsco.html>

"Reports." *The War of the Rebellion: A Compilation of the Official Records of the Union and Confederate Armies.* Series 1, Vol. 19, Pt. 1. Washington, D.C.: Government Printing Office, 1887.

"Savannah Republican, 1862." *The University of Texas at Tyler/UT Tyler/News, Events, Admissions, Academics*. 24 Nov. 2010. <http://www2.uttyler.edu/vbetts/savannah_republican_1862.htm>

"The Second Confiscation Act, July 17, 1862." *History*. 6 Jan. 2012. <http://www.history.umd.edu/Freedmen/contact2.htm>

"Southern Confederacy (Atlanta, GA), 1861-1863." *The University of Texas at Tyler/UT Tyler/News, Events, Admissions, Academics*. 22 Nov. 2010. <http://www2.uttyler.edu/vbetts/southern_confederacy.htm>

"An Undelivered Speech on Executive Arrests: Ingersoll, Charles, 1805-1882: Free Download & Streaming: Internet Archive." *Internet Archive: Digital Library of Free Books, Movies, Music & Wayback Machine*. 3 Jan. 2012. <http://archive.org/details/undeliveredspeec00inge>

"The Vacant Chair." *Poetry and Music of the War Between the States*. 22 Dec. 2011. <http://ww.civilwarpoetry.org/union/songs/chair.html>

"Valley of the Shadow: Civil War-Era Newspapers." *The Valley of the Shadow: Two Communities in the American Civil War*. 18 Nov. 2011. <http://valley.lib.virginia.edu/news/vs1862/pa.fr.vs.1862.04.30.xml>

"Valley of the Shadow: Valley Personal Papers. Benjamin S. Schneck to Margaretta S. Keller, September 12, 1862." *The Valley of the Shadow: Two Communities in the American Civil War*. 18 Nov. 2011. <http://valley.lib.virginia.edu/papers/F6081>

Welles, Gideon. *The Diary of Gideon Welles, Secretary of the Navy under Lincoln and Johnson.* New York: Houghton Mifflin Co., 1911.

Wheeler, Samuel P. "The Prayer of the Twenty Millions." *LincolnStudies.com*. 5 Jan. 2012. <http://www.lincolnstudies.com/archives/80>

Wingate, George W. *History of the 22nd Regiment of the National Guard of the State of New York*. New York: Edwin W. Dayton, 1896.

Acknowledgments

Thirty years ago, when I was a youthful and impressionable historian, I heard Dr. Richard McMurry lecture at Jerry Russell's annual Congress of Civil War Round Tables on Southern newspaper editors and the underutilization of newspapers as a primary source by Civil War historians. As an avid reader of current newspapers and a sponge for current events, I believed Richard was on to something, and I determined to launch my own investigation of Civil War news sources.

That venture proved terribly frustrating. I discovered most newspapers were accessible only through far-flung archives repositories or copied poorly on illegible microfilm. No wonder Civil War historians avoided newspapers. They were painful to locate, and even more painful to read.

So, second to Dr. McMurry for his inspiration, I must thank the countless creators of computers and digitization for making it possible to read Civil War newspapers on the internet. In addition, I express gratitude to the dozens of curators and archivists who comprehended the potential of newspapers and worked hard to make these remarkable resources accessible to the world.

In addition to Dr. McMurry, I am indebted to academicians who have taken personal interest in me and guided and influenced my understanding and presentation of history. Dr. James I. "Bud"

Robertson taught me to humanize history. Dr. Millard K. Bushong helped me visualize the past. William C. "Jack" Davis challenged me to write, and to write some more. Dr. James McPherson made me appreciate historical context. Dr. Gary Gallagher inspired me to ground-truth personal recollections. Dr. Richard Sommers made me realize the smallest detail may be the most important one. Dr. Joseph Harsh encouraged me to question other historians. Dr. Allen Guelzo expanded my theories as a sparring partner. Dr. Peter Carmichael preached outreach to a broader audience. Dr. Mark Snell helped me understand military intricacies. And Dr. Tom Clemens, my close friend and fellow Antietam scholar, challenged me with spirited debates. To my academic mentors and friends, I express gratitude for the broad approach presented in this book.

My colleagues in public history have been a consistent source of inspiration. Not enough words can describe what I've learned from the great masters Edwin C. Bearss, Chief Historian emeritus of the National Park Service, and Michael Musick, the Civil War oracle of the National Archives. My friends Ted Alexander of the Antietam National Battlefield, John Hennessy at Fredericksburg and Spotsylvania National Military Park, Robert K. Krick at Fredericksburg and Spotsylvania National Military Park, and Jim Ogden of Chickamauga/Chattanooga National Military Park, for years have offered fresh sources and encouragement. NPS ranger historians Paul Lee, Todd Bolton, John King, Catherine Bragaw, Melinda Day, Jeff Bowers, John Powell, David Fox, David Larsen, and Kyle McGrogan willingly shared exciting discoveries, spanning several decades. NPS curators Hilda Staubs, Michelle Hammer, Pam West, and Trudy Kelly carefully cared for the papers of the past in local repositories. NPS archeologists Dr. Stephen Potter, John and Cari Ravenhorst, and Mia Parsons amazed me with discoveries that enriched my paper trail exploits.

Special kudos to Superintendent Rebecca Harriett at Harpers Ferry National Historical Park who champions my work as a public historian and grants me days upon days of personal leave to practice my profession. As a NPS manager, my job permits me no time to research and write history; but Rebecca gave me the opportunity to accomplish that mission on my own time. Her predecessor, Superintendent Donald W. Campbell, also granted me countless personal days to indulge in history pursuits. I've been blessed with great bosses.

This book would not have been possible without the expertise and hand-holding of my friends in the publishing world. How fortuitous for me that Beth Rowland had just sold her publishing company (that she owned for 27 years) and she needed a hobby — my book! Beth patiently guided me through the maze of publishing; and in addition to managing this project (and me), she handled the design, cover art, and final editing, all in record speed. Ably assisting Beth was husband Tim Rowland — columnist, humorist, and editorial page editor for the *Hagerstown Herald Mail* newspaper. Tim has a rare ability of combining brilliance and common sense, and his grip of the English language improved this book immeasurably. I offer special appreciation to primary editor Cathy Baldau who permitted September, 1862 to interrupt her 21st century duties and functions. I am indebted to Cathy for her diligence, efficiency, and editorial expertise. Her professional input crafted a much improved product.

Any writer with a spouse knows the demands of time required by writing. My wife, Sylvia, is absolutely the foremost champion of my pursuits in Civil War history. Sylvia grants me the solitary asylum that I need to venture into the past and to be creative about its presentation. She is respectful of the disciplined demands of an author, and she appreciates the legacy of historical scholarship. I am grateful and fortunate to have Sylvia as my understanding and supportive companion. My Boston Terriers, Mr. Lincoln and Bonnie Blue, share my historian's life, but they demand momentary lapses for ball playing and tug-of-war.

All of us, in fact, should adopt the rule of the canines, and have time to play or pursue our favorite interests.

Index